In the Meantime

In the Meantime
Toward an Anthropology of the Possible

Edited by
Adeline Masquelier and Deborah Durham

berghahn
NEW YORK • OXFORD
www.berghahnbooks.com

First published in 2023 by
Berghahn Books
www.berghahnbooks.com

© 2023, 2025 Adeline Masquelier and Deborah Durham
First paperback edition published in 2025

All rights reserved. Except for the quotation of short passages for the purposes of criticism and review, no part of this book may be reproduced in any form or by any means, electronic or mechanical, including photocopying, recording, or any information storage and retrieval system now known or to be invented, without written permission of the publisher.

Library of Congress Cataloging-in-Publication Data
Names: Masquelier, Adeline Marie, 1960- editor. | Durham, Deborah Lynn, 1958- editor.
Title: In the meantime : toward an anthropology of the possible / edited by Adeline Masquelier and Deborah Durham.
Description: [New York] : Berghahn Books, 2023. | Includes bibliographical references and index.
Identifiers: LCCN 2022045274 (print) | LCCN 2022045275 (ebook) | ISBN 9781800738867 (hardback) | ISBN 9781800738874 (ebook)
Subjects: LCSH: Time--Social aspects. | Social change. | Civilization, Modern--21 century.
Classification: LCC HM656 .I6 2023 (print) | LCC HM656 (ebook) | DDC 304.2/37--dc23/eng/20230202
LC record available at https://lccn.loc.gov/2022045274
LC ebook record available at https://lccn.loc.gov/2022045275

British Library Cataloguing in Publication Data

A catalogue record for this book is available from the British Library

EU GPSR Authorized Representative
LOGOS EUROPE, 9 rue Nicolas Poussin, 17000, LA ROCHELLE, France
Email: Contact@logoseurope.eu

ISBN 978-1-80073-886-7 hardback
ISBN 978-1-83695-080-6 paperback
ISBN 978-1-83695-220-6 epub
ISBN 978-1-80073-887-4 web pdf

https://doi.org/10.3167/9781800738867

Contents

List of Illustrations   vii

Acknowledgments   viii

Introduction.   1
Minding the Gap in the Meantime
Adeline Masquelier and Deborah Durham

Chapter 1.   26
"*Just* Waiting": Korean Chinese Mobility and Immobility in Transnational Migration
June Hee Kwon

Chapter 2.   43
In the Meanplace: Traversing Boom and Bust in China's High Growth/Ghost Town
Michael Alexander Ulfstjerne

Entretemps.   63
"A Lot of Standing Around in the Dark": Specters of Waiting in Paranormal Research
Misty L. Bastian

Chapter 3.   69
Raising Consciousness in the Costa Rican Seasonal Low
Sabia McCoy-Torres

Chapter 4. 91
Stranded in Decolonization: The Attritional Temporality of
Sahrawi Activism in Moroccan-Occupied Western Sahara
Mark Drury

Entretemps. 115
Machine-Made Time: Dialysis and the Complexities of Waiting
and Planning
Janelle S. Taylor and Ann M. O'Hare

Chapter 5. 124
Waiting for Thieves: Nighttime Capital and the Labor of Sitting
in Niger
Adeline Masquelier

Chapter 6. 148
Waiting to Heal in "Crip Time": Temporalities of Chronic Skin
Wounds among Gunshot Survivors in New Orleans
Daniella Santoro

Entretemps. 168
Urgency, Boredom, and Pandemic Mean/Time(s)
Martin Demant Frederiksen

Chapter 7. 172
African Time, Waiting, and Deadlines in Botswana
Deborah Durham

Chapter 8. 194
Waiting Out the Rush: On the Durability of Wealth in Kenya's
Coastal Sex Economies
George Paul Meiu

Afterword. 219
In Slow Time
Thomas Hylland Eriksen

Index 224

Illustrations

Figure 5.1.	A wall adorned with the name of the *fada* that meets there. Niamey, Niger, 2018. © Adeline Masquelier.	131
Figure 5.2.	"Couloir Danger" (Corridor Danger) is the name some *fadantchés* gave to a *fada* to keep away potential trespassers and thieves. Niamey, Niger, 2015. © Adeline Masquelier.	139
Figure 5.3.	The *fada*'s name, "22H00," is painted on the wall against which members gather in Dogondoutchi, Niger, 2015. © Adeline Masquelier.	140
Figure 8.1.	The rush of life in Mtwapa, Kenya, 2017. © George Paul Meiu.	203
Figure 8.2.	House fortified with a concrete brick fence and a large gate, Mtwapa, 2017. © George Paul Meiu.	211
Figure 8.3.	Graffiti mural: "Development: plan the budget." Mombasa, Kenya, 2017. © George Paul Meiu.	213

Acknowledgments

This book began with a series of discussions at Tulane University in March 2018. We thank the Newcomb College Institute, the New Orleans Center for the Gulf South, and the Department of Anthropology at Tulane for supporting these discussions. Although not all the participants could contribute chapters to the edited publication, the papers they presented and the discussions that centered on those papers enriched our understanding of how anthropologists deal with stalled temporalities. We thank João Felipe Gonçalves, Nicole Katin, and Carolina Sanchez Boe for their participation. The four discussants Laura-Zoë Humphreys, Sabia McCoy-Torres, Paul Naylor, and Allison Truitt offered illuminating comments and we gratefully acknowledge their feedback. Thanks are owed to Thomas Hylland Eriksen for writing the Afterword. As editors and authors, we express gratitude to the two anonymous reviewers for their invaluable editorial suggestions. We also want to thank our editor at Berghahn Books, Tom Bonnington, for his support and encouragement. Special thanks to Caroline Kuhtz for her expert assistance in the final preparation of the manuscript. Michael Garvey copyedited all the chapters with great care and improved them immeasurably. Finally, we are indebted to our contributors for producing rich ethnographic accounts of what it means to live in the meantime.

Introduction

Minding the Gap in the Meantime

Adeline Masquelier and Deborah Durham

This book has taken shape in one of the most dramatic "meantimes" of recent history, and that experience has indeed shaped the book. Although initiated well before, it came together during the Covid-19 pandemic, a time when many of us were living a suspended life, locked down in our homes, our exterior lives put on hold as we waited for the pandemic to loosen its grip as a result of the emergence of a vaccine or through simple exhaustion. Some of us lived almost entirely alone during that time; others crowded into bubbles of constant, sometimes too-close interaction. We learned, in that time, how waiting is filled with anticipation of pleasures to come but also dread of the deaths of loved ones, as well as anxieties over lost jobs or careers put on hold and the seeming impossibility of recovery. Was life postponed—weddings, holidays with family, reunions with old friends, fieldwork and in-person conferences for anthropologists like us, or just drinks and dinner out—or was a "new normal," which was certainly not normal, lurking in our future? We learned, too, how differently different people managed the forms of waiting that were new to us and old forms that had been newly recast: waiting in lines for Covid tests, waiting to purchase basic foodstuffs or necessities that disappeared from store shelves, waiting for and watching medical data ranging from global daily case and death counts to the oxygen levels and bloodwork of hospitalized relatives. We discovered not only the camaraderie—the communitas—of patient waiting as we stood together in lines at testing or vaccine clinics, but also the fractiousness, anger, and violence that erupted when people competed for scarce toilet paper or refused to wear masks on planes. And at this moment, as we revise our final draft, it looks like there is no return to "normal"; instead, the pandemic, with its ever-mutating Omicron variants, is endemic, and the experience of the meantime has reshaped our futures in unanticipated ways, as well as reshaping the final form of this book.

If the current moment has taught us anything, it is that such "meantimes" rarely, if ever, amount to a period of stilling or stasis—waiting is not a "dead" moment when nothing happens. Indeed, in a flurry of sometimes too many activities (rediscovering cooking, reconfiguring the home, renegotiating domestic relations, starting home-based businesses, devising new ways of working and teaching on Zoom), people reorganized their lives, renavigated their relationships to the past, and rethought possible futures. As close relationships were reworked—parents homeschooling their children, families adopting pets, survivors living with losses that could not be managed through traditional forms of mourning and support—broader fields of empathy, disinterest, and solipsistic possessive individualism were also refigured. If the wait was partly filled with purpose and direction, people also contended with restlessness, frustration, a loss of former purpose, and boredom. Many lost the sense of scheduled time produced by work commutes, school hours, appointments, and other temporal rigors of capitalism, yet found little relief in unscheduled but demanding needs. The meantime was filled with divergent feelings and temporalities, where the dynamics of reworking the everyday were combined with devising what was now possible for the future. With the suspension of temporalities, people reevaluated what it means to live in a society whose sociality is finding, and indeed in need of, new alignments (Ulfstjerne 2020).

The wait that was more than a wait—for it was also a conflation of times between suspension, overwork, emptiness, frustration, and anticipation—revealed itself as a space of potential. It is precisely the potential nested in that space of deferment, the gap between what is suddenly past and an unknown future—elusive, promising, or feared, but possible—that this edited collection wishes to scrutinize through a series of ethnographic case studies of what we call "the meantime." Waiting is usually understood to be a gap, a space between the past and the future where activity might flourish, but where all that doing is ancillary to a desired, or possibly dreaded, future. The past is pushed aside or is now envisioned as, indeed, past; the future is rife with expectation, discernable through its promises, even when it is known to bring surprises as well as that which is anticipated. We extend that idea with the meantime, usually understood as the gap between promise and affirmation, the wished for and the actual; it is also a space in the convergence of, and not just the divergence from, the past, the present, and the future. The contributions in this book see this gap as a space of experimentation, "of reconfigurations of the conditions of possibility for the afterlives of now time" (Fischer 2018: 3). As the contributors attend to the temporalities of emergence, they explore the meantime as a space of "the possible" in which calculation coexists with uncertainty, imminence with deferral or delay, and where the now must be brought into conversation with the past and the possible. By focusing on the possible, they put the stress on the potentialities of waiting—the temporal tactics, social commitments, material connections, dispositional orientations, and "affective circuits" (Cole and Groes 2016) that emerge in—but also make—the meantime even in the most desperate times.

Some waiting is directed, as in waiting *for* something, suggesting a clear anticipated or unwanted event that marks the end of waiting. AbdouMaliq Simone (2008) has suggested, by contrast, that when the moment that has been waited for is not easily demarcated, waiting emerges as an attitude or predisposition rather than a clear trajectory, dispositional and affective at once. We see the meantime as characterized by its own kind of temporality, an ever-shifting tangle of past, present, and future, and we are interested in the multiple, intersecting, and often cross-cutting, modalities of engagement that waiting entails—the overlapping affective temporalities ranging from longings for ever-receding horizons of possibilities to efforts to keep life projects alive to more ordinary struggles to navigate uncertainties, to stitch together discordant temporal regimes, or, in the meantime, to "mind the gap." Recognizing the multiplicities of temporality that intersect in that gap, we see it neither as a "suffering slot" nor as a bright space in which to locate "the good" (Robbins 2013), but as a space to be approached through rich ethnographic engagements offering careful, critical understanding of a complex world (Ortner 2016). And we are aware that this gap, the gap of not-quite-understanding and of revising and reworking the past with the now and with what is possible, is also a gap that allows anthropological ethnography to take place and, indeed, grow, an issue we return to below.

Scholars have argued that it is in the gaps, pauses, and contradictions that the otherwise can be contemplated, unfettered from classic teleologies and other tools designed to predict and prophesize. In this way, they press far beyond the "liminal" space popularized in Victor Turner's work—a liminality that operated only to reassert the core social values that kept society functioning, where "the eternally rebellious individual is converted . . . into a loyal citizen" (Turner 1967: 43). In *The Mushroom at the End of the World*, Anna Tsing (2015: 20) writes that "indeterminacy, the unplanned nature of time, is frightening but thinking through precarity makes it evident that indeterminacy also makes life possible."

How indeterminacy makes life possible—how the seeming suspension of a predicted future is what allows undetermined futures to emerge—is what the volume sets out to trace through a consideration of waiting as an experience "kept open by the presence of futuristic possibilities within it" (Hudson, in Anderson 2004: 750).

Writing against dominant productivist narratives that privilege speed, movement, strategic plans and assessments, and progress, the contributors attend to the meantime of waiting, the period before the future and after the past, a phase that is temporally more marked than the simple present, as an object with its own affordances and constraints, its own subjectivities, temporalities, and ecologies. At a time when large swaths of the world's population, including refugees, irregular migrants, flexibly employed workers, entrepreneurs whose small business ventures fail, the sick, the unemployed, and those living in war zones, feel excluded from the progressivist time of modernity and its associated project of (capitalist) growth, tracking how people inhabit "slow time," how they navigate delays and disruptions, and how they engage with the institutional structures and temporal regimes that consign them to a meantime is itself a matter of urgency. In the remainder of this Introduction, we situate our approach to this distinctive temporality within the existing body of anthropological literature on time, waiting, duration, and futurity, relating it to recent anthropological concerns with thwarted life courses and precarious futures, elaborating on the modest contribution we make to the field, and discussing how each contributor deals with the gap as a form of engagement and a space of possibility.

Awaiting Wait Times

At the dawn of twentieth-century anthropology, in *Argonauts of the Western Pacific*, Bronislaw Malinowski stressed that a Kula gift that a Trobriand man gave to his trading partner and the counter-gift he received could not be exchanged at the same time. The two transactions must be "distinct in time" (Malinowski [1922] 1961: 353). Even if a gift exchange took place during the same Kula event, Malinowski noted, "there must be an interval between the two gifts, of a few minutes at least" ([1922] 1961: 353). The interval was what distinguished the Kula from *gimwali*, ordinary trade, and what allowed Kula items, the armshells and necklaces that went on circulating into the future, to accrue value. By setting the gift apart from the counter-gift, the "time between" framed the two transactions as discrete *happenings*. Since the partnership uniting two men was a lifelong affair and ownership of Kula valuables was invariably momentary, each transaction was inscribed in a larger pattern of give and take that encompassed numerous island communities. The so-called Kula ring could be pictured as two flows of equivalent objects streaming in opposite directions, even though it was composed, for the participants, of a series of individual strategies and events.

Temporality, it is worth noting, was not one of Malinowski's concerns, and yet it pervades his monograph, in the discussion not only of Kula, but also of gardens and their magical encouragement. The "time between" remained an unscrutinized dimension of the Kula, even if the waits were described as being filled with variously directed activities, all aimed at forging and reworking socialities in time and space. Malinowski was more interested in documenting the reasonableness of Trobriand lives, their love of display, their use of magic, their ambitions, and "the substance of their happiness" ([1922] 1961: 25), yet one cannot read *Argonauts* without picking up on the omnipresence of waiting in Trobriand lives, its relational character, and its directionality. A Kula expedition to another island, we learn, was the culmination of months of planning. Long before the scheduled visit, communities were "alive with preparations" ([1922] 1961: 149). These preparations began in the gardens, where surplus yams were planted and carefully fostered with industry and magic ahead of the next Kula season; they engaged affines, kin, and other partners, redirecting those relationships in their particular overlapping spatiotemporal spheres. Festive dresses were fashioned. New canoes were built and old ones repaired: the painstaking process, blending social networking, technical effort, artistic talent, and magical rite, concluded with a ceremonial launching and a trial run. Months before a party was set to sail, Malinowski ([1922] 1961: 148) wrote, "the hopes and anticipations grew bigger and bigger." Men caught up in the excitement of their next expedition talked of traveling further than anyone else had before, even though, in the end, they never did. In sum, ordinary life seemed to revolve around planning, forecasting, and speeding up, or, alternatively, delaying, Kula.

Though Malinowski did not set out to examine temporality, he hinted at the centrality of anticipation in the experience of Kula: people waiting for a fleet of canoes to turn up on their shore, loaded with goods; a man planning to relinquish a Kula valuable while enjoying the prestige derived from its temporary ownership; a sailing party feverishly preparing to depart for a distant island, and so on. Much of this waiting was hopeful, agentive. It corresponds to *kairos*, the Greek term for the time of opportunity, when conditions are right for action. In other words, it was lived time, unconstrained by clock or calendar. On the other hand, when a man held on to his Kula valuable for too long, leading to spats, perhaps even a feud, with a trading partner, the waiting endured by the frustrated partner was more akin to dead time, or what the Greeks called *chronos*, that is, the (frequently long) stretches of sequential time that feel empty, ordinary, burdensome. Put simply, waiting was and is unevenly experienced. While Trobrianders manipulated time, delaying expeditions, taking their time to hand over a valuable, and so on, they were also forced to cope with the delays imposed by others.

In the following half-century, anthropologists examined the temporalities of anticipation, planning, postponing, and passing time, but waiting was rarely the focus of their analyses. Since it often signaled a lack of agency—a mode of doing nothing, with action being taken by other agencies—waiting belonged to that part of human experience that went unremarked because it was deemed unremarkable (Ehn and Löfgren 2010). Owing perhaps to the discipline's predilection for exposing the cultural basis of that which seemed only natural, there was limited anthropological interest in a human experience as ubiquitous and universal as waiting. This remains an entrenched perspective in some quarters. When, in 2017, we applied for funding from a national organization to hold a conference on "waiting," we were told that the exhaustiveness of the concept, its capacity to include not only a plurality of experiential phenomena but also diverse affective states ranging from hope to doubt and dread to boredom and much more, made it impossible to pin down as an object of analysis. Put bluntly, waiting was not a "serious" topic of anthropological investigation in the way that more clearly defined problems, such as exchange, migration, precarity, or even futurity, were. And yet it is precisely the multiplicity of temporalities entailed in the meantime, including those that sort out a past, a present, and a future as well as those that overlap and converge in the moment, and the sheer diversity of its affective and dispositional character that make waiting a compelling, and serious, topic.

Ironically, the idea that waiting, the gap between things, is a fundamental constituent of human experience, the exploration of which can yield important insight into the workings of society, has long been present in social anthropology. It was Marcel Mauss who initially suggested that by attending to practices of anticipation and speculation, and other modes of future-making, analysts would be able to contemplate social facts not as static elements but rather "in motion," just as "we observe octopuses or anemones in the sea" (1967, in Reinhardt 2018: 117) Though Mauss (2016) recognized that there are countless ways to invest in the future, he turned his attention to gift exchange, showing that time stabilized what was essentially an open-ended, future-oriented form of relational engagement by giving it a cyclical dimension (in the process, he critiqued

Malinowski's focus on the individual rather than social dimension of the exchange). In sum, time was the substance of reciprocity.

Pierre Bourdieu later fastened on this gap—the necessary gap in which the return or outcome was always uncertain, in which things could happen, and in which relationships and values could be extended or suspended—to discover a history that included not only a "genesis amnesia" (1977: 79) (of those "structuring structures") but also space for improvisation. Annette Weiner (1976) and Nancy Munn (1986) traced how, in the Kula ring, these gaps were orchestrated by men striving to insert themselves into a transformed future space that needed constant planning and maintenance, lest they disappear into an unremembered and unexpansive past. Nevertheless, Mauss's major insight into the temporal economy of society—his recognition that anticipation and future-making were critical dimensions of human experience—was largely ignored by anthropologists, for whom, until recently, "time was the handmaiden to other anthropological frames and issues" (Munn 1992: 93), as is well exemplified by E. E. Evans-Pritchard's (1940) subordination of Nuer history, ecological time, and life trajectories to an atemporal structure. There was especially limited acknowledgment that to live in society is to wait for and with others and, circumstances permitting, to make others wait, as part of temporal social dynamics.

Things are changing. Perhaps it was the "end of history" announced by Francis Fukuyama (1992; he has since recanted the idea)—at the very least, the end of a structured history and the concomitant limitation of ideas like "social reproduction"—that woke us up to the complex ambiguities and open-endedness of waiting, as opposed to waiting for the inevitable. If the flurry of recently edited collections on suspension, anticipation, and chronopolitics (Jacobsen, Karlsen, and Khosravi 2021; Janeja and Bandak 2018; Kirtsoglou and Simpson 2020; Singer, Wirth, and Berwald 2019) is any indication, there is a growing recognition that waiting is implicated in some of the important issues of our time. When deployed as an analytical device, Ghassan Hage (2009b: 5) argued, waiting has the capacity to shed new light on dimensions of human experience that might otherwise be overshadowed or entirely hidden. Studies on the politics of waiting have yielded valuable insight into the temporality of hope (Miyazaki 2004), the ethics of anticipation (Gaibazzi 2012), the capacity to focus on long-term aspirations (Appadurai 2013), the economics of emotion (Illouz 2007), and the reworking of problematic pasts (Vigh 2006), among other issues. By attending to the ways that people wait, anthropologists have produced illuminating analyses of the experiences of refugees and migrants (Bendixsen and Eriksen 2018; Ibañez-Tirado 2019; Turner 2015), the sick (Lee, James, and Hunleth 2020; Ferrie and

Wiseman 2016), and the dying (Kaufman 2006). Whether experienced as an existential crisis (Ralph 2008), a sense of being-in-the-world (Chua 2011), a preemptive action (Fox 2019), a pious watchfulness (Robbins 2004), or a form of unpaid labor (Kwon 2015), waiting contains the seeds of transformational praxis. In this edited volume, we take another look at the "time between," which we call the meantime, focusing on often-ignored aspects of waiting—the tensions that emerge between different temporal demands, the diverse modalities of "time work," the forms of sociality it produces, the contingencies or dependencies it yields, and the ways in which it customizes temporal experience (Flaherty 2003)—to determine what they tell us about the contradictions of living.

The meantime is frequently referred to as "waiting," a designation that reduces it to a period of suspension to be endured. By contrast, we understand it as a temporal space of possibilities to be managed, a present to be lived in one way or another, and a way of relating to the past. Recognizing that living in the meantime is "the human condition" (Arendt [1968] 1993), we argue it cannot be reduced to frustrated hope or the forlorn hollowness of waiting for Godot (Beckett [1954] 1982). Building on the recent interest in waiting as a social experience characteristic of late modernity (Hage 2009a; Jeffrey 2010; Sharma 2014), the contributors to this edited volume consider the meantime, not in the straightforward and obvious sense of how people fill the gaps between the events of their lives, but as a more complex, capacious, and variable space in which time is constituted in the act of waiting and by the world around. In using the term "meantime," we draw attention to how waiting is a mode of inhabiting—and constituting—a temporality that is often cross-cut with diverse temporal orientations and projects, and how, within it, waiting in its various forms is socially produced. As Munn (1992, 2013) made clear, we live simultaneously in a myriad of temporal modes, from the existential and phenomenological to the institutional and structured to the imaginative. As a mode of engagement in and with time, waiting is necessarily entangled with other temporalities and other projects, thereby contributing to the occasionally puzzling complexity of the meantime. How waiting coexists with, but also rubs against, other experiences, what is produced (or conversely erased) from these social and material entanglements, and what textures time takes on in the space of the "not-yet" even as other things are happening are the central analytical concerns of this collection.

Possibility in the Meantime

The "time between" has long been described in anthropology as a critical period for the making of hegemonies and creativity. Perhaps most familiar is Turner's corpus on liminality (1967, 1969), a period of "betwixt and between" necessary to effect a transition between social states. Turner (1967: 99) described the liminal as a period of structural invisibility, detachment, and ambiguity during which a person "is neither this nor that, and yet is both." While Turner's model celebrated the communal anti-structure of between-times, found in rites of passage, millenarian movements, carnival festivals, and hippie communities, it was essentially redressive, resolving social contradictions and stabilizing structure: the liminal suspension was the necessary companion to predictable structure, the meantime the necessary companion to standard time, inverted spaces of uncertainty the necessary companion to conviction. Yet, Turner did also suggest that liminality was a "realm of pure possibility" (Turner 1967: 97), though he did not pursue that possibility.

Bourdieu (1977, 2000) turned his attention to the ways people created the gap, intentionally "playing" with time. "Quite the opposite of the inert gap of time ... [where] nothing *but* time is going on" (Bourdieu 1977: 6, 7), the meantime was the product of work and strategy. Holding back a gift, putting off a payment, delaying revenge—in short, making the recipient wait—were tactics of temporal gamesmanship, critical to the unfolding of power between individuals and collectives, a power we all feel when, forced by another to wait, we experience "nothing but time." From this perspective, time was a resource rather than an impediment to action, and "to abolish the interval [was] to abolish the strategy" (Bourdieu 1977: 6)—and to proscribe the possible.

While Turner looks at liminal space as something that is created by circumstances external to the agent, and Bourdieu examines the way in which agents create the gap, we see the meantime as encompassed by both, where a time frame is imposed upon the agent who then makes and remakes it in order to aspire to, and perhaps achieve or suffer, a future. Making time and experiencing time is also work on the self, a form of self-making perhaps closer to Turner's vision than Bourdieu's. Valeria Procupez (2015) describes how the demeanor of "patience" was cultivated among activists and families living through a housing crisis in Buenos Aires, how recognition of one's "in-between" position was fostered among unemployed young people, and how some created or confronted the routinization of waiting. Occupying the meantime, making it into a gap or a wait, hinges on socialized dispositions, which might restrain people from queue-jumping in particular contexts or allow such queue-jumping for certain kinds of persons. While Vincent Crapanzano (1986) described long waits under circumstances beyond one's control (such as White South Africans resignedly awaiting the end of apartheid) as a kind of "existential waiting," people also can, as Hage (2019c) describes, "wait out the crisis" in a test of valued fortitude and perseverance. Because other things go on in such gaps—feeding oneself and others, awaiting the imminent release of a popular movie or book, celebrating a calendrical date (birthdays, Eid al-Fitr, the victorious end of a war)—meantimes are dense times for configuring a multiplex and multitemporal selfhood.

Making Time

In this volume, we address the relationship between individual experience, on the one hand, and collective engagement on the other. The contributors look at how the condition of waiting, not as suspended animation but as living in a meantime, is socially constructed as ordinary or abnormal, productive or thwarted, and filled with possibilities that are rewritten as they are anticipated. In probing the meantime, we treat waiting as a "total social fact," a phenomenon that is enmeshed in all domains of social life yet is also intimately experienced by individuals (Mauss 2016; Valeri 2013). This is not simply a move to valorize waiting as an analytical object. It also stems from a recognition that the experience of waiting, enmeshed as it is in wider configurations of power and production, can shed light on how capitalist and other techniques of time enact and continually reinforce the boundaries of inclusion and exclusion, and of becoming and belonging. Mauss understood social life to be inherently dynamic. In his formulation, the concept of "total" gestures not to a positivist vision of society but to "a perpetual state of becoming" (2006, in Kasuga 2010: 103). As we shall see, it is precisely that sense of emergence that we seek to foreground through situated ethnographies of how people in occupied territories, dialysis centers, tourist towns, haunted buildings, and countless other contexts variously apprehend the meantime.

The equation of waiting with inactivity can be traced to changes that, in modern Europe, led to the perception of time as both a fixed grid, which regulated human activity, and a finite property, to be carefully budgeted, saved, and spent, like money. These changes were not just technological but also moral. Not to make good use of one's time was essentially to waste it (Graeber 2018; Thompson 1967; Weber [1905] 2009). Punctuality was thus an important dimension of working lives while inactivity constituted failure, failure to produce things. The equation of idleness with wasted time still permeates our language. In legal terminology, "dead time" is the length of time a defendant has been institutionalized, which cannot be deducted from that person's sentence. Its literal French translation, "*temps mort*," refers to the pause during athletic competitions to allow athletes to rest or receive advice from their coaches. In English, that pause is referred to as "time out," to mark it as time outside of game play. By the same token, the lives of irregular migrants waiting in refugee camps or detention centers are said to be "on hold," suggesting that their futures have been suspended. In contrast, speed, mobility, access, and constant productivity are associated with progress and valued accordingly.

Following the same logic, late modernity has been characterized as a period of "compressed space-time" (Harvey 1990; Massey 1994) in which technology and global capitalism have radically transformed the experience of both space and time, speeding things up and yet forming horizontally shared experiences of time. Recent years have witnessed the glorification of "creative destruction" associated with neoliberalism, corporate raiding, and the heady exuberance of Silicon Valley's "disruptions," in which patience and experience of the present—indeed, the gap—is forgone. The introduction of time-saving technology has led to the fragmentation of experience: time, divided into ever-decreasing units, eventually ceases to exist as duration, turning instead into a jumbled array of deadlines (Eriksen 2001).

Yet modernity is not all quicksteps. Capitalist growth inescapably coexists with the regimentation and bureaucratization of time. Rejecting models that view movement, access, and speed as hallmarks of modernity, scholars (Leccardi 2003; Parkins 2004) have examined how waiting is intricately "woven through the fabric of the mobile everyday" (Bissell 2007: 277), producing diverse temporal regimes and yielding diverse modes of productivity. People wait in lines to buy goods or apply for things that they must then wait to receive; commuters sit on buses and trains—catching up on sleep, dreaming, observing, using their devices; patients wait for the doctor to examine them. The end of the month with its paycheck looms farther away as due dates for outstanding bills pass by; patients count the days until results from a biopsy are delivered; grandparents await the longed-for visit of teenaged grandchildren whose time is devoted to racking up activities that will get them into college. Americans wait to turn sixty-five, when they become eligible for Medicare, government-sponsored health insurance, and entire nations wait for the result of elections or for legislation that is promised but never passed.

Although everyone waits, some people wait more than others. Business-savvy kinetic elites zoom through VIP spaces, avoiding lines and making "efficient" use of their time. On the other hand, economic liberalization and the creation of "spaces of exception" and zones of exclusion from dominant expectations of development have had a catastrophic impact on people's livelihoods, trapping many in situations of chronic waiting (Appadurai 2013; Biehl 2005) and turning them into disempowered "patients of the state" (Auyero 2012). For most of these people, the hope that functions to keep people in a state of suspension, orienting them toward the future (Miyazaki 2004), has turned into despair or quiet resignation. This has generated experiences of longing or boredom as "suspended" time (O'Neill 2017) and led to the relative evacuation of the near future in evangelical Christianity (Guyer 2007). Meanwhile, asylum seekers and undocumented migrants who are subjected to repeated, endless waiting, as if their time were somehow less valuable than the time of citizens, struggle to engage in future-making even as they try to avoid becoming stuck (Khosravi 2021). There, as Madeleine Reeves (2019) shows in her ethnography of un- or insufficiently documented Kyrgyzstani migrant workers navigating Russian bureaucracy, waiting is sometimes less about making things happen than it is about maintenance, a "keeping-things-going" form of engagement in the face of deep uncertainty.

Indeed, waiting seems to have become a sign of our times. Currently, entire nations, such as Syria, Myanmar, or even Scotland, are waiting for an elusive future (Bayart 2007; Wirth 2019). Yet, even in the face of dark political horizons, people continue to build homes, have children, and send them to school, even if they must do so in the most precarious conditions, in refugee and migrant camps, for instance (Mountz 2011). Whether people choose to "wait out" crises (Hage 2009c), retreat into nostalgia (Ferguson 1999), use waiting time to build skills and networks (Masquelier 2019), make plans for futures that will never be realized (Chu 2010), or actively plan to avoid dreaded futures (Samimian-Darash 2016), the meantime is an important site in people's struggle to grant meaning to lives caught between precarious presents and expectations of progress. By turning our attention to stalled life trajectories and suspenseful states, we seek to recover temporalities that have been flattened by the propensity to assess contemporary experiences strictly through the lens of mobility, productivity, and intensity.

Waiting as Becoming

Recent anthropology has asked that we shift our attention from forms of "being" to ongoing "becomings" (see Biehl and Locke 2017). We argue, following Michael Fischer (2018: 4), that coming to terms with the multiple, entangled temporalities and orientations of waiting necessitates inhabiting the meantime, for only an anthropology in the meantime can attend to the emergent, that gap between "visions and implementations, . . . , theory and practice, . . . speculation and artistry," which we cannot always see, despite confident predictions and expert models. In this volume, we approach waiting as a mode of becoming to "see what happens in the meantimes of human struggle and daily life" (Biehl and Locke 2017).

A focus on becoming can assume different forms and inflections. Age categories have often been looked at as states of being (childhood, youth, adulthood, old age), each with its own distinctive character. At the same time, studies of youth sometimes contrast a period of "becoming" with the "being" of adulthood: although the becoming was frequently seen as period of experimenting with possible selves, people "knew" the endpoint, adulthood and its structural inscriptions of marriage, house, and career (see Durham 2017). A shift in focus from structure to practice, the predictable to the indeterminate, "the fixed conditions of possibility" to "lines of potential" (Stewart 2007: 2, 11) helps us recognize how the "becoming" reforms not just the moment but the multiple possibilities to be contemplated. As people devise possibilities, in conditions of poverty or rapid social change, they reinvent futures, including creating new forms of adulting in the place of adulthood (Durham 2021). Michael Jackson (2013) writes of how African migrants living in Europe engage in strategic shapeshifting, stitching together various parts of their past and present selves to become "others" as they navigate impossibly complex bureaucratic rules.

Writing against the commonalities of "waithood" that inform countless studies of youth in the Global South—its "stuckedness" (Hage 2009c: 97), its boredom (Honwana 2012; Singerman 2007)—Claire Dungey and Lotte Meinert (2017) show that in Ugandan schools, waiting is not a waste of time but a moral disposition, cultivated precisely for its capacity to prepare young men for the uncertainties of adulthood. Attending to the temporalities of the "loaned life" in Chile, Clara Han (2012: 31) traces the entanglements of debt, dependency, and care to reveal how the poor continuously strategize to preserve the future, however precarious. Anna Eisenstein (2021) describes how Ugandan women deliberately punctuate their movement through the life course with periods of patient waiting, delaying marriage and motherhood in order to improve their economic opportunities. Her work recalls Jennifer Johnson-Hanks's (2002) study of how Cameroonian women move into and out of life stages instead of progressing through them. Creating the wait, delaying, is not limited to youth, of course. In a discussion of Japanese elders who prepare for death by getting rid of material possessions, Anne Allison (2018: 185) characterizes the affective and practical strategies taken to minimize the possibility of "dying badly" as "active not waiting" to stress that it is the future, not the present, that these elders wish to be freed from.

Whether they examine the tempo of social engagements or the potentialities nested in the liminal, these studies highlight people's capacity to act even in the face of severe hardship and limited autonomy. On the other hand, seemingly productive and purposeful forms of waiting may lead nowhere and may be retrospectively assessed as wasteful. Indeed, for some, the sense of "doing nothing" (or nothing "productive") may define the wait, while others may realize that they were waiting as much in retrospect, or through the lens of the anticipated future, as in the experience of the moment.

Attending to the contingent and the possible, the relation of the past to the future, through a focus on meantimes reveals how interstitial spaces "overflow with shifting aggregates of desire and power" (Biehl and Locke 2017: 6) as people strive to realize their dreams and aspirations. Put differently, waiting is not just a "gap" but also a critical path to the unfolding of possible futures and, as in the case of the Japanese elders, the reorganization of the past. Rather than seeing waiting as an intermission, an interruption between events anticipated as a sequence of events, it can be studied as part of "duration," the experiential aspect that involves a range of emotive orientations (Dalsgård et al. 2014). Setting their sights on the domains of the unforeseen, the unexpected, the incomplete, Achille Mbembe and Janet Roitman (1995) discussed how people in structurally adjusted Cameroon confronted hardship and privation in contexts in which "crisis" no longer referred to an emergency of circumscribed duration, with a beginning and hence an end, but was instead synonymous with an endless temporal horizon. When crisis becomes normalized, "emergency" takes on a double meaning. It refers to the seemingly never-ending period of suspension in which people find themselves when the futurity previous generations took for granted dissolves. Paradoxically, it also gestures toward *emergent* life forms and practices aimed at rescuing the future, what Mbembe and Roitman describe as the "routinization of a register of improvisations" (1995: 326), widely known as entrepreneurship.

The concept of entrepreneurship, we note, derives its signification from its embeddedness in the contingent and the unplanned. If capitalism is all about business plans, carefully rational investments, and hedges against loss, the new fad of entrepreneurship draws attention to its instabilities and creativity and focuses on the individual instead of corporations and (infra)structures. A loan word from the French, it refers to opportunistic forms of engagement at the intersection of risk-taking and innovation. The term *entrepreneur* was allegedly coined by Jean-Baptiste Say, a liberal economist who expounded the doctrines of Adam Smith and advocated for free trade and competition, to describe those intermediaries in the production process who anticipate needs while bearing the market's uncertainty. Composed of *entre*, "between," and *prendre*, "to catch, to take, to grasp," and derived from the Latin, the related verb *entreprendre* hints at the importance of the interval, as a space of potentiality, for the undertaker who is ready to try something new. In this regard, it shares with Michel de Certeau's (1984: 37) "tactics" a willingness to act by "seizing on the wing the possibilities that offer themselves at any given moment." Like tactics, entrepreneurship depends on the judicious use of time, or, more precisely, the interval of time that seems ripe for intervention, as George Paul Meiu and Michael Alexander Ulfsterne make clear in their respective chapters.

In contexts of economic uncertainty and labor flexibilization, many people are forced to operate within unpredictable time frames and engage in a wide array of small projects to ensure that at least some of them will come to fruition—a form of entrepreneurship Craig Jeffrey and Jane Dyson call "zigzag capitalism" (2013: R1) to call attention to the multidirectionality of the meantime. Characterized by an improvisational approach and frequent goal recalibration, zigzag capitalism relies on tactics of improvisation to secure "interstitial livelihoods" (Jones 2014: 223) and is evident in the "gig economy" emerging in the United States. People navigate a risky landscape of fluctuating opportunities, running from one short-term goal to another and calculating how to make the most of the gaps, or *kairos*, that inevitably open between such goals. Indeed, as described in Deborah Durham's chapter, the tempos of the entrepreneurial zigzag do not all move toward an optimistically transformed future, yet the interstices of planning and doing can be better than the "deadline"; people sustain many crisscrossing waits, which run counter to each other, and make a life.

Tracking waiting at the intersection of microdynamics and macro-forces requires that we attend to the tentative, nonlinear ways in which people, confronted by arbitrariness and contingency, orient themselves in uneven, shifting landscapes of opportunity, projecting their paths, crossing thresholds, encountering dead ends, making breakthroughs, holding onto the meantime in the face of an unwanted ending, or languishing in waiting spaces, physical or otherwise. A focus on the meantime, as both a temporality and an analytical device, helps us remain attuned to the plasticity and promise of people's projects, small and large, by paying close attention to the emergent, the becoming, the unresolved and, at times, by acknowledging less obvious "empirical" findings. Even as they aim to clarify the qualities and textures of human engagements with the "not yet," our ethnographic works cannot, and should not, be definitive. They must remain, of necessity, partial, open-ended. At the same time, their very raison d'être springs from the recognition that "while these openings may ultimately lead nowhere, and futurity always struggles with futility and a sense of the inevitable, people can simultaneously be stuck and do things, and this is not nothing" (Biehl and Locke 2017: 21). As we look at the not-nothings people do, as they carve out a meantime between what now seems like a past and that uncertain future, we must be careful in our diagnostics of "cruel optimism" (Berlant 2011) not to allow belief in futility to override their hope, creativity, resolution, and unforeseen attainments.

Orientations

Anthropology, Marilyn Strathern (2022) reminds us, takes place in gaps: our field research is always at some distance from our writing about it, spatially, socially, and temporally, and ethnography is the space between. This is especially true of collective projects like this one. The present collection emerges out of "Waiting," a series of discussions held at Tulane University in March 2018. One of the outcomes of this was a coalescence around the concept of the "meantime" through a critical examination of waiting as "emptiful" duration (Hudson, in Anderson 2004: 750) whose open-endedness gestures to the possible, the otherwise. *In the Meantime* reflects the contingent nature of human projects, including editorial ventures. Some participants did not contribute a chapter to the volume. Several scholars joined the project at a later stage. We opted to include essays of different lengths, interspersing succinct works among longer analytical pieces, with the shorter works offering the reader many possibilities and the longer ones moving the ethnography toward analytical conclusions.

The short essays function, too, as interruptions, while reminding us of the fullness of the meantime. We refer to them as *entretemps* to mark their interludic role, while also gesturing to Gilles Deleuze and Félix Guattari's equation of the meanwhile (*entretemps*) with *devenir*, becoming ([1991] 2005: 149). These interludic pieces are situated more closely in the moment of waiting, where the meantime is full of the possible, anticipations, unknown temporalities, and the uncertainty that comes with these. If anthropology and ethnography take place in a temporal gap, as Strathern wrote, the gap is closer in these interludes; although written after the events described, they focus on the experiential, the feeling of the moment. While the longer chapters seek to resolve the dilemmas of the meantime with reference to an array of phenomena and contexts, as anthropology does, the *entretemps* return us to the irresolution of life in the meantime.

June Hee Kwon, in her chapter, analyzes the intersecting life trajectories of two Korean Chinese men caught up in "the Korean Wind," the massive migration of Korean Chinese to South Korea for better employment opportunities. Kwon traces the divergent pathways of the two men's waiting, illuminating the legal and political temporal regimes structuring the experience of migration. Though distinct, the two men's meantimes spring from historically specific forms of hope and fear—collective aspirations emerging from the Korean Wind, as well as concerns that dwelling on possible futures may erode these futures' promises.

Michael Alexander Ulfstjerne shows that the boom and bust in Ordos, China, is not necessarily correlated with hardship and uncertainty, the predominant concerns of anthropologies of waiting, and does not have easily demarcated temporalities. Though prolonged waiting did become a hallmark of the city's bust, as financially strapped residents waited for debts to be repaid, businesses to reopen, and life to return to normal, people had, even before the bust, been waiting, planning, scheming, and strategizing how they could make the most of seemingly inexhaustible urban growth. By attending to the places made through waiting, which he calls the "meanspace," Ulfstjerne traces the materialities of waiting that are reoriented but not given up in conditions of both certain boom and uncertain bust.

In the first *entretemps*, Misty L. Bastian describes how paranormal researchers in the United States convene in rumored haunted locations, set up complex technological equipment, and wait for ghosts to make their presence known. "Ghost hunting" requires patience and an ability to sustain attentiveness through the meantime. Some researchers wait for years for evidence of paranormal activity. Waiting is so embedded in the pursuit itself that most ghost hunters consider the ability to wait a sign of true commitment to the field.

Sabia McCoy-Torres, through an analytical focus on the intersecting temporalities of waiting in Puerto Viejo, a Costa Rican beach town, traces how the mostly Afro-Caribbean residents navigating the ebb and flow of the tourist economy "make time." When the tourists are gone, cash levels are low, and time is plentiful, local residents play with the configurations of social temporality, bending them to suit their needs, even when temporal agency is in short supply. Smoking marijuana in the downtimes and composing music, intrinsic forms of Rastafari world-making, they "overstand" their past and their present, with conflicting hopes and expectations of the future.

Mark Drury discusses how Sahrawi militants mobilized for an elusive political future are effectively suspended between war and peace. Since a ceasefire was signed in 1991 between Morocco and the Polisario Front, the politico-military organization opposing Moroccan control over the former Spanish territory of Western Sahara, little has happened to move the Sahrawi Arab Democratic Republic, a state-in-exile based in Algeria, closer to self-determination. Many Sahrawis are committed to the nationalist cause even if the end goal—Sahrawi sovereignty—seems unattainable, sustaining a meantime directed toward a highly unlikely future.

In the second *entretemps*, Janelle S. Taylor and Ann M. O'Hare discuss how dialysis prolongs life, but the time patients with kidney failure gain involves much waiting, including waiting for the machine to filter their blood. For providers, kidney failure is an "end stage" of a disease with low rates of long-term survival. It requires anticipating the worsening of patients' health. Yet, this is precisely the kind of future many patients try to avoid. The time they spend on dialysis is a wait for a healthier future, as they wait for organs to become available.

Adeline Masquelier has spent much time waiting with jobless young men in Niger. Though they often claim to be "just sitting" as they wait for stable jobs that do not materialize, a closer examination of the forms their waiting takes at the *fadas* (tea circles) they join reveals how social immobility, through time management, is deployed as an asset. Masquelier discusses the *fadas* as infrastructures of anticipation where waiting has its own rules, regulations, and rewards. Through a focus on the nocturnal side of *fada* activities, she describes how young men, by branding themselves as neighborhood sentinels, turn the act of sitting, which elders denounce as a sign of slothfulness, into a form of labor.

Antibiotic-resistant wounds may take months, even years to heal, if they ever do, defying the promise of biomedical curative technology. Through a focus on the meantime of the chronic skin wounds of disabled gunshot-injured patients, Daniella Santoro shows how living with chronic wounds is a place of strained mobility experienced in the protracted state of waiting to heal. By examining the management of these wounds through the lens of "crip time," a temporality that unsettles the hegemony of curative time, Santoro alerts us to the need for slower-paced, nonjudgmental approaches to human experience.

During the Covid-19 pandemic, the impending lockdown in Denmark initially produced a sense of urgency before giving way to boredom as lockdown routines set in. In the third *entretemps*, Martin Demant Frederiksen compares these temporalities with the early days of the 2008 Russo–Georgian war, when Georgians were readying themselves, and the post-war period, when young men left jobless experienced boredom. Though not as economically disruptive as elsewhere, the Covid meantime in Denmark nevertheless shares similarities with the meantime of jobless young Georgian men waiting for things to happen, even as nothing changed.

Deborah Durham discusses how the time of waiting in Botswana is connected with—and connects—past, present, and future, and how, for youth especially, it is a time of things happening and opportunities being created. In Botswana, people spend a lot of time waiting for things to happen, from waiting for people to show up for events to waiting for debts to be secured or called in. Yet these delays, referred to locally as "African time," are not experienced as deprivation or frustrated anticipation to be endured. They are moments to be enjoyed, sought out, or expanded for the promises they offer.

George Paul Meiu, in his contribution, examines what waiting practices reveal about the production of value when "the rush," the urge to make things happen fast, shapes life. Mtwapa, a coastal town known as Kenya's "Sin City," has witnessed a rush of investments, commodification, and people. But one cannot grasp the rush, Meiu argues, without examining how people inhabit "slow time." Besides waiting *for* the rush, people devise new ways to *wait* it *out*. Since "rushed money" never lasts, they engage in diverse projects "to make the money wait," extending its durability and waiting out the urgency.

In his Afterword, Thomas Hylland Eriksen summarizes some of the key concerns of this edited collection, ranging from the concept of the entrepreneur navigating temporal gaps, to the relation between fast and slow time, to the potentialities embedded in the uncertainties of the meantime.

This volume was not rushed once the discussions ended; since then, many of us have learned more about the recently popular temporalities of "slow living" during the pandemic. We remember rush-hour commutes, the flights that took us back and forth in the course of our work, the insistent calls from children needing to be picked up *now*, stopping to pick up takeaway because we had no time to cook. We developed new ways of temporal living, less tied to clock time but often with multiplying demands of home and (at-home) work. We also found the meantime to be rich with rethinking and revising, as a consequence of which the results of our project, as they came to fruition, were more resonant and insightful than anticipated. We can use the meantime to reorient our temporalities and extend our empathies to a larger social space. At the very least, we hope that this volume makes it abundantly clear that in the meantime, convergent and divergent temporalities are the very means of living.

Adeline Masquelier is Professor of Anthropology at Tulane University. She has conducted extensive research on gender, religion, and health in Niger. She has authored three books, including *Women and Islamic Revival in a West African Town* (Indiana University Press, 2009), which received the 2010 Herskovits Award and the 2012 Aidoo-Snyder prize, both from the African Studies Association. Her latest book *Fada: Boredom and Belonging in Niger* (University of Chicago Press, 2019) was a finalist for the Best Book Prize from the African Studies Association. She has edited three books, including *Critical Terms for the Study of Africa* (University of Chicago Press, 2019). She is coeditor of *HAU: Journal of Ethnographic Theory*.

Deborah Durham has engaged in research in Botswana since 1989 and has published many articles and chapters based on that work, covering issues from minority life in a liberal democracy, to love and jealousy, to bodiliness and civic virtue, to youth. She has also published more generally on youth and "adulting." Having been a professor of anthropology at Sweet Briar College for many years, she currently teaches at the University of Virginia, is an editor at HAU Books, and is deputy editor of *HAU: Journal of Ethnographic Theory*.

References

Allison, Anne. 2018. "Not Waiting to Die Badly: Facing the Precarity of Dying Alone in Japan." In *Ethnographies of Waiting: Doubt, Hope and Uncertainty*, ed. Manpreet K. Janeja and Andreas Bandak, 191–203. New York: Bloomsbury.

Anderson, Ben. 2004. "Time-Stilled Space-Slowed: How Boredom Matters." *Geoforum* 35(6): 739–54.

Appadurai, Arjun. 2013. *The Future as Cultural Fact: Essays on the Global Condition*. New York: Verso Books.

Arendt, Hannah. [1968] 1993. *Between Past and Future: Eight Exercises in Political Thought*. London: Penguin Books.

Auyero, Javier. 2012. *Patients of the State: The Politics of Waiting in Argentina*. Durham, NC: Duke University Press.
Bayart, Jean-François. 2007. *Global Subjects: A Political Critique of Globalization*, trans. Andrew Brown. New York: Polity.
Beckett, Samuel. [1954] 1982. *Waiting for Godot: A Tragicomedy in Two Acts*. New York: Grove Press.
Bendixsen, Synnøve, and Thomas Hylland Eriksen. 2018. "Time and the Other: Waiting and Hope among Irregular Migrants." In *Ethnographies of Waiting: Doubt, Hope and Uncertainty*, ed. Manpreet K. Janeja and Andreas Bandak, 87–112. New York: Bloomsbury.
Berlant, Lauren. 2011. *Cruel Optimism*. Durham, NC: Duke University Press.
Biehl, João. 2005. *Vita: Life in a Zone of Social Abandonment*. Berkeley: University of California Press.
Biehl, João, and Peter Locke. 2017. "Introduction: Ethnographic Sensorium." In *Unfinished: The Anthropology of Becoming*, ed. Biehl, João and Peter Locke, 2–38. Durham, NC: Duke University Press.
Bissell, David. 2007. "Animating Suspension: Waiting for Mobilities." *Mobilities* 2(2): 277–98.
Bourdieu, Pierre. 1977. *Outline of a Theory of Practice*, trans. Richard Nice. Cambridge, UK: Cambridge University Press.
———. 2000. *Pascalian Meditations*, trans. Richard Nice. Stanford, CA: Stanford University Press.
Certeau, Michel de. 1984. *The Practice of Everyday Life*, trans. Steven Rendall. Berkeley: University of California Press.
Chu, Julie. 2009. *Cosmologies of Credit: Transnational Mobility and the Politics of Destination in China*. Durham, NC: Duke University Press.
Chua, Jocelyn. 2011. "Making Time for the Children: Self-Temporalization and the Cultivation of the Antisuicidal Subject in South India." *Cultural Anthropology* 26(1): 112–37.
Cole, Jennifer, and Christian Groes, eds. 2016. *Affective Circuits: African Migration and the Pursuit of Social Regeneration*. Chicago: University of Chicago Press.
Crapanzano, Vincent. 1986. *Waiting: The Whites of South Africa*. New York: Random House.
Dalsgård, Anne Line, et al., eds. 2014. *Ethnographies of Youth and Temporality: Time Objectified*. Philadelphia, PA: Temple University Press.
Deleuze, Gilles, and Félix Guattari. [1991] 2005. *Qu'est-ce que la philosophie?* [What Is Philosophy?] Paris: Editions de Minuit.
Dungey, Claire Elisabeth, and Lotte Meinert. 2017. "Learning to Wait: Schooling and the Instability of Adulthood for Young Men in Uganda." In *Elusive Adulthoods: The Anthropology of New Maturities*, ed. Deborah Durham and Jacqueline Solway, 83–104. Bloomington: Indiana University Press.
Durham, Deborah. 2017. "Elusive Adulthoods: Introduction." In *Elusive Adulthoods: The Anthropology of New Maturities*, ed. Deborah Durham and Jacqueline Solway, 1–38. Bloomington: Indiana University Press.
———. 2021. "Adulting and Waiting: Doing, Feeling, and Being in Late Capitalism." *Sosyoloji Dergisi* 41–42: 1–23.

Ehn, Billy, and Orvar Löfgren. 2010. *The Secret World of Doing Nothing*. Berkeley: University of California Press.

Eisenstein, Anna. 2021. "On Waiting Willfully in Urban Uganda: Toward an Anthropology of Pace." *Cultural Anthropology* 36(3): 458–83.

Eriksen, Thomas Hylland. 2001. *Tyranny of the Moment: Fast and Slow Time in the Information Age*. London: Pluto.

Evans-Pritchard, E. E. 1940. *The Nuer: A Description of the Modes of Livelihood and Political Institutions of a Nilotic People*. Oxford: Clarendon Press.

Ferguson, James. 1999. *Expectations of Modernity: Myth and Meaning on the Zambian Copperbelt*. Berkeley: University of California Press.

Ferrie, Jo, and Phillippa Wiseman. 2019. "'Running out of Time': Exploring the Concept of Waiting for People with Motor Neurone Disease." *Time & Society* 28(2): 521–42.

Fischer, Michael. 2018. *Anthropology in the Meantime: Experimental Ethnography, Theory and Method for the Twenty-First Century*. Durham, NC: Duke University Press.

Flaherty, Michael G. 2003. "Time Work: Customizing Temporal Experience." *Social Psychology Quarterly* 66(1): 13–33.

Fox, Elizabeth. 2019. "Beyond Reciprocity and Obligation in the *Ger* Districts of Ulaanbaatar, Mongolia." *The Cambridge Journal of Anthropology* 37(1): 32–46.

Fukuyama, Francis. 1992. *The End of History and the Last Man*. New York: The Free Press.

Gaibazzi, Paolo. 2012. "God's Time Is the Best: Religious Imagination and the Wait for Emigration in The Gambia." In *The Global Horizon: Expectations of Migration in Africa and the Middle East*, ed. Knut Graw and Samuli Schielke, 121–35. Leuven: Leuven University Press.

Graeber, David. 2018. *Bullshit Jobs*. New York: Simon & Schuster.

Guyer, Jane I. 2007. "Prophecy and the Near Future: Thoughts on Macroeconomic, Evangelical, and Punctuated Time." *American Ethnologist* 34(3): 409–21.

Hage, Ghassan, ed. 2009a. *Waiting*. Melbourne: Melbourne University Press.

——. 2009b. "Introduction." In *Waiting*, ed. Ghassan Hage, 1–12. Melbourne: Melbourne University Press.

——. 2009c. "Waiting Out the Crisis." In *Waiting*, ed. Ghassan Hage, 97–105. Melbourne: Melbourne University Press.

Han, Clara. 2011. "Symptoms of Another Life: Time, Possibility and Domestic Relations in Chile's Credit Economy." *Cultural Anthropology* 26(1): 7–32.

Harvey, David. 1990. *The Conditions of Postmodernity*. Hoboken, NJ: Blackwell Publishers.

Honwana, Alcinda M. 2012. *The Time of Youth: Work, Social Change, and Politics in Africa*. Boulder, CO: Lynne Rienner.

Ibañez-Tirado, Diana. 2019. "'We Sit and Wait': Migration, Mobility and Temporality in Guliston, Southern Tajikistan." *Current Sociology* 67(2): 315–33.

Illouz, Elizabeth. 2007. *Cold Intimacies: The Making of Emotional Capitalism*. New York: Polity.

Jackson, Michael. 2013. *The Wherewithal of Life: Ethics, Migration, and the Question of Well-Being*. Berkeley: University of California Press.

Jacobsen, Christine, M., Marry-Anne Karlsen, and Shahram Khosravi, eds. 2021. *Waiting and the Temporalities of Irregular Migration.* New York: Routledge.
Janeja, Manpreet K., and Andreas Bandak, eds. 2018. *Ethnographies of Waiting: Doubt, Hope, and Uncertainty.* New York: Bloomsbury.
Jeffrey, Craig. 2010. *Timepass: Youth, Class, and the Politics of Waiting in India.* Stanford, CA: Stanford University Press.
Jeffrey, Craig, and Jane Dyson. 2013. "Zigzag Capitalism: Youth Entrepreneurship in the Contemporary Global South." *Geoforum* 49: R1–R3.
Johnson-Hanks, Jennifer. 2002. "On the Limits of Life Stages in Ethnography: Toward a Theory of Vital Conjunctures." *American Anthropologist* 104(3): 865–80.
Jones, Jeremy. 2014. "'No Move to Make': The Zimbabwe Crisis, Displacement-in-Place and the Erosion of 'Proper Places.'" In *Displacement Economies in Africa: Paradoxes of Crisis and Creativity,* ed. Amanda Hammar, 206–29. New York: Zed Books.
Kasuga, Naoki. 2010. "Total Social Fact: Structuring, Partially Connecting, and Reassembling." *Revue du MAUSS* 36(2): 101–10.
Kaufman, Sharon. 2006. *And a Time to Die: How American Hospitals Shape the End of Life.* Chicago: University of Chicago Press.
Khosravi, Shahram. 2021. "Afterword: Waiting, a State of Consciousness." In *Waiting and the Temporalities of Irregular Migration,* ed. Christine M. Jacobsen, Marry-Anne Karlsen, and Shahram Khosravi, 202–7. New York: Routledge.
Kirtsoglou, Elisabeth, and Bob Simpson, eds. 2020. *The Time of Anthropology: Studies of Contemporary Chronopolitics.* New York: Routledge.
Kwon, June Hee. 2015. "The Work of Waiting: Love and Money in Korean Chinese Transnational Migration." *Cultural Anthropology* 30(3): 477–500.
Leccardi, Carmen. 2003. "Resisting 'Acceleration Society.'" *Constellations* 10(1): 34–41.
Lee, Amanda A., Aimee S. James, and Jean M. Hunleth. 2020. "Waiting for Care: Chronic Illness and Health System Uncertainties in the United States." *Social Science & Medicine* 264 (113296). Accessed 20 December 2021. https://www.ncbi.nlm.nih.gov/pmc/articles/PMC7435333/pdf/main.pdf.
Malinowski, Bronislaw. [1922] 1961. *Argonauts of the Western Pacific.* New York: E. P. Dutton.
Masquelier, Adeline. 2019. *Fada: Boredom and Belonging in Niger.* Chicago: University of Chicago Press.
Massey, Doreen. 1994. *Space, Place, and Gender.* Minneapolis: University of Minnesota Press.
Mauss, Marcel. 2016. *The Gift,* trans. Jane I. Guyer. Expanded edition. Chicago: HAU Books.
Mbembe, Achille, and Janet Roitman. 1995. "Figures of the Subject in Times of Crisis." *Public Culture* 7(2): 323–52.
Miyazaki, Hirokasu. 2004. *The Method of Hope: Anthropology, Philosophy and Fijian Knowledge.* Stanford, CA: Stanford University Press.
Mountz, Allison. 2011. "Where Asylum-Seekers Wait: Feminist Counter-topographies of Sites between States." *Gender, Place & Culture: A Journal of Feminist Geography* 18(3): 381–99.

Munn, Nancy. 1986. *The Fame of Gawa: A Symbolic Study of Value Transformation in a Massim (Papua New Guinea) Society*. Cambridge, UK: Cambridge University Press.

———. 1992. "The Cultural Anthropology of Time." *Annual Review of Anthropology* 21: 93–123.

———. 2013. "The 'Becoming-Past' of Places: Spacetime and Memory in Nineteenth-Century, pre–Civil War New York." *HAU: Journal of Ethnographic Theory* 3(2): 259–80.

O'Neill, Bruce. 2017. *The Space of Boredom: Homelessness in the Slowing Global Order*. Durham, NC: Duke University Press.

Ortner, Sherry. 2016. "Dark Anthropology and Its Others: Theory since the Eighties." *HAU: Journal of Ethnographic Theory* 6(1): 47–63.

Parkins, Wendy. 2004. "Out of Time: Fast Subjects and Slow Living." *Time and Society* 13(2/3): 363–82.

Procupez, Valeria. 2015. "The Need for Patience: The Politics of Housing Emergency in Buenos Aires." *Current Anthropology* 56(11): S55–S65.

Ralph, Michael. 2008. "Killing Time." *Social Text* 97, 26(4): 1–29.

Reeves, Madeleine. 2019. "The Queue: Bureaucratic Time, Distributed Legality, and the Work of Waiting in Migrant Moscow." *Suomen Antropologi* 44(2): 20–39.

Reinhardt, Bruno. 2018. "Waiting for God in Ghana: The Chronotope of a Prayer Mountain." In *Ethnographies of Waiting: Doubt, Hope and Uncertainty*, ed. Manpreet K. Janeja and Andreas Bandak, 113–38. New York: Bloomsbury.

Robbins, Joel. 2004. *Becoming Sinners: Christianity and Moral Torment in a Papua New Guinea Society*. Berkeley: University of California Press.

———. 2013. "Beyond the Suffering Subject: Toward an Anthropology of the Good." *Journal of the Royal Anthropological Institute* 19(3): 447–62.

Samimian-Darash, Limor. 2016. "Practicing Uncertainty: Scenario-Based Preparedness Exercises in Israel." *Cultural Anthropology* 31(3): 359–86.

Sharma, Sarah. 2014. *In the Meantime: Temporality and Cultural Politics*. Durham, NC: Duke University Press.

Simone, AbdouMaliq. 2008. "Waiting in African Cities." In *Indefensible Space: The Architecture of the National Security State*, ed. Michael Sorkin, 97–110. New York: Routledge.

Singer, Christoph, Robert Wirth, and Olaf Berwald, eds. 2019. *Timescapes of Waiting*. London: Brill.

Singerman, Diane. 2007. "The Economic Imperatives of Marriage: Emerging Practices and Identities among Youth in the Middle East." Working Paper 6, Wolfensohn Center for Development, Washington, DC.

Stewart, Kathleen. 2007. *Ordinary Affects*. Durham, NC: Duke University Press.

Strathern, Marilyn. 2022. "The Ethnographic Effect I." In *Property, Substance and Effect: Anthropological Essays on Persons and Things*, ed. Marilyn Strathern, 1–26. Chicago: HAU Books.

Thompson, E. P. 1967. "Time, Work-Discipline, and Industrial Capitalism." *Past & Present* 38: 56–97.

Tsing, Anna Lowenhaupt. 2015. *The Mushroom at the End of the World: On the Possibility of Life in Capitalist Ruins*. Princeton, NJ: Princeton University Press.

Turner, Simon. 2015. "'We Wait for Miracles': Ideas of Hope and Future among

Clandestine Burundian Refugees in Nairobi." In *Ethnographies of Uncertainty in Africa*, ed. Elizabeth Cooper and David Pratten, 173–91. New York: Palgrave Macmillan.

Turner, Victor. 1967. *The Forest of Symbols: Aspects of Ndembu Ritual*. Ithaca, NY: Cornell University Press.

———. 1969. *The Ritual Process: Structure and Anti-structure*. Piscataway, NJ: Transaction Publishers.

Ulfstjerne, Michael Alexander. 2020. "Songs of the Pandemic." *Anthropology in Action* 27(2): 82–86.

Valeri, Valerio. 2013. "Marcel Mauss and the New Anthropology." *HAU: Journal of Ethnographic Theory* 3(1): 262–86.

Vigh, Henrik. 2006. *Navigating Terrains of War: Youth and Soldiering in Guinea Bissau*. New York: Berghahn Books.

Weber, Max. [1905] 2009. *The Protestant Ethic and the Spirit of Capitalism*, trans. Talcott Parsons. New York: W. W. Norton.

Weiner, Annette. 1976. *Women of Value, Men of Renown: New Perspectives in Trobriand Exchange*. Austin: University of Texas Press.

Wirth, Robert. 2019. "Scotland: A Nation-State in Waiting." In *Timescapes of Waiting: Spaces of Stasis, Delay and Deferral*, ed. Christopher Singer, Robert Wirth, and Olaf Berwald, 155–75. London: Brill.

Chapter 1

"*Just* Waiting"
Korean Chinese Mobility and Immobility in Transnational Migration

June Hee Kwon

In 2009, I sat down in a KFC in Yanji, the capital city of Yanbian, China, with two Korean Chinese men who had been caught up in "the Korean Wind," the massive migration of Korean Chinese to South Korea for the better wages they found there. Both were back in Yanbian, but for different reasons. Mr. Yun had been deported as an illegal Korean Chinese migrant worker and was therefore ineligible to return anytime soon. Mr. Shin, on the other hand, had registered under the new regulations and was spending a year at home, as the regulations required, before being allowed to work in South Korea for three years as a legal labor migrant. Though they were both waiting to return to South Korea, their respective waiting was framed by distinct contingencies. Whereas Mr. Shin was confident he would be back in South Korea within a year, Mr. Yun was uncertain as to when he would be able to return there for he had to wait until his "black stamp" (*Kŏmŭn dojang* in Korean, a record for the deported) expired and the bar to his reentry into South Korea was lifted. The divergent trajectories of the two migrants' lives were rooted in their responses to the South Korean government's legal shift back in 2005, when a large-scale amnesty was granted to undocumented Korean Chinese migrants.

Both men had worked as undocumented migrants in South Korea for a decade. Since the South Korean government did not issue proper work visas to Korean Chinese from the early 1990s to 2005, many of them used illegal brokers to travel to South Korea. They ended up living in South Korea as undocumented laborers and risked being arrested and deported back to China. Under South Korea's deportation regime, those who were arrested were caught in a legal limbo; they waited in detention centers, hoping a South Korean guarantor would turn up and support their stay in South Korea. Meanwhile, those who were not detained continued to work without being able to make future plans while desperately hoping for legalization in the near future. Mr. Yun and Mr. Shin, like other undocumented Korean Chinese, endured this deportation regime for years, finding refuge in churches that sheltered undocumented migrants from the state.

However, the situation was dramatically upended in 2005, when the South Korean government granted amnesty to undocumented Korean Chinese migrants and recognized them as overseas Koreans. Formerly undocumented Korean Chinese could clear their "illegal" record *if* they registered their status and left South Korea for a year in order to return to work under a five-year work visa time frame. But if they did not follow this protocol, they could be caught and deported, losing the amnesty opportunity. Mr. Shin and Mr. Yun made different choices. Mr. Shin reported to the government and left South Korea, while Mr. Yun chose to remain undocumented and was eventually caught and deported. Both men were forced to wait, but their experiences of waiting were in striking contrast. When I asked the two of them about their waiting during our conversation at KFC—how they were waiting, why they were waiting, or what they were actually waiting for—they both said they were "just waiting" (*Kŭnyang kidarinda* in Korean), a response I frequently received from my interlocutors. The term *Kŭnyang* (just) translates as "no more changes, leaving things as they are," or "expecting no special reward, condition, or meaning." In Korean, the use of *Kŭnyang* implies that you have no special reasons for performing an action and no special expectation of what might happen as a result, and it suggests that you are not making any particular or concerted effort to plan for the future. But were Mr. Shin and Mr. Yun really just waiting? What made them *just* wait? How can we understand their use of "just" to describe their long and frequent waits? What were they ultimately waiting for?

The periods of waiting endured by the two men typify what many Korean Chinese people experience in Yanbian. The divergent pathways that their waiting took allow me to capture the power of specific temporal regimes that structure mobility and immobility, the flow of money, and the making of future economic and life plans. Waiting, I argue in this chapter, is a liminal condition that connects mobility and immobility, a temporal incubator in which the future is materialized in a collective manner. The forms of Korean Chinese waiting I discuss here share similarities with the "chronic waiting" experienced by patients, the urban poor, the unemployed, asylum seekers, and migrants in detention camps

(Appadurai 2013; Auyero 2011; Jeffrey 2008). This mode of anticipation is not a passive state, but rather a basis for thought and political actions (Jeffrey 2008). Most of all, it is an expression of collective aspiration, a future-making mode of being or acting. Shedding light on such experiences thus necessitates exploring how widely waiting has been adopted as an embodied and naturalized temporal mode of being in Yanbian.

This chapter unravels the meaning of "just" in "just waiting," a phrase that has come to characterize an accepted, shared, and normalized mode of Korean Chinese living in the midst of socioeconomic upheaval. The Korean Wind that has swept through Yanbian has generated hopes for a better future, often imagined in the form of bigger houses, fancy cars, better education, additional cash, and expanding business ventures. Though waiting can be painful, especially when accompanied by boredom or loneliness, it is usually considered to be worth enduring since it can yield material rewards: long waits can lead to employment in South Korea, the return of a loved one, or remitted cash. In sum, time spent "just waiting" is productive.

In what follows, I analyze the act of "just" waiting as shared practice and collective aspiration in close conversation with Arjun Appadurai's discussion of how people imagine the future. Aspirations, Appadurai argues, are never individual, but are always formed in interaction with others, in the thick of social life (2013: 180). While aspiration emerges from systems of local ideas, the capacity to aspire is not evenly distributed. Humans make the future based on culture; culture appears as a dialogue between aspirations and sedimented traditions (195). In this sense, the notion that "just" waiting is a collectively shared mode of Korean Chinese aspiration can be considered a legitimate cultural fact. The Korean Wind was generated by the same transformation in political economy that shaped this cultural fact—the intersection between post-socialist China and post–Cold War South Korea. The Korean Chinese migration experience reminds us that studies of waiting must attend to both the politics of waiting, "an engagement with structural and institutional conditions that compel people to wait," and the poetics of waiting, that is, "the existential affordances of being placed in temporal relations, gaps, and intervals where the outcome is uncertain" (Janeja and Bandak 2018: 3).

This chapter considers waiting as a value-producing activity through an exploration of what might be called the economy of waiting. The value of waiting is both visible and invisible, tangible and intangible. Waiting is not always appreciated, nor is it necessarily considered work, since it involves a very ordinary process—the passing of time that often goes unnoticed. However, as I have argued elsewhere in the context of the experience of Korean Chinese migrant couples that are separated as one spouse waits in Yanbian for the return of the other, who works in South Korea, waiting is itself work (Kwon 2015). Waiting is shaped not only by the conditions created by the Korean Wind but also by the intentions, needs, and actions of those who wait. Korean Chinese who wait in Yanbian do not earn money themselves, but they sustain an affective thread between the mobile and the immobile through their management of the remittances they receive and their maintenance of households. Waiting is work because the act of waiting keeps the two parties together and committed as part of a larger circuit of migration.

There is an additional dimension of waiting to consider. After enduring a decade of legal limbo as undocumented migrant workers in South Korea, some Korean Chinese, such as Mr. Shin, were granted amnesties. They became documented subjects able to move "freely" between China and South Korea under the 1-3-2 regime (Kwon 2019): returning to China for a year in order to be allowed allowed to work in South Korea for three years; then returning to China again to be granted the right to work in South Korea for a further two years. The five-year work visa regime was specifically designed to break up migrant tenures in South Korea into two- and three-year blocs. The resulting peculiar migratory rhythms have introduced intermittent periods of immobility within the rampant and relentless mobility of the Korean Wind. My interlocutors' claims that they were "just" waiting allow me to consider how the future is imagined in dialogue with the deep uncertainty and long-standing doubt structured by collective aspirations and the Korean Wind, but most of all by the actual waiting endured by those who navigate the circuits of transnational migration. By attending to the multiple meanings of "just" (*Kŭnyang*) in the omnipresent phrase "just waiting," I demonstrate that, far from denoting a lack of expectations or purpose, the term captures a cultural fact as well as something of a collective, future-oriented aspiration, helping us grasp how, in the wake of the Korean Wind, waiting has become a natural and accepted mode of being.

End Waiting, Begin Waiting

My research on Korean Chinese migration began at the peak of the deportation regime in 2004 in a church where dozens of undocumented Korean Chinese congregated and lived together. I first visited the church to meet Minister Lim, a leader in the pro-democracy movement of the 1980s who had recently led a year-long series of demonstrations to demand the reform of the Overseas Korean Act (which defines the category of overseas Korean) and the legalization of undocumented Korean Chinese workers. At first sight, the church seemed ordinary, offering services on Sundays and Wednesdays for South Koreans. A closer look revealed that it also functioned as a camp, housing fifty or sixty undocumented Korean Chinese men who were unable to go out freely to work. These were ethnic Koreans whose ancestors had migrated from the Korean peninsula to China a century or so ago. Beginning in the early 1990s, these people had moved to South Korea in search of better wages. Instead, they were living a "bare life" (Agamben 1998), exposed to the threat of deportation back to China and lacking any legal protection. Seeking to avoid possible arrest, they had sought refuge in the church. Now they were waiting for their prospects to improve. Specifically, they were waiting for a reform of the Overseas Korean Act that would initiate more favorable treatment of Korean Chinese as ethnic Koreans.

The Overseas Korean Act was enacted in 1998 to identify members of the Korean diaspora who might invest in the troubled South Korean economy, which was struggling as a result of a large-scale, neoliberal economic restructuring aggressively pushed by the International Monetary Fund and the World Bank. The Act promised overseas Koreans great benefits, such as free entry, the right to stay and work, medical insurance, and property ownership. However, Korean Chinese were excluded from the category of overseas Korean, even though they were (and have remained) the largest group of diasporic Koreans living and working in South Korea. The reasons for this exclusion were rooted in their affiliation with socialist China and the potential threat of a sudden Korean Chinese influx that could disrupt the South Korean labor market. From the early 1990s, Korean Chinese had been living "bare lives" in South Korea in the sense that they lacked legal protections. As George Agamben (1998: 11) writes, "bare life remains included in politics in the form of the exception, that is, as something that is included solely through an exclusion." Despite having entered South Korea without proper work visas, Korean Chinese migrants were initially welcomed as overseas Korean who had returned to their ethnic homeland. They were later excluded from the category of overseas Korean by the newly enacted Act. Since most of them had relied on illegal brokers and fake documents to get into South Korea, they were reduced to the status of undocumented workers.

The scene of the undocumented Korean Chinese workers stuck in the church helps us grasp the impact of this "legal limbo." During three months of intense demonstrations, Minister Lim and other NGO activists made the case that the Overseas Korean Act was unconstitutional. In the end, the South Korean government admitted that the Act was flawed and accepted the need for revision—although, at that point, it was unclear when revisions would actually be implemented and Korean Chinese would gain a legal status. By then, Korean Chinese were "just" waiting for the reformed Act to take effect and for their undocumented status to be resolved. During my visits to the church in July 2004, the "refugees" often shared their recollections of the demonstrations. "It's hard to express in words how much we suffered during those three months of cold winter," one former demonstrator told me. "We slept on the cold concrete floor, shared the room with dozens of other Korean Chinese, ate only small amounts of distributed food, and rarely got to take a shower." During the demonstration, some of them got sick. Others left for work. Yet others returned to China or were deported there. One person died in an accident. Most expressed how tired they were during these unsettling times and how frustrated they became afterwards in the absence of a meaningful resolution. Since their legal status as undocumented migrants remained unchanged, they still faced the risk of arrest and deportation.

Korean Chinese participants in the demonstration had gathered in the church hoping to find a community that would protect them in case they were caught by the police. They treated the church as if it were a camp, a space of exception—"a hybrid of law and fact in which the two terms have become indistinguishable"[1] (Agamben 1998). During this liminal and uncertain period, the undocumented migrants experienced a paradoxical combination of inclusion and exclusion. Inside the church, they felt safe and did not have to worry about deportation. Outside, on the other hand, they were vulnerable to arrest. The church effectively became a zone in which the law was suspended. Until the reforms took effect and the South Korean government determined how to handle the problem of half a million undocumented Korean Chinese, the church continued to function as a space of exception. If the long wait for the recognition of the rights of undocumented migrant workers had ended, another wait had begun, this time having to do with the legalization of their status as migrant workers.

In 2005, the Korean Constitutional Court eventually found the Overseas Korean Act to be unconstitutional because it unjustly discriminated against some overseas Koreans on the basis of their nationalities and their demographics. The Overseas Korean Act was rewritten to include those who had previously been excluded, granting the same rights to *all* overseas Koreans (through the F-4 visa). There was a notable exception, however. Unskilled laborers—precisely the category to which most Korean Chinese belonged—would be excluded. Hence, Korean Chinese who worked in the service and construction sectors could not secure F-4 visas, which permitted free entry and lengthy stays in South

Korea. Instead, the South Korean government addressed the needs of these particular Korean Chinese workers through the institution of the H-2 visa, the Overseas Korean Visit-Work Visa. Although this visa was designed for any overseas Koreans in low-skill jobs, in practice, it has mostly been used by Korean Chinese and Koreans from the former Soviet Union.[2] The H-2 visa was effective for five years only and renewal was not automatic.[3] It operated under the rhythm of "1-3-2," as I described earlier. Former undocumented Korean Chinese were now "free" to move back and forth between China and South Korea as long as they reported their undocumented status and left South Korea for one year, as stipulated, in order to "clean" their undocumented status. Yet while the amnesty technically allowed the free movement of Korean Chinese workers across borders, Korean Chinese workers still had to follow the migration rhythm imposed by the new visa regulation. Within this new temporal framework, Korean Chinese workers became mobile as well as immobile—free but trapped. The old waiting—punctuated by the omnipresent fear of being deported—had ended. Another kind of waiting had begun under the regime of "free" movement.

"Free" but "Trapped"

Yanbian, the Korean Chinese Autonomous Prefecture in Jilin Province, China, has experienced remarkable economic development and social change as a result of the "Korean Wind." Yanbian has a population of around two million, 30 percent of which is Korean Chinese. The prefecture has its own ethnic schools, newspapers, broadcast networks, and government. Bilingual signs—first in Korean and second in Chinese—are standardized across the region. Education in Korean ethnic schools has enabled Korean Chinese to maintain their ethnic identity as well as fluency in the Korean language. Thus, most Korean Chinese are grateful for and proud of the ethnic minority policies implemented by the Chinese Communist Party.

To understand the effects of the Korean Wind on this ethnic borderland, one must also consider the rapid privatization that has occurred in the rest of China. Layoffs from work have become common. In this context of newly precarious employment and the mounting cost of living, some Korean Chinese "plunged into the ocean" (下海 Xiahai: enter the ocean by going from government work to the private sector) to open and run their own businesses, becoming entrepreneurs—laoban in Chinese. At the same time, Korean Chinese found that they possessed a useful currency: Korean language skills and cultural affinities that allowed them to advantageously navigate the South Korean labor market. In the service sector, Korean Chinese were a cheap source of quality labor for restaurants, care providers, cleaning services, and construction industries. It is the synergistic relations between the South Korean labor market and Korean Chinese migrants that have generated the Korean Wind over the last three decades.

Most Korean Chinese believe that Yambian's much-vaunted development would have been impossible without the introduction of "Korean money," remittances sent by Korean Chinese migrants working in South Korea. Time and again, I heard Yanbian locals saying: "Thanks to Korean money, we have made *this* much." Despite the desolate and depressing portrayal of the effects of the Korean Wind by some—for example, "everybody is gone with the Korean Wind and thereby Yanbian becomes empty" or "the sharp Korean Chinese population decrease may cause Yanbian to be taken over by Han Chinese"—half a million people (both Korean Chinese and Han Chinese) still live in Yanbian, and the economy has burgeoned. What is significant is that migrants are constantly moving back and forth between Yanbian and South Korea, or other regions of China.

My doctoral research and follow-up research have traced the back-and-forth trajectory of Korean Chinese migration since 2005. While in South Korea, I was especially close to Mr. Shin and Mr. Yun, having spent a great deal of time in the church (mentioned in the previous section) where they had sought refuge from the grasp of the South Korean state. We reunited in Yanbian three years later. Both men recalled their time in South Korea in contrasting ways.

> Mr. Shin: China has changed a lot. It's now much better off than when I left. People don't worry about having enough food anymore. But, however good China has gotten to be, I still want to go back to South Korea as soon as possible. I just miss the feeling when the flight lands at Incheon Airport. It smells different and it feels so good to be in Seoul.
>
> Mr. Yun [*in a grumpy tone*]: What's good about it? I was deported from South Korea. I am still full of anger toward South Korea. It's a bad country, which kicked out its own ethnic people. There are no basic human rights. The law sucks. The discrimination was unbearable. The exploitation was extreme. I would not even want to piss toward Korea [*in a very angry voice*].
>
> Mr. Shin: What are you talking about? You say you hate South Korea, but you still want to go back, don't you? I know you're getting ready to go back.
>
> Mr. Yun: It's not because I like it, but only because I can't make as much here as in South Korea. I just want to use the opportunity. I need money.
>
> Mr. Shin: You're fooling yourself. We have to admit that South Korea has offered great opportunities for Korean Chinese. Without the advantages from South Korea, how could Yanbian be economically improved this much and this fast? Look at the Han Chinese farmers. They are still poor.

Mr. Yun: Not really. The policy of the Chinese government has become better. Now, Han Chinese farmers are better off than Korean Chinese who went to South Korea. There is no worry about starvation. They are well off and well fed, and they've never been to South Korea.

Mr. Shin: Are we pigs? Whenever I hear people say that China is the best country due to plentiful food and free time, I get really pissed off. Food is not enough for life. We are not animals. We should have a life. I cannot find the life in China that I had in South Korea. Yes, the work was very hard and tiring. But I had a great time there and learned a lot. I took exercise, yoga, and computer classes run by the local government.

Mr. Yun: Where did you find time to do all that? The police were tracking me down all the time. I was always nervous about deportation—that, and money.

Mr. Shin: You must not have managed your life there well, then. We were all in the same situation. I was illegal and the police were after me, too. Even with the risk, I liked being in South Korea. Here I can't get used to the way people spend so much time eating and drinking. I feel I am wasted here, without producing anything special.

Mr. Yun: If we have money or power in China, it will be the best place to be. China will be the greatest economic power in the world, exceeding even America. It'll happen in just a few years.

Mr. Shin: China and some Chinese might have a lot of money. But there's no civility, no politeness. Look at the Han Chinese spitting all over the world. It's really gross. Public space is very dirty. Nobody really takes care of it. Chinese are way behind in cultural manners (*suzhi*). Do you remember how clean the streets were in Seoul? We are human beings. Life should have more to it than just eating and drinking. I want to get back to the life I had in South Korea—I just miss it.

Let me pause Mr. Shin and Mr. Yun's discussion. By this point, it had nearly degenerated into a fight. In fact, I was embarrassed at the loud, angry tirades that had erupted in public space despite my best attempts to mediate between my two interlocutors. I also wondered what had sparked their intense disagreement. Did they have such different interpretations of their experiences as undocumented migrant workers in South Korea? Did it have to do with their contrasting situations—Mr. Yun stuck in China, unable to return to South Korea, while Mr. Shin traveled back and forth between the two countries after the amnesty took effect?

Having gotten to know Mr. Yun well, I understood why he was upset. Yet it also seemed that there was an odd contradiction between what he said and what he actually wanted (to return to South Korea). Mr. Yun did not benefit from the amnesty, unlike countless other undocumented Korean Chinese workers, including Mr. Shin, because at the time he could not decide whether to stay in South Korea longer or not. To apply for amnesty, he would have had to leave South Korea for one year before being eligible to return. However, he needed money more than ever: his wife was very ill at the time and his daughter was preparing for college. Leaving South Korea would have put the family in serious financial jeopardy. The remittances he sent were the family's sole source of income. While he was trying to figure out what to do, Mr. Yun was arrested at work and deported back to China.

By contrast, Mr. Shin, having applied for amnesty on time, became a free-moving subject who could enjoy the "smell" and "feeling" of being in Seoul. He said, "Whenever I remember the moment that the airplane hits the ground of Incheon Airport, I become excited. I cannot wait for the moment to happen again." Mr. Shin was proud of and happy with his experience of work in South Korea, although his friends in China looked down on him because in South Korea, he had a "low-wage" construction job. Some of his friends, despite never having gone to South Korea, had done very well in the wake of China's global rise. Indeed, he was shocked at the amount of money they were making. In his view, his humble achievements were not comparable to those of his friends who ran their own businesses and rode the current economic boom in China. They were experts at mobilizing networks and raising back-door capital, neither of which he would have been capable of doing. Nevertheless, Mr. Shin felt confident in himself. He believed he had learned "lessons" from South Korea that his wealthy friends, who had stayed in China, would never learn.

The most important of these lessons, Mr. Shin said, had to do with manners—not spitting in public, refraining from littering, lining up for the subway. Knowledge of such manners enabled Mr. Shin to judge who was "cultured" and who was not. Moreover, he liked what he considered the South Korean habit of speaking in milder tones and listening respectfully to others, which was contrasted by the louder and more boisterous way of talking in Yanbian. As he told me, in a confessional tone,

> I would not want to be known as Korean Chinese, as I don't act or speak like other Korean Chinese. I have made a special effort to embody manners and orderliness because I would like to be seen as cultured and civilized. That is why I was very displeased about the uncultured manners in China—spitting, shouting, taking their shirts off in public. They have no manners, whether they have money or not.

Mr. Shin's testimony, specifically his conviction that "[w]e are not pigs," suggests that his search for "something else" went beyond money and free time. Mr. Shin seemed to lean toward South Korean manners, accepting them as politer, more modern. But not all his memories of South

Korea were positive. While there, he had to put up with harsh discrimination. His South Korean employers were often exploitive, forcing him to work long hours and treating him as a second-rate citizen. There was no job security and he did not know a single person in South Korea whom he could trust. Before he legalized his status as a migrant worker, he had no health insurance. When he got sick, he had to nurse himself back to health without access to a doctor, since he could not afford the high cost. Regardless of the adversity, hardship, and insecurity of working in South Korea, however, Mr. Shin said he could not overestimate the satisfaction of making money and gradually increasing his savings. Sometimes he received raises, occasionally big ones, in recognition of his labor. All in all, Mr. Shin said it was not all bad being in South Korea and he was able to draw some meaningful lessons from his time there:

> I have learned how South Koreans divide hours into minutes to use time in an effective way and how every hour is converted into money. In South Korea, one minute and even one second is counted as money, unlike in China, where time is too loose and too plentiful. There is nothing free in South Korea. Even South Koreans older than sixty or seventy are still working, still leading their lives. You know what? There are many more poor people in South Korea than in China. In China, most people own houses and there are few beggars seen in the streets. But because South Korea is a capitalist country, there is less support from the government. It is very obvious in South Korea; if there is no work, there is no life. It is a brutal and competitive society. I was the only one I could rely on. I had to take care of myself. Now, I have nothing sacred in my life—I will do whatever it takes to survive.

The argument was intense, emotional, and explosive, and his confession was compelling. At the end of the conversation, Mr. Shin told us that he was preparing to go back to South Korea. After growing accustomed to construction work in South Korea, he had come up with a new concept of life: "If there is no work, there is no life."[4] He said that he was good at disciplining himself in terms of handling time, money, and his body, and he also enjoyed organizing his life around work. Contrary to the assumptions of the discourse of entrepreneurship, Mr. Shin, a proud *dagong* (physical worker), has also developed methods of governing himself and internalized these principles in order to become a proper worker in South Korea. More importantly for him, he has adopted civility and cultural manners as the core principles of a good life. As he steadfastly maintained, "We are not pigs."

"Those who never went to South Korea don't know about *the world*," Mr. Shin insisted confidently. "They're just big frogs in a small pond." It is true that migration was a channel through which he learned about the world, in a form of "social remittance." After the amnesty, he became a frequent traveler between China and South Korea, in contrast to Mr. Yun, for example, who lacked the freedom to go to South Korea because of his previous deportation. But Mr. Shin's life was still caught up in the five-year rhythm of circulation, "1-3-2," a rhythm that was and is subject to change under the fluctuating migration policy of the South Korean government. He was waiting between the rhythms; he stayed in South Korea for three years and had to return to China for a while in order to be able to avail of the final two years with his work visa. Mr. Shin was both free and trapped, mobile but also immobile between rhythms, following the regulation of "free" movement.

Stuck in Waiting

When I met Mr. Yun again in Yanbian in 2009, he was barely making ends meet, working at a local restaurant. He was considering every possible way he could leave China—including going to Australia as a farm worker or traveling to the United States as a simple manual laborer. At the same time, and despite professing hatred for the place, he was still trying to get into South Korea. After a big dinner on a piercingly cold day in January, Mr. Yun suggested that I stay over in his daughter's room instead of going back in the dark and cold to Yanji—where my place was located. His daughter was eighteen years old and attended a Han Chinese school. She could barely speak Korean, although she did communicate with her parents and grandmother in that language. When I entered her room, she was studying for an English admission exam to an Australian university. If she got in, Mr. Yun would have the opportunity to go to Australia as a parent of a student. This was another one of Mr. Yun's strategies for getting out of China. As he had previously told me, his wife was too sick even to walk around the house. She had suffered complications after back surgery a few years before. The doctors could not tell exactly what was wrong with her. Their dining table was covered with bottles of different medications she was taking to mitigate her pain and other symptoms. The medicines took up a considerable portion of the monthly household budget. Mr. Yun's mother-in-law also lived in the house, and she helped with the cooking and cleaning.

Although I originally planned to stay just one night at Mr. Yun's place, I ultimately stayed another couple of days at his insistence. "When will we meet again?" he exclaimed. During my stay, I helped his daughter prepare for the English exam and hung out with her, watching her favorite TV shows and listening to her favorite music. The days I spent with Mr. Yun's family helped me see how their time was spent, structured, and planned. I came to understand Mr. Yun's anger better. He was truly desperate to leave China, where he was trapped without the ability to make much money and without much of a future. He kept saying, "I am doing nothing but just waiting."

He certainly tried everything he could to get out. His usual morning routine included calling various brokers in the migration business. If the possibility of securing a visa to another country arose, he went down to the office to see if he was eligible. But it was apparently very hard for him to obtain anything, even faked or manipulated visas, let alone one to South Korea. I noticed that he obsessively played the lottery (彩票 *caipiao*) every night. It seemed like far more than a mere hobby for him. Every night after dinner, he went to the lottery store, where a crowd of people gathered to see which numbers would be the winner. One night, Mr. Yun took me there and explained how it worked. I understood only vaguely, even after he repeated his explanation. He exchanged greetings and information with the men in the store. After we got back home, I found out that lottery-related "research" kept him up until 2 AM. I asked, "Don't you sleep?" He said, "I have something to study." He laughed, but he was serious about his "studies." In his financial desperation, Mr. Yun was trying to crack the logic of the lottery, by working on all the possible number combinations that would deliver a winning number.

As I have written elsewhere, Korean Chinese migrants suffer from "split bodies and split time" as they juggle between "too-much-time" in China and "too-little-time" in South Korea (Kwon 2019). Half of Mr. Yun's life was lost after he was deported back to China; he had been very busy with work in South Korea. Now that he was back in Yanbian, he could do nothing but wait. In contrast to Korean Chinese migrant workers, who, like Mr. Shin, move back and forth between China and South Korea under the amnesty and the "1-3-2" rhythm, Mr. Yun was trapped in China, unable to travel to South Korea, due to his unlucky and untimely deportation. Unlike returnees who have become *laoban* (business owners) after saving every penny earned in South Korea, Mr. Yun had limited savings. Most of the money he had earned in South Korea had gone toward supporting his household, including paying for his wife's medication and his daughter's tuition.

Now he watched his friends and relatives make better money than he ever did. "I am really pissed off whenever I think of the moment I got caught for deportation and see other people freely moving around. It doesn't matter whether they're working as a lower-class *dagong* under South Korean bosses. They're working in South Korea and making better money than me in China." The missed opportunity to apply for the amnesty exposed him to the wide disparity between those who can move about and those who cannot. Stymied by unpredictable and fluctuating visa regulations, Mr. Yun became ever more depressed and dejected as he was confronted by his intractable situation every single moment, with no way out except through "studying" the logic of the lottery while "just" waiting.

In fact, he had tried very hard to find work since being deported from South Korea. Whenever he got paid, however, he could not avoid comparing the wages and asking himself, "What if I had worked the same kind of job for the same hours in South Korea?" While he cursed the South Korea that had inhumanely deported him, I also found that he lived on his memories of the place—how much he had made per day, the good friendships he had developed there, how hard-working he had been there, and so forth. His constant remembrances of his time in South Korea ultimately prevented him from working in China, by increasing his desire to leave China as soon as possible. His body was caught in China while his mind was in South Korea. Like other deported Korean Chinese, Mr. Yun was trapped, neither living in nor leaving China. He did not have enough capital to invest in or open a new business as a *laoban*. Nor did he want to get paid the very low wages that Chinese *dagong* (physical worker) receive. His future, like the lottery, had become too contingent, dependent on random luck and unpredictable timing, and it ultimately had little to do with his own strivings and hard work. He was stuck "just" waiting.

"*Just* Waiting"

This essay has analyzed "just" waiting as an expression of collective aspiration and a future-making mode of being in the context of the Korean Wind for the last three decades. Those experiencing ubiquitous, chronic waiting have been discussed as "paused subjects" (Elliot 2016), "stuck in the middle" (Turnbull 2011), "waiting in the liminal space" (Sutton, Vigneswaran, and Wels 2011), "waiting in the asylum" (Rotter 2016), or "out of time" (Griffiths 2014). Temporal uncertainty and ceaseless liminality always afflict those who wait in detention camps and those who wait in queues to gain legal status. An unstructured and unpredictable temporality consolidates the permanent temporariness faced by the powerless on the margins of transnational migration, while at the same time creating opportunities for new political agency and reshaping the politics and poetics of waiting in migration.

Methods of coping with chronic and endless waiting vary according to local contexts, collective aspirations, and cultural facts, as Appadurai

(2013) notes. Here, waiting accompanies the not-yet-consciousness across the liminality between the present and the future and it produces a particular image of the future (Adams, Murphy, and Clarke 2009).[5] The anticipation not only belongs to individual bodies, but is also provoked and distributed in the form of mass fear and hope, thereby creating an "affective economy" (Ahmed 2004), which I referred to as the economy of waiting: work that produces actual or virtual value and perpetuates the circuit of migration. Waiting entails a value-making temporal process. Especially in the context of transnational migration, waiting bridges mobility and immobility through legal processes and a liminal limbo until things are stamped and approved on paper.

Here, Mr. Yun's case requires an extended explanation. When I last met him, he was waiting at home (Yanbian, China) as if he were in a detention center—"just" waiting for the moment when he could regain transnational mobility. Later, I heard that he was able to return to Seoul to work when his "black stamp" (a symbol of deportation) expired after five years had passed. In 2014, I finally saw Mr. Yun—and others I had met at the church in Seoul—again. Mr. Yun was now a documented migrant, working as a restaurant chef and living with his wife in Seoul. He looked very happy and said, "I survived after 'just' waiting for so long in China. I want nothing more." He told me about Mr. Shin, who was doing business between China and South Korea, still moving back and forth. Mr. Yun, like other Korean Chinese migrant workers who benefited from the amnesty, had become a "free" moving subject. While I have explored "just" waiting and "studying" the logic of the lottery—which may have turned out to be good luck for Mr. Yun after all—my ethnographic focus has been on how unknown and unpredictable futures are imagined into a more knowable present material reality, and how waiting migrants cope with a present life that embraces future uncertainty.

The idea that migrants are "just" waiting is indicative of an inability to find an exit from their particular form of immobility. But waiting also happens in the midst of mobility, as a consequence of following the rhythms of migration. Either way, the stories of Mr. Shin and Mr. Yun tell us that waiting reflects a shared mode of being or acting conditioned by the collective aspirations emerging from the Korean Wind. The "just" in "just waiting" represents not only a studied casualness that combats the uncertainty of post-socialist China, but also a strong willingness to live and thrive within the fluctuating present. The use of "just" accepts the impact of the Korean Wind and insists on the cultural facts that those who wait have themselves been shaping all along. In that sense, far from being the equivalent of "simply" or "merely," the "just" in "just waiting" provides evidence of a constantly structured and naturalized mode of being and acting among Korean Chinese.

June Hee Kwon is an assistant professor in the Asian Studies Program at California State University, Sacramento. In her research and teaching, she focuses on migration and diaspora, borderland and development, gendered labor and class formation, conflict and reconciliation/redress, human suffering and memories, and humanitarianism and human rights. Her area of expertise spans contemporary Korea (North and South), China, and Japan. Her articles have appeared in *Cultural Anthropology*, *Journal of Ethnic and Migration Studies*, and *Critique of Anthropology*. Her book, *Borderland Dreams: The Transnational Lives of Korean Chinese Workers*, is forthcoming from Duke University Press.

Notes

1. The arrested undocumented Korean Chinese were put in detention centers. Some cases showed that Korean guarantors used bail money to have arrestees released on the basis of personal relationships or trust.
2. The Overseas Korean Act did not include Korean Chinese, (some) Korean Japanese, or Korean Russians, all of whom were associated with socialism. Even since the revision took effect, there have been several cases of Korean Japanese not being permitted to enter South Korea due to possible relationships with North Korea, even though these accusations are often unfounded. Korean Chinese and Korean Russians have used H-2 visas to work in South Korea since the revision of the Act.
3. Korean Chinese work visa regulations have changed frequently. More steps and kinds of visa have been introduced for Korean Chinese: C-3-8 (prequalification for education in skilled labor), H-2 (labor visa for limited fields), F-4 (professional visa), F-5 (prequalification for green card).
4. In *The Problem with Work*, Kathi Weeks analyzes work not as a simple economic practice, but as the primary means by which individuals are integrated into social, political, and familial modes of cooperation. She also views work as an essential part of life that transforms subjects into the independent individuals of the liberal imaginary; it is construed as a basic obligation of citizenship (2011: 7–8). I have partially followed her definition of work as an ontological condition of life that enables people to participate in economic activities and meaningful social relationships.
5. In their article "Anticipation: Technoscience, Life, Affect, Temporality," Vincanne Adams, Michelle Murphy, and Adele E. Clarke (2009) sum up the anticipatory regime as follows: 1) it is formed by seeing the future as palpable in the present; 2) it has epistemic value for knowledge production and ethnicized value for subjects; 3) it is formed through modes of prediction and instrumentality; and 4) it has an affective dimension binding subjects in affective economies of fear, hope, salvation, and precariousness in relation to futures already made real in the present. Here, anticipation seems like

a group- or community-specific future-making attitude that operates with collective binding force.

References

Adams, Vincanne, Michelle Murphy, and Adele E. Clarke. 2009. "Anticipation: Technoscience, Life, Affect, Temporality." *Subjectivity* 28(1): 246–65.
Agamben, Giorgio. 1998. *Homo Sacer: Sovereign Power and Bare Life*, trans. Daniel Heller-Roazen. Stanford, CA: Stanford University Press.
Ahmed, Sara. 2010. *The Promise of Happiness*. Durham, NC: Duke University Press.
Appadurai, Arjun. 2013. *The Future as Cultural Fact: Essays on the Global Condition*. New York: Verso Books.
Auyero, Javier. 2012. *Patients of the State: The Politics of Waiting in Argentina*. Durham, NC: Duke University Press.
Griffiths, Melanie B. E. 2014. "Out of Time: The Temporal Uncertainties of Refused Asylum Seekers and Immigration Detainees." *Journal of Ethnic and Migration Studies* 40(12): 1991–2009.
Elliot, Alice. 2016. "Paused Subjects: Waiting for Migration in North Africa." *Time & Society* 25(1): 102–16.
Janeja, Manpreet K., and Andreas Bandak, eds. 2018. *Ethnographies of Waiting: Doubt, Hope and Uncertainty*. New York: Routledge.
Jeffrey, Craig. 2010. *Timepass: Youth, Class, and the Politics of Waiting in India*. Stanford, CA: Stanford University Press.
Kwon, June Hee. 2015. "The Work of Waiting: Love and Money in Korean Chinese Transnational Migration." *Cultural Anthropology* 30(3): 477–500.
———. 2019. "Rhythms of 'Free' Movement: Migrants' Bodies and Time under South Korean Visa Regime." *Journal of Ethnic and Migration Studies* 45(15): 2953–970.
Rebecca Sutton, Darshan Vigneswaran, and Harry Wels. 2011. "Waiting in Liminal Space: Migrants' Queuing for Home Affairs in South Africa." *Anthropology Southern Africa* 34(1–2): 30–37.
Rotter, Rebecca, 2016. "Waiting in the Asylum Determination Process: Just an Empty Interlude?" *Time & Society* 25(1): 80–101.
Turnbull, Sarah. 2016. "'Stuck in the Middle': Waiting and Uncertainty in Immigration Detention." *Time & Society* 25(1): 61–79.
Weeks, Kathi. 2011. *The Problem with Work: Feminism, Marxism, Antiwork Politics, and Postwork Imaginaries*. Durham, NC: Duke University Press.

Chapter 2

In the Meanplace
Traversing Boom and Bust in China's High Growth/Ghost Town

Michael Alexander Ulfstjerne

> You can get so confused
> that you'll start in to race
> down long wiggled roads at a break-necking pace
> and grind on for miles cross weirdish wild space,
> headed, I fear, toward a most useless place.
> The Waiting Place...
> ... for people just waiting...
> *Everyone is just waiting.*
> —Dr. Seuss, *Oh, the Places You'll Go!*

Introduction

In July 2012, I returned to the city of Ordos in China's Inner Mongolia after a year-long absence. Much had changed in the intervening year. The city's economy, which once boasted some of China's highest growth rates, had collapsed. A new district once bustling with life had been emptied of its many investors, entrepreneurs, credit institutions, and luxury restaurants. Construction in new districts, which had, until recently, been taking place on an unprecedented scale at great speed, had stopped entirely. Millions of square meters of real estate—commercial and residential complexes, monumental plazas, and towering government buildings—now stood half finished. In neighborhoods intended to accommodate hundreds of thousands of new residents, the residential buildings and shopping malls were as empty as the streets. Property prices, soaring months before, had plummeted, and the spectacular, fast-paced expansion that had previously animated Ordos and fueled its economy seemed to have paused indefinitely.

Though the economic collapse affected everyone, those who had previously benefited from the city's rampant growth were particularly impacted. They had invested in new constructions and new businesses, hoping to cash in once the district became a hub of commerce and tourism. However, their hopes were short-lived and soon replaced by a feeling of great uncertainty. For many people I came to know, the city's trajectory from boom to bust marked a period of profound disorientation and incessant waiting: creditors, who included people across the social spectrum, waited for debtors to pick up their phones and repay their loans, everyone waited for life to return to normal, for investments to make good, for the 24-7 noise of construction to pick up again, and maybe for another boom to materialize (Woodworth 2019).

Yet, I argue in this chapter, even before the bust, many people were already waiting. Their waiting cannot be accounted for in the way it is generally depicted in recent anthropological accounts: they were not overwhelmed by doubt or operating in conditions of uncertainty. Rather, people were sure that urban growth would continue, property prices would at least double, and business endeavors would yield windfall profits. Their confidence was anchored in a range of tangible facts and figures ranging from growth projections in official charts and urban development strategies to the ubiquitous real estate advertisements that engulfed the city's many budding developments. New theme parks and spectacular convention and sports centers were in the early stages of construction. Luxurious banquets and lavish wedding celebrations were key to solidifying the interpersonal promises and debts made in the heyday of the city's spectacular growth. Against the backdrop of these master plans, schemes, and strategies, the present stretched in foreseeable ways into the future and the question was not whether the boom would last but how to make the most of it.

In this volume, the editors advance the idea of "the meantime" to stress how waiting is about the ways we inhabit a certain time rather than simply being a passive state or experiential realm. But what about the *mean*place, that is, *where* we wait? The coeval dimensions of time and space are often considered together in analyses of heritage, memory, ruins, epochs, and their architectures. Yet, the spatial aspects of temporal interludes have attracted less attention in the literature,[1] even though time is often conceptualized in spatial terms: whether short or long, events "take place" before or after something. They constitute stretches of time. Time and places are thus inextricably linked. In the words of philosopher Edward Casey (2009: 21, emphasis in original), "there's *no (grasping of)* *time without place*; and this is so precisely by virtue of place's actively delimiting and creatively conditioning capacities. Time arises *from* places and passes (away) *between* them." From this perspective, things not only happen in time but also to time—literally. As Casey (2009: xxv) writes, "things happen *in [place]*, but *it happens too*." Places, in this regard, are not neutral containers for people, activities, or events, but serve to anchor certain orientations. We live "*through* them" (Casey 2009: 23).

The configuration of places, things, and rhythms has implications for how we wait: during Ordos's boom period, this played out in anticipation, a steady move toward preconfigured goals in perfect synchrony with the expansion of the city. Later, as the real estate-driven economy collapsed, waiting took place among abandoned and unfinished construction projects marked by a general sense that time had fallen out of joint. The aim of this chapter is to analyze the collusion of space and things in distinct experiences of waiting through a focus on how the city's built-in environment mediated the residents' experience of time. If, as the editors note in the Introduction, waiting emerges as a predisposition, how does this correlate with the radical changes residents experienced in their immediate surroundings? To frame these considerations, I draw on observations and notes from my research on the booms and busts of contemporary Chinese urbanization. The argument put forward in this chapter is based on eight months of fieldwork conducted in the city of Ordos between 2011 and 2014. While the initial period of fieldwork took place in early 2011, during the peak of the city's boom, the rest of it was conducted in 2012 and in 2013, following the sudden collapse of the local economy. I was able to trace the experience of several individuals through the city's boom and bust. Many of those who initially accumulated wealth had assumed urban growth would continue. The bust took them by surprise. Faced with significant financial losses by 2012, they were engaged in precarious and uncertain forms of waiting. I argue that by traversing different scenes of waiting across boom and bust, we may gain insight into the materiality of such temporal dispositions, specifically how temporalities are both felt and made. By attending to the collusion of things implicated in the ways we inhabit meantimes, we may complicate anthropological accounts of waiting time that focus strictly on structural inequalities and illuminate other ways of waiting or related dispositions of anticipating, deterring, or postponing.

The Waiting Bias

Waiting is often held to be a central part of what it means to be human. Franz Kafka's writings bring out the absurdity of endless waiting in bureaucratic systems, while Samuel Beckett's (2011) dramas suggest that the waiting itself may turn out to be all there is. As Dr. Seuss's verse from this chapter's epigraph proposes, we all wait. More philosophically, waiting is part of a general "human condition" in which we are permanently suspended between "past and future" (Arendt in Janeja and Bandak 2018: 1). Regardless of whether we consider it a necessary evil, a most useless place, a revelation about the ultimate meaningless of life, or a meaning-laden space of imaginative potentiality, there is no escaping waiting.

Even though everyone routinely waits, there is a tendency in anthropology and humanistic studies to address waiting in contexts of crisis or precarity. Here, waiting has proved to be not only an important empirical phenomenon but also a useful analytical device to interrogate marginalization and the intolerable conditions experienced by powerless people who are stuck in institutional limbo, forced to rummage for the right paper or stamp, or who find themselves wedged between places of departure and hoped-for destinations (Gaibazzi 2012; Hage 2009; Malkki 1992). Attention to such liminal positions has shed light on prevailing forms of inequality and (im)mobility but it may also have served to generate what I call a "waiting bias," that is, a tendency to ignore experiences of waiting that are not associated with precarity and uncertainty. One purpose of my inquiry into Ordos's various *meantimes*, then, is to spur methodological reflexivity in relation to this bias. In this chapter, therefore, I ask whether waiting still counts as waiting if there is no doubt or uncertainty involved? Is such waiting merely calculated anticipation? And, by implication, is anthropology more prone to analytically valorizing some forms of waiting over others?

Another identifiable feature of the waiting bias is an inclination to locate forms of waiting in relation to structural positions (outside national orders, in between categories or "proper" places). The result is a relative silence on how *concrete* locations, transformations in the environment, or particular objects serve to mediate temporal orientations. Fieldwork in Ordos drew my attention to how particular places and things were generally perceived, populated, and configured as "approximations" of temporal orders (or disorders) (Bjerregaard, Rasmussen, and Sørensen 2016). Scholars have pointed to the active role that things play in *meantimes* by mediating the experience of how one moment anticipates the arrival of another. Focusing on the experiences of mostly young employed young men, Adeline Masquelier (2019) sheds light on a number of everyday objects and rituals that saturate experiences of *idle* time in the *fadas* (sites of sociality) of Niger. Looking beyond common tropes of "stuckedness" (Hage 2009: 97) and marginality, she shows that *fadas* are places for tactical waiting, for establishing relationships, and for appropriating central locations in the city. Yael Navarro-Yashin's (2009) work explores how, in the wake of the 1974 war and subsequent partition of Cyprus, displaced Greek and Turkish Cypriotes were forced to inhabit the homes and live among the belongings of the community construed as the "enemy." Others have documented how broken or decaying everyday objects may serve to suspend, postpone, or deter time (Frederiksen 2019). In Ordos, both boom and bust were strongly experienced as an affect that was generally conveyed through the materiality of things: luxury cars, undeveloped land, real estate, pieces of jotted paper indicating debts owed, and empty spaces that all animated different ways of inhabiting the *meantime*.

In what follows, I show how the meantime in Ordos took widely different forms across boom and bust. First, I outline the high-paced, anticipatory forms of waiting that characterized the city's tremendous economic boom and urban expansion, examining the differences between official temporal maps and the ways in which people create time through material engagements. Second, I discuss places in the city that were closely connected to waiting in the post-boom period: inactive worksites, empty office spaces, and particularly a special office set up to work with debt settlement in informal lending. This period resonates with other ethnographic accounts of waiting in contexts of uncertainty and crisis. In the final section, I disrupt the clear distinction between boom and bust through a focus on the myriad ways in which people inhabited the downturn of the local economy through their occupation of one of the city's high-rises. I show that it was difficult to determine whether the building was under construction or simply decaying and whether people were living in ruins or building a future. I argue that, in the way it permitted people to reconfigure their lives amidst debt and uncertainty, the building was itself a *mean* between boom and bust and a space for reinvention. But first, let me briefly locate the ethnography within a broader historical and geographic setting.

Leapfrogging Development

Anticipating that millions of rural Chinese inhabitants would move to cities in search of opportunities, China began implementing an ambitious master urbanization plan at the turn of the millennium that would reshape the country. As the government rushed to turn massive chunks of the countryside into functioning metropolises, hundreds of new districts, cities, and neighborhoods emerged. Between 2003 and 2014, around 100 billion square feet of floor space was added across China (National Bureau of Statistics of China 2014). Office buildings, residential complexes, monumental infrastructure, and road systems were built at breakneck space, fueling an economic boom that attracted investors. However, the tempo of construction was so rapid that the supply of built space often outpaced in-migration, leaving much of the space unoccupied. The surge of built space relative to population is often described as the main factor in the emergence of "ghost cities"—urban developments whose sprawling commercial and residential complexes, parks, and streets remain startlingly empty. Yet, as we shall see, the surge in construction is but one cause of these real estate debacles.

Kangbashi District, which sits on the edge of the desert, is an example of such hastily planned urban development. Located 27 kilometers southwest of Dongsheng District, it originally consisted of small, scattered settlements and barren lands. Development was supposed to turn it into a bustling district of the city of Ordos, complete with museums, parks, and convention centers. Indeed, the construction boom initially fueled intense activity. Yet, by 2011, the 35-square-kilometer area that had been envisioned as a home for more than one million residents was practically empty—which is how it earned the moniker of "China's modern ghost town."[2] To understand how an urban district that was once dubbed China's answer to Dubai could emerge so rapidly and just as rapidly turn into a ghost city, some context is necessary.

A large part of Ordos's territory is desert. Water resources are generally scarce, creating a serious challenge for farming and urban development (Erdos Urban Development Strategy 2005: 17). But the Ordos Plateau contains large coal and natural gas reserves (ibid. 25). As the demand for energy rose, municipal revenue generated from licenses and taxes in the coal industry alone tripled between 2002 and 2010 (OBS 2011; see also Zhang 2007: 30). Ordos became an energy boomtown. Urban expansion projects, financed by coal profits, further spurred economic growth. Local officials and regional development reports described the city's trajectory as an economic success story that demonstrated a path forward for China's less-developed in-land regions.

In 2001, Ordos underwent an important administrative change when it transitioned from Yeke Juu League (*Yikezhao meng*) to Ordos Municipality (*E'erduosi Shi*), a prefectural-level city. The region had previously been composed of an urban core—Dongsheng District—surrounded by mainly minor rural settlements. Despite spanning a large territory of mostly sparsely populated rural land, the nominal change to Ordos Municipality served to recalibrate the entire region as distinctly urban. The change effectively expanded the local government's regulatory and fiscal ambit, endowing it with the authority to stipulate new construction-friendly policies and effectuate land conversions while enabling new forms of financialization.[3] Lax regulation of the building sector spurred a rash of construction.

The urban built-up areas grew from 16 km^2 in 2000 to 250.21 km^2 in 2012 (Woodworth 2015: 118). The Dongsheng District itself underwent massive transformations as waves of modernization spread across the city. Citizens displaced by urbanization projects and extractive industries were compensated and rehoused in modern apartments in the newly urbanized areas. The most prominent of these areas was the Kangbashi New District. Resource revenues were funneled into comparatively high compensation payments[4] for citizens whose land was being expropriated for the extractive industries or the city's expansion. Officials held up Ordos as a paradigmatic example of how growth and urbanization could be accelerated through a more horizontal distribution of profits from the region's extractive resource industry.

Sensing opportunities, people invested their new wealth in real estate, igniting a frenzied process of speculation that led to overinflated property prices. Lack of financial oversight and regulation enabled a streak of informal lending arrangements. Although the terms of these lending arrangements varied, most were uniformly referred to as *gaolidai*, literally high-interest lending. Thus, rather than being solely the result of a glut of construction, the collapse of the property sector was also intimately linked to a breakdown in these informal lending networks that had come to define the city throughout the 2000s, until the time of the crisis (Woodworth and Ulfstjerne 2016).

Waiting in the Boom

In 2010–11, the Ordos municipal government's party office and board of management released a short promotional video of the municipality's new flagship development, the Kangbashi New District. The video was distributed to future investors and prominent visitors to the city. It was housed in an ornamental cardboard box, the front cover of which featured the words "Kangbashi" written in Chinese and Mongolian characters and "The city of quality" written in English characters. The footage and narrative conveyed a sense of the official temporal articulations of development in Ordos, one that largely coincided with citizens' anticipations of growth in the time of the boom. Let me recap some of the video's highlights.

Approaching from outer space, the gaze of the viewer drifts across ice-covered lands. The camera zooms in on a bronze statue of Genghis Khan. The statue fades slowly, morphing into a burning flame, while a Chinese voiceover narrates the great Khan's cultural legacy and the geological and cultural origins of the Ordos plateau. Pages on a calendar move us forward in time to the sound of a Mongolian string instrument, the Khuuchir (*sihu*). A young woman in Mongolian clothing walks across vast dunes; a single green plant stands out in the yellow sand. The narrator tells of "green dreams" as the vast desert suddenly transforms into a lush forest. Everything blooms. Forests, trees, and small yellow flowers stretch upwards. Once more, the calendar brings us forward. The voice explains how we have now reached a "new era." Planes fly over farmland, modern irrigation systems emerge, and landscapes become greener and lusher.

An urban grid comes into view in the slipstream of a large eagle drifting across Ordos's blue skies. It is the Kangbashi New District. The blueprint magically transforms into a view of the real city. The sound of the Mongolian string instrument fades away, replaced by electronic reggae music. Modern office buildings spring up from the ground. New residential housing, large blue lakes, and busy construction sites appear. People draw, plan, and calculate. A high-speed train cuts across the screen on an elevated railway line. Building cranes stretch toward the sky against orange sunsets. We see science parks, modern industrial sites, airplanes, and children flying kites. Kangbashi manifests itself through both cultural institutions and modern architecture, as captured by the sight of hundreds of tai chi practitioners moving in synchrony in Genghis Khan Square. The narrators continue: "Kangbashi doesn't turn its back on its future generations, nor does it ignore the opportunities to come . . . Modern, green, ecological, civilized, livable. Such perfect environments are not a fairytale here . . . If you imagine a city's development as the growth rings of a large tree, Kangbashi is one of modernization's most beautiful rings." The video concludes with the widely circulating slogan: "City—make life even better" (*chengshi—rang shenghuo geng hao*).

The eleven-minute-long promotional video affords the spectator a glimpse of the developmental rationale underpinning state-led urbanization in Ordos. It depicts a version of time that is progressive—moving forward in calendric time toward ever more developed stages—but also organic in the sense that the envisioned development is somehow naturally connected to the region's cultural and environmental history, its landmarks, and its people. As implied by the image of a large tree's growth rings, development is presented as preordained growth, extending like an inevitable force of nature. There is no indication of rupture or pause; development has taken place smoothly across generations. Having swapped the hardships of rural life for the convenience of urban life, citizens have found their places among modern-day architecture. Meanwhile, references to traditional minority culture (Mongolian string instruments, clothing, Genghis Khan) allude to the harmonious coexistence of ethnic groups in China's frontier regions (Bulag 2010). Technology creates the illusion of urban planning's smooth and undisturbed pace. By tracing development from deserts and barren lands to farmed fields and then modern urban infrastructure, the video suggests that such infrastructure entails massive, yet inescapable changes to the environment. The video collapsed the past and future into the present tense.

The "progress" depicted, however, was not simply conjured up by city officials and real estate prospectors with rich imaginations. Much of the infrastructure was already in place: the poor housing and infrastructural conditions of the Yeke Juu League had in large part been replaced by modern cityscapes and grand infrastructural developments. Before 2000, there were no express roads. By 2009, Ordos had constructed 658 km of public express roads and was one step closer to becoming a central node in a wider metropolitan region that included the urban centers of Baotou and Hohhot. Railway infrastructure showed similar advances. Meanwhile, Ordos Airport, which had been shut since 1983, reopened in 2007 after it was renovated and redesigned in the shape of an eagle hovering over the vast grasslands of Ordos. Other infrastructural advancements included the establishment of industrial zones, cultural infrastructures, and a massive administrative complex in Kangbashi New District. At the time of Kangbashi's inauguration in July 2006, the district included 749 kilometers of underground pipes for water, electricity, Internet, sewerage, gas, and steam heat provision (Woodworth 2015: 126–27).

Infrastructural booms play an important role in mediating the temporal orientation of citizens, though not always in the ways intended (cf. Appel 2018; Gupta 2018; Hetherington 2004; Laszczkowski 2016). As Kregg Hetherington (2004: 42) observes in his study of rural land reform in Paraguay, infrastructures may serve to arrange the present and the future into coherent narratives in an "unfolding anticipation."[5] Unlike the Paraguayan case of land reform, however, the temporal sensibility of infrastructural development in Ordos was not perceived as "a suspended tense." It was not anticipating some different, "better future" (Hetherington 2016: 40; see also Laszczkowski 2016). Instead, it collapsed the open-endedness and uncertainty of the future into what I have elsewhere called the "present continuous" to designate a particular temporal sensibility that implies continuity as the only possible kind of change (Ulfstjerne 2019: 579). It gave citizens a sense that the future was anything but uncertain: "Of course more people will come," was how civil servants working in the new Kangbashi New District often put it. Those who patrolled the mostly empty streets had no doubt about the bustling city life that was almost already there. "It's only a matter of time before we surpass Beijing," a librarian working in the mostly empty five-story Kangbashi library told me.

Although the improved infrastructure and roads were welcomed by local residents, few considered how the city itself would "make life better," as proclaimed in the video. Most of those I met had no intentions of becoming particularly urban or "civilized" (*wenhua*) citizens. What did emerge was an interest in the material and economic gains afforded by development. A common pastime that people took up was surveying increases in real estate prices so they could enter the market at the right moment. This came with the additional benefits of allowing them to participate in new spectacular real estate developments. In many cases, these were developments that had yet to start construction or even be granted building licenses. What was for sale were mostly imaginary apartments in buildings that did not yet exist.

The temporal sensibility of the "present continuous" sparked a rash of speculative property investments between 2001 and 2012. But these investments were far from speculative in the eyes of investors. As one of my closest interlocutors assured me, "buildings—they can never lose value." For these investors, the aim was simply to obtain as much real estate as quickly as possible. This required liquidity. As few had access to sufficient formal banking credit, everyone I knew—even bankers and state employees—would either borrow funds from informal lenders to invest in real estate or deposit private funds into informal lending arrangements with generous returns. In sum, many of these individuals were simultaneously debtors and creditors. Judging from the scores of investments in the real estate sector, the future seemed *certain*. The temporal sensibility made it seem as though waiting time in Ordos was characterized by a strange absence of chance. Radical changes in the built environment of Ordos and the investments they spawned were reflective of the pervasive modality of waiting before the bust.

By 2012, fluctuations in resource prices had severely affected the local economy. The city's burgeoning real estate sector collapsed alongside with the *gaolidai*, the local system of private high-interest loans that had fueled it. Unpaid debts proliferated, leading to an altogether different experience of the meantime.

Waiting in the Post-Boom

I first encountered Mr. Liu, a 26-year-old man, in March 2011 in Honghai, a small rural site from which he would soon be evicted to make space for the city's expansion. Honghai was in the Ejin Horo Banner, an area bordering Kangbashi that would be almost completely rebuilt and modernized in the course of a few years. When I returned less than a year later, I spent a considerable amount of time trying to make contact with Mr. Liu. When I finally reached him, I learned that he had deliberately avoided me as he felt too ashamed to tell me about the financial mess that he was in. I learned that while Mr. Liu had initially been skeptical about forced relocation, he came to appreciate the generous relocation funds he had received from the government. Hoping to secure his future, he decided to invest his new wealth in a development venture. He had been busy enjoying what he termed his "new life" (*xin shenghuo*) when the crisis hit, the developer went bankrupt, and all the money people like him had invested in the venture was lost.

One morning, the two of us visited one of Ordos's new institutions for debt settlement. I wanted to learn more about the impact of so many "failed" new-town projects on the lives of those who had invested in urban development. Mr. Liu had his own reasons for visiting. As we reached the twenty-one-story building, we were greeted by an official signboard that announced the "Dongsheng District's Security Bureau for Striking Down on Illegal Fundraising" (*daji feifa jizi bangongshi*), often just referred to as the "Dafeiban." Although it was still early in the day, the entrance was already filled with people, all of whom hoped to solve their financial problems, whether they owed or were owed money. Initially, Mr. Liu and I stayed away from the crowded entrance. People gathered there were engaged in loud arguments. Many carried purses with paperwork, identification documents, and, as I later learned, small (frequently handwritten) notices that served as lending agreements. As we waited, we observed more people arriving. A few individuals emerged from new luxury vehicles and quickly disappeared into the office's upper sections. The great majority stepped out of cheap Chinese minivans known as "bread trucks" (*mianbao che*). They lived beyond the urban fringe, in newly built high-rise residential areas now occupied by large numbers of landless, resettled peasants.

In China, relatives and close friends commonly pool their savings and funds to invest in ventures offering *gaolidai* (informal high-interest lending), based upon the advice of someone they know or by following the example of others. Earlier that year, Mr. Liu, along with two friends, had decided to invest some of his compensation funds in a coal truck repair service. He had also bought a black Toyota Land Cruiser and was living off the interest coming in from another collective "investment" he and his family had made in a developer's project, a *gaolidai*. After going bankrupt, the developer could no longer disburse interests to Mr. Liu, much less repay the capital. And things got worse for Mr. Liu. Despite the long hours he put into it, the coal truck repair business was losing money. To spare himself the embarrassment of having to inform his family about his financial problems, as well as to save money on transport, Mr. Liu moved into a small shabby room close to his worksite. As he explained it to me:

> Headaches. I can't get my money back. Nothing to do but wait. He [the developer] probably wouldn't even repay us if he had the money. At least, we would surely not be first on the list of people to repay. And there's really nothing I can do. Wait, and wait. If you push a developer too far, he might commit suicide, or run away. And in neither case do you get your money back. It's a difficult balance.

The financial loss Mr. Liu had suffered also meant that he had to postpone his wedding indefinitely, which preoccupied his future parents-in-law.

Mr. Liu had considered every option he could think of to retrieve his investments. He had little confidence that bringing his case to the Dafeiban would help. The constant flow of people stepping out of "bread trucks," the frustration many of them seemed to be feeling, the squabbles that arose in some groups, and the tense atmosphere overwhelmed him. In the end, he decided not to press his case with the Dafeiban and we left.

The sense of a predictable future, so pervasive just months before, had quickly vanished and given way to a sense of helplessness and a form of chronic waiting bordering on inertia. For many, the bust translated into a feeling of being cast back in time; people were often faced with the necessity of doing hard and demeaning labor. The reversal of fortune was felt as a kind of time reversal.

Mr. Liu's trajectory from resettlement to a life as a creditor enjoying high investment returns to financial failure and a return to poverty and uncertainty was an experience shared by many in Ordos at the time. The crowds that gathered daily at the Dafeiban attested to this. While property titles would often be offered as compensation for outstanding debts, creditors typically refused such deals, arguing that they had little use for them in the current market. Many of them were convinced that powerful debtors were hiding their wealth and repaying fake debts or secretly investing funds elsewhere.

The apparently irreversible trajectory of organic growth and escalating property prices had reversed and the uncertainty that had been momentarily clouded by the "present continuous" tense of the infrastructural boom had inverted into a prevailing sense of what Ghassan Hage has termed "stuckedness" (2009: 97). Halted construction expressed the city's predicament, resulting in an eerie silence compared to the 24-7 noise of the boom; fancy architecture in the new district no longer signaled that Ordos had finally caught up with China's coastal regions, but spoke of excess and corruption. Empty apartments no longer translated into future wealth but rather into unpaid debts, irreversible and concrete reminders that families were falling apart.

In March 2013, Mr. Liu introduced me to the two friends who had invested in the "mobile truck repair" joint venture. Located at a dirt road stop off the side of the eastern entry road to Dongsheng, the repair facility mostly serviced coal freight trucks. It consisted of a small van in which Mr. Liu and his friends kept tools and spare parts and a second-hand caravan in which they could stay warm, play cards, eat, and pass the time in between clients. When we arrived, Mr. Liu's two associates rested on a small bed in the rear of the caravan. "Doing nothing really," they explained. At the entrance was a battered coal stove, on top of which the young men cooked meals. To keep the place warm, the windows were covered with homespun insulation materials. Empty bottles and cigarette boxes, oil, tools, and advertisements for spare parts were scattered about. Ever since coal prices had declined the previous year, their business only yielded small sporadic profits. The three men knew they would sell the van, the caravan, and the rest of the equipment at a loss in the current market. They had already been forced to sell some of their repair tools, though they hoped to repurchase them if and when the market turned.

Personal experiences of waiting had their spatial counterparts, often reflecting citizens' class and financial dispositions. The Dafeiban was central to many, but there were others. Petitioning institutions that served as the administrative systems for dealing with citizens' complaints and grievances were flooded with complaints from citizens who had left their homes having been promised free resettlement and high compensation but who had received neither due to developers' bankruptcies. The new institutions with their extraordinary legal measures set up to preempt escalation of debt-related violence and social unrest were concrete locations for the meantime that, in the view of disadvantaged creditors such as Mr. Liu, would most likely lead nowhere. Creditors were stuck, left with no option but to wait or to use extra-legal means to put additional pressure on their debtors. Waiting in the meantime of the post-boom, while almost the inverse of the infrastructural temporality of the boom, paints a bleak picture that resonates with accounts of urban crisis and dispossession.

Waiting in the Coal Tower

Waiting spaces in Ordos, however, were not stably positioned within either boom or bust; some were far more ambiguously situated within a complex geography with differential temporal orientations. A ten-minute walk southwest of the Dafeiban leads you to the Coal Tower, an office building located in the "old" urban core of Ordos, where I regularly met with a group of young entrepreneurs.[6] The tower itself is an ordinary office building. Before the crisis, the units were subleased to scores of small and large enterprises: restaurants, insurance offices, micro-lending companies, IT service stations, a liquor business, and so on. Now the building was largely empty. Though much of the space was crammed with construction materials, no human activity could be detected in the building during working hours. The renovation of many of the floors, initiated during the "Ordos miracle," appeared to have stopped midway through the work, making it difficult to determine whether the units were still undergoing renovation or had gradually fallen into disarray. On the seventh floor, most of the office spaces were vacant, except for one suite that was furnished with expensive office décor: ivory bookcases, a pristine wooden desk displaying a family picture, a large iMac desktop computer. A collection of exhibit samples and advertisements suggested that the company that once leased the space had specialized in high-end Chinese liquor. On almost every floor, messages scribbled on the wall advertised rental space available at a cheap rate. They offered a clue as to how low real estate prices had dropped since the previous year. The eighteenth floor had no tenants—yet another sign of how abrupt and far-reaching the change of fortune had been for many. Toilet facilities had been sealed off, yet one could see traces of excrement everywhere, as well as small pieces of paper and cigarette butts—signaling that the socially stranded made use of the building.

It is tempting to conclude that the Coal Tower vacancies served as an accurate measure of the real estate crisis. Yet a closer look revealed that the building was far from abandoned. I noticed that small improvements had recently been made on some floors. There were also a handful of new subleases, primarily on the ground level, suggesting that, for some people, the building still had some potential.

I visited the Coal Tower several times: on one of my visits, I encountered new leaseholders on the nineteenth floor. One of them was a family from Ordos whose rented space functioned as both a home and an office. They supplied black tea to local shops and kept a small room in their home for private tea tastings. The entire place was nicely furnished. When they went down the top staircase to the lift, the family had to walk across a floor covered with trash and feces, but they seemed to pay little heed to such signs of decay. Though they were reluctant to explain why they had moved there in the first place, the father of the family recounted that leaseholders had met recently and had decided to fund basic maintenance in the building—perhaps in an effort to improve the appearance the floor below.

On the sixth floor, space was unevenly used. On the north side of the building, the offices were mostly empty and no one seemed to be around. The southern side, which had a similar floor plan, was more densely occupied. There, people had transformed the offices into living spaces. One unit featured a double bed complete with colorful linen. A wedding picture sat atop an open cupboard in which clothes were stored, giving the place a homey feel. Next to this unit, a small space had been converted into a dining room and featured small plastic chairs, a table, and a cooking stove. An electric bike was parked next to several large plants in the office hallway in a fashion that was reminiscent of courtyard aesthetics in traditional residences. The occupants, a migrant family from Xian, Shaanxi (central China), had moved in six months previous: a three-year-old boy, his parents, and the boy's grandmother, who was mostly responsible for seeing to the child while parents were chasing—once abundant but now scarce—day-laboring jobs in the service and construction sectors. Like other families living in what were once offices in the Coal Tower, this family had negotiated a low rent for the square footage they had converted into a residential space. Indeed, nearly half of the sixth floor was occupied by families who considered the place their home.

For most of the entrepreneurs who lived and/or worked there in the post-boom era, the Coal Tower was intimately linked to the experience of default loans, failed business ventures, and crushing debts. But for others, the meantime of this space—its liminality—presented an opportunity to reconfigure the space into living and commercial quarters, and in some cases into high-rise migrant worker communities complete with parking space for electric bikes.

The Coal Tower space reflected the *meantime* in two senses of the term: first, it exemplified an oscillating *mean* or middle ground between boom and bust, one that shifted from floor to floor and from one form of occupation to another, and that, for some families, encompassed both retrenchment and recovery in one space. Each floor in the building had a distinct physical and temporal topography: some floors, abandoned and falling into disrepair, were in sync with the general state of the economy, stopped, as it were, in its tracks, while others had been newly reconfigured through combinations of family life and hopeful entrepreneurial ventures. Second, and in line with this edited collection's exploration of the meantime as a space of "the possible," the surfeit of construction brought about by the boom allowed for a radical reconfiguration of surplus office space, with such space being inhabited in entirely new ways, almost echoing Anna Tsing's (2015) exhortation to explore "the possibility of life in capitalist ruins."

Conclusion

In this chapter, I have shown how Ordos residents inhabit the *meantime* on either side of the financial crisis in distinctly spatial terms. During the boom, this was evidenced in the way the vertical and horizontal expansion of the city, the circulating property titles, and the monthly interest payments aided in collapsing the future into the present tense, as if to eradicate any future uncertainty. Such orientations, I have argued, were like the official temporal articulations of the city's "organic" development, as exemplified by the promotional video. In the same way that seemingly irreversible growth was inferred from the environment in the time of Ordos's infrastructural building frenzy, the post-boom waiting was conveyed by the state of urban built forms: high-rises whose construction was halted were labeled *lanweilou*, literally, "buildings with rotten tails," suggesting the failure of the mode of organic development previously hailed local developers and city officials. At Mr. Liu's truck repair site, things played differential roles in the meantime: some things, like cigarettes, magazines, and the deck of cards, helped pass the prolonged stretches of time between trucks. Insulation material and the stove helped the three young men cope with the cold during longer waits. Tools that had been sold off but could potentially return if the market changed occupied a more ambiguous space. As such, Ordos's trajectory from boom to bust provides ample grounds to consider the widely different ways in which *meantimes* are inhabited: from descriptions of the pre-boom time as a standstill characterized by a lack of speed and development to the "Ordos speed," the rapid pace at which the city embarked on its wholesale transformation. This was indeed also a time of the possible. Finally, as the city plunged into crisis, time slowed down again, and for some of my interlocutors, including Mr. Liu, the moment was experienced as an uncomfortable return to the poverty of the pre-boom era.

I have discussed how my interlocutors experienced a return to uncertainty in both spatial and temporal terms, indexing a relapse to the standstill and the kinds of waiting characteristic of life on the periphery of development. The profound reconfiguration of people's temporal and material orientations from boom to bust could partly be understood through the vocabulary of dispossession. But dispossession conveys a feeling of loss rather than the sense of return that interlocutors and friends expressed in their testimonies. Many described the crisis as a retreat to a familiar topography of being or going "nowhere": they were "doing nothing, really."

I have argued that analytical takes on waiting reflect a methodological and disciplinary bias, one that is likely reinforced by our resolve to study waiting in its more precarious forms. Moving into the debt settlements of the post-boom, I entered a terrain that is familiar to readers of anthropologies of waiting and the thwarted future. My fieldnotes at the time were filled with descriptions of endless waiting, despair, violence, debt settlement, and uncertainty that resonate with the anthropological literature on crisis. As Manpreet Janeja and Andrea Bandak (2018: 4) observe, waiting is often dealt with ethnographically through a focus on "the destitute and disadvantaged." Anthropologists have minutely documented how asylum seekers are put on hold or find themselves stuck in perpetual transit, both existentially and physically (Malkki 1992; Missbach 2015). Such a focus has yielded important insights into how marginalized groups are disempowered by contemporary techniques of governance or bureaucracy and sustained in perpetual states of waiting as they turn into "patients of the state" (Auyero 2012; see also Appadurai 2013; Jeffrey 2010; Khosravi 2014). Yet it provides limited understanding of how people inhabit less precarious meantimes. By this measure, the affective atmospheres and anticipations of the *boom* were far more difficult to discern, calling into question whether such dispositions should be understood as waiting at all.

The bias may very well have something to do with the conditions of doing fieldwork. People who wait are more accessible to the anthropologist than those who go from business meeting to business meeting and for whom things tend to turn out as planned. Ethnographic writing may therefore more readily reflect critically upon the precarious *meantime* of the post-boom than the high-paced sociality and *present continuous* tense of the boom. As my discussion of the Coal Tower suggests, however, the spatial and temporal inhabitation of both boom and bust are not entirely preconfigured or absolute. Recalling the diverse forms of occupation that I encountered inside a single office tower, I try to make sense of how the variation does not simply follow what Stef Jansen (2015: 49) has termed "prevailing regimes of temporal reasoning." While Ordos's sudden downturn did not go unnoticed, the range of different ways in which spaces in the tower were occupied may afford glimpses into a more contested topography of meantimes: how different modalities of waiting are distributed across the city and across different groups; how they are experienced and made spatially; and how conflicting dispositions or orientations could coexist.

Michael Alexander Ulfstjerne has a background in anthropology and is currently employed as a part-time lecturer in the Department of Culture and Learning at Aalborg University, Denmark. His research focuses on the emergence of new economies and the resulting spatial effects. His publications cover diverse topics, such as architecture, spatial planning, economic booms and busts, humanitarian innovations, displacement, and margins.

Notes

1. As Jon May and Nigel Thrift (2001) argue, spatial analyses tend to forget about time. Conversely, it seems that the bulk of research into waiting time devotes less attention to the significance of things and space.
2. The term was allegedly first coined in a report by *Al Jazeera* on 10 November 2009. Subsequent research into the Chinese "ghost town" phenomena relates excess urban construction to a variety of phenomena, including informal lending schemes (Woodworth and Ulfstjerne 2016), fiscal and political incentives on the local level (Hsing 2010), and an ideological commitment to urban growth (Bulag 2002).
3. Municipal-level governments increasingly leverage local developments by establishing limited liability companies that can borrow money, and, through reforms of the Chinese bond market, even issue debt (Walter and Howie 2011: 134).
4. According to China's "Land Administration Law," compensation fees for land expropriation include resettlement subsidies, compensation for land, and compensation for produce or crops on the land. This model often calls into question the fairness of compensation because of the significant gaps between levels of compensation and the market value of the land. In Ordos, however, most eviction and new construction happened at a brisk pace due to the high-level compensation commanded by what was later termed "the Ordos model."
5. Kregg Hetherington observes a similarly progressive temporality in both infrastructural development and developmental thinking: "the tense of infrastructure, like any development project, is therefore the future perfect, an anticipatory state around which subjects gather their promises and aspirations" (2016: 40). One central effect of infrastructural developments is the way their linear temporality serves to rearrange different aspects of landscapes into a "natural past and civilized future" (2016: 41–42). This yields effects for the populations who oversee infrastructural upgrades as they exist in what Hetherington terms a "future perfect . . . a suspended tense that will someday have been the past of a better future" (2016: 40).
6. Ethnographic descriptions of the Coal Tower constitute a condensed account of my earlier work on vacancy and excess in China's ghost cities (Ulfstjerne 2017).

References

Appadurai, Arjun. 2013. *The Future as Cultural Fact: Essays on the Global Condition*. New York: Verso Books.
Appel, Hannah. 2018. "Infrastructural Time." In *The Promise of Infrastructure*, ed. Nikhil Anand, Akhil Gupta, and Hannah Appel, 41–61. Durham, NC: Duke University Press.
Auyero, Javier. 2012 *Patients of the State: The Politics of Waiting in Argentina*. Durham, NC: Duke University Press.
Beckett, Samuel. 2011. *Waiting for Godot: A Tragicomedy in Two Acts*. New York: Grove Press.
Bjerregaard, Peter, Anders Emil Rasmussen, and Tim Flohr Sørensen. 2016. *Materialities of Passing*. Farnham: Ashgate.
Bulag, Uradyn E. 2002. "From Yeke-Juu League to Ordos Municipality: Settler Colonialism and Alter/native Urbanization in Inner Mongolia." *Provincial China* 7(2): 196–234.
——. 2010. *Collaborative Nationalism: The Politics of Friendship on China's Mongolian Frontier*. New York: Rowman & Littlefield Publishers.
Casey, Edward. 2009. *Getting Back into Place: Toward a Renewed Understanding of the Place-World*. Bloomington: Indiana University Press.
Erdos Urban Development Strategy. 2005. *The Erdos Urban Region Development Strategy: A Report to the Municipal People's Government of Erdos*. Developed in collaboration with The World Bank (EASUR) and The Cities Alliance and prepared by Chreod Ltd, www.chreod.com.
Frederiksen, Martin Demant. 2019. "In the House of Un-Things: Decay and Deferral in a Vacated Bulgarian Home." In *Repair, Brokenness, Breakthrough: Ethnographic Responses*, ed. Francisco Martínez and Patrick Laviolette, 73–86. New York: Routledge.
Gaibazzi, Paolo. 2012. "God's Time Is the Best: Religious Imagination and the Wait for Emigration in The Gambia." In *The Global Horizon: Expectations of Migration in Africa and the Middle East*, ed. Knut Graw and Samuli Schielke, 121–35. Leuven: Leuven University Press.
Gupta, Akhil. 2018. "The Future in Ruins: Thoughts on the Temporality of Infrastructure." In *The Promise of Infrastructure*, ed. Nikhil Anand, Akhil Gupta, and Hannah Appel, 62–79. Durham, NC: Duke University Press.
Hage, Ghassan, ed. 2009. *Waiting*. Carlton South: Melbourne University Press.
Hetherington, Kregg. 2016. "Surveying the Future Perfect: Anthropology, Development and the Promise of Infrastructure." In *Infrastructures and Social Complexity: A Routledge Companion*, ed. Penny Harvey, Casper Bruun Jensen, and Atsuro Morita, 40–50. London: Routledge.
Hsing, You-tien. 2010. *The Great Urban Transformation: Politics of Land and Property in China*. Oxford: Oxford University Press.
Janeja, Manpreet K., and Andreas Bandak, eds. 2018. *Ethnographies of Waiting: Doubt, Hope, and Uncertainty*. New York: Bloomsbury.
Jansen, Stef. 2015. *Yearnings in the Meantime: "Normal Lives" and the State in a Sarajevo Apartment Complex*. New York: Berghahn Books.

Jeffrey, Craig. 2010. *Timepass: Youth, Class, and the Politics of Waiting in India*. Stanford, CA: Stanford University Press.
Khosravi, Shahram. 2014. "Waiting." In *Migration: A COMPAS Anthology*, ed. Bridget Anderson and Michael Keith, 66–67. Oxford: COMPAS.
Laszczkowski, Mateusz. 2016. *City of the Future: Built Space, Modernity and Urban Change in Astana*. Oxford: Berghahn Books.
Malkki, Liisa H. 1992. "National Geographic: The Rooting of Peoples and the Territorialization of National Identity among Scholars and Refugees." *Cultural Anthropology* 7(1): 24–44.
Masquelier, Adeline. 2019. *Fada: Boredom and Belonging in Niger*. Chicago: University of Chicago Press.
May, Jon, and Nigel Thrift, eds. 2001. *Timespace: Geographies of Temporality*. Abingdon, UK: Routledge.
Missbach, Antje. 2015. *Troubled Transit: Asylum Seekers Stuck in Indonesia*. Singapore: ISEAS-Yusof Ishak Institute.
National Bureau of Statistics of China. 2014. *China Statistical Yearbook*. http://www.stats.gov.cn/tjsj/ndsj/2014/indexeh.htm.
Navarro-Yashin, Yael. 2009. "Affective Spaces, Melancholic Objects: Ruination and the Production of Anthropological Knowledge." *Journal of the Royal Anthropological Institute* 15(1): 1–18.
OBS. 2011. *E'erduosi Tongji Nianjian 2011* [Ordos Statistical Yearbook 2011]. Ordos: Ordos Bureau of Statistics.
Tsing, Anna L. 2015. *The Mushroom at the End of the World: On the Possibility of Life in Capitalist Ruins*. Princeton, NJ: Princeton University Press.
Ulfstjerne, Michael A. 2017. "The Tower and the Tower—Excess and Vacancy in China's Ghost Cities." In *Emptiness and Fullness: Imaginaries of Lack and Dynamics of in Contemporary China*, ed. Susanne Bregnbæk and Mikkel Bunkenborg, 67–84. Oxford: Berghahn Books.
———. 2019. "Iron Bubbles: Exploring Optimism in China's Modern Ghost Cities." *HAU: Journal of Ethnographic Theory* 9(3): 579–95.
Walter, Carl E., and Fraser J. T. Howie. 2011. *Red Capitalism: The Fragile Financial Foundation of China's Extraordinary Rise*. Hoboken, NJ: Wiley.
Woodworth, Max D. 2015. "City Profile: Ordos Municipality: A Market-Era Resource Boomtown." *Cities* 43: 115–32.
———. 2019. "Boomtown in Ruins: Ordos and Ruination." International Institute for Asian Studies, Newsletter, Spring (28). https://www.iias.asia/the-newsletter/article/boomtown-ruins-ordos-ruination.
Woodworth, Max D., and Michael A. Ulfstjerne. 2016. "Taking Part: The Social Experience of Informal Finance in Ordos, Inner Mongolia." *Journal of Asian Studies* 75(3): 649–72.
Zhang, Zhanlin. 2007. *Shouru Kuozhang Zhong de Difang Caizheng Kunnan: Shizheng Lunyao* [Difficulties of local finance amid increasing income: A discussion of evidence]. Beijing: Minzhu yu jianshe chubanshe [Democracy and reconstruction publishing house].

Entretemps

"A Lot of Standing Around in the Dark"
Specters of Waiting in Paranormal Research

Misty L. Bastian

Harold Schweizer tells us, "The very familiarity of waiting has obscured it. Its uselessness has made it an economic liability. Its unpredictability has rendered waiting the precarious condition for unexpected self-encounters. Nobody likes to wait" (Schweizer 2008: 15). This meditation on waiting frames the discussion of waiting in paranormal research below. Paranormal researchers, however, might take issue with Schweizer's dictum that "nobody likes to wait." The pleasure to be had from waiting is very much the point in paranormal research work, as I hope to demonstrate below.

"You want to know what it's like to be a ghost hunter?" Jon grinned, first at the digital recorder on the table between us and then directly at me. "Well, it's a lot of standing around in the dark, waiting for something to happen." Jon was not the first paranormal researcher to tell me this, but he was probably the most genial. Turning what most of my interviewees would say into a joke was very much his style—which did not, however, mean that Jon saw the practice he described in a frivolous way. Standing around in the dark was serious business in paranormal research, as was the waiting that scripted posture and temporality implied. It was also mundane, often boring, and a space for joking behavior among researchers. Every ghost hunter has to stand around in the dark; every ghost hunter has to wait—but so, in a sense, does every ghost. Neither the living nor the dead are immune to what Harold Schweizer above calls "the precarious condition for unexpected self-encounters."

I have been engaged in ethnographic research with paranormal researchers (ghost hunters, in everyday parlance) throughout the 2010s.

In that period, I interviewed over two hundred researchers in the Mid-Atlantic region of the United States and carried out participant observation with the researchers during formal and informal ghost hunts, "ghosting" conferences, ghost tourism events, and more ordinary social activities (like Halloween and birthday parties with a paranormal theme). I have traveled with the researchers and I have visited them in their private homes. I have also stood around in the dark with them for hours on end, waiting to see/hear/smell/feel something that might be characterized as ghostly. Which brings me to the questions I will concern myself with in this brief interlude: what happens when paranormal researchers wait, and what sorts of "unexpected self-encounters" ensue when the waiting bears fruit? What kind of possibilities does the meantime afford to those who make waiting their business, and often, their vocation (in the Weberian sense), as they seek contact with ghosts?

Most paranormal researchers I have met are patient people when it comes to their "work in the field," as they like to describe ghost hunting. Serious researchers tend to be meticulous and precise: setting up technological equipment with great care, taping down meters and meters of electrical cords so that people will not trip over them after the lights go out, using digital, infrared cameras that offer the maximum coverage of the space of investigation, envisioning all parts of the space like a stage manager with his stage, directing one another in relation to exactly where to stand and how to move through the set-up space economically and effectively. Handheld devices are used deliberately, batteries stowed in pockets or backpacks for quick access as needed, and the parameters of the research are agreed upon beforehand so that everyone in the team has a task, or a group of tasks, to perform once the waiting begins—for the wait for spiritual connection is not passive and it has its disciplines and techniques. This is, indeed, hunting in its oldest sense: social in nature, well planned, deeply prepared, and characterized by vigilant waiting. For, as in the ancient art of hunting, the devil is in every detail, and the hunters may only get one shot at their swift-moving prey.

Schweizer opines that "[n]obody likes to wait," as I noted above, but that is not particularly true in the context of paranormal research (or, one suspects, hunting of the more usual sort across the United States). The temporality of hunting and waiting is filled with sensations and meaning. Once the technology and the researchers are in place, standing around in the dark has a rhythm. The artificial lights go out, excepting some on the non-visible spectrum, and people begin to make themselves comfortable, preparing to wait effectively. There are certain conventions to be observed: people may identify themselves, by voice, on digital recorders that now stand ready to record any slight noise; they may cough softly and shuffle their feet, finding the right position in which to stand; they may make a few joking remarks, "lightening" the atmosphere and shaking off any nervousness. Soon, however, the milieu becomes more professional and largely silent, except for the attempts of permitted, authoritative speakers to summon or invoke a spectral presence by rote query. ("If anyone is here, we would love to speak with you tonight. Please don't be afraid to come near, to touch us, or to talk into the red lights on these small boxes.")

Unless paranormal researchers are doing EVP work—that is, asking spirits direct questions and giving them space to whisper or to speak into the digital recorders—standing around in the dark is pretty much what it sounds like. A researcher holds out his/her handheld device or operates a camera and waits. This waiting is freighted with significant silence, since even ordinary breathing can be readily detected on the recording devices all around. The waiting is also freighted with significant expectation. Any untoward noise or movement will require the group to pivot in the direction of the disturbance, and attention will be instantly centered on whatever seems to be anomalous. (Indeed, for some paranormal researchers, any hint of ghostliness is referred to as "an anomaly.") Waiting together helps the group to cohere and to develop the capacity to make this pivot. One "centers" oneself during the wait, readying oneself for that brief possibility of contact or engagement.

Darkness is not an absolute requirement for paranormal research, nor is quietude, but both are thought to be particularly helpful because spirit communication is so ephemeral, contingent, and downright elusive. Few researchers have been privileged to see ghosts (the "full body apparition" is considered to be the greatest, and the most wished-for, rarity in the field), so they do not usually choose to depend on sight as the primary sense for experience. Taking away sight through darkness enables the other senses to attune during the waiting period, especially hearing and touch. Waiting opens the sensorium, usually too dependent on vision in the view of most paranormal researchers, and prepares it for a broader reception of whatever might come.

Sometimes—but not always—something happens while ghost hunters stand around in the dark. This "something" might be a small sound or a light touch on the arm of a researcher; it could be a glimpse of a shadow in the ambient light; it might be the welcomed ping of a motion sensor or a cascade of lights on the K-2 (a handheld object that measures fluctuations in electromagnetic energy). Such short interruptions of the waiting cause the researchers to momentarily forget their weary feet and aching backs. Everyone galvanizes into action, trying to encourage a repeat of the anomalous event or an extension of it. ("Please walk by that black box with the green light on top of it again." "If you can, come close to this little box with the green light on it, here in my hand, and see if you can make the lights change colors.") When the purported spirit performs, the quiet, meditative waiting ceases and another sort begins: an anxious and even more purposive waiting, with researchers hoping to see another anomaly or to be drawn further into the drama of communication. What usually happens is that there is a cessation of action in a very short time and a return to standing around in the dark, preparing for the next opportunity. Eventually, the researchers decide (non-ironically) that "the room is dead" and discuss which space would be fruitful to try next. With good-natured jokes and comments about the experience, flashlights are lit, they move on, and the work begins again.

Many of the ghost hunters with whom I spoke over the years admitted to being quite bored during parts of their investigations, but said that the boredom is "the price you pay" for those moments of excitement and engagement with what may—or may not—be ghosts. For them, boredom is transactional and productive; one reaps rewards from it that far surpass the small pain associated with it. They do not try to mask the boredom by checking their phones, moving their bodies, humming, or engaging in any of the hundreds of other mannerisms we all cultivate to distract ourselves in more ordinary moments. The paranormal researchers spend considerable amounts of time and money in preparation before they find themselves in a space where they may do their research with other members of their group. They often talk about how hard it has been to wait for the evening of the ghost hunt to begin, how much they have looked forward to it, and how ardently they have planned to spend the night standing around in the dark in a hopefully haunted location. When they are there, at last, even the boredom of research is prized because it is part of the expected narrative of ghost hunting. An impatient researcher will, in those narratives, invariably miss some important clue or ignore a tentative gesture on the part of his/her quarry. Boredom done right, however, will keep the researcher on point and ready for any challenge. (As one researcher, acting as a docent at a staged ghost event, told a bored teenager who kept trying to take out his phone and look at it: "You can stare at your phone and text your friends anytime! How often do you get to try to talk to eighteenth-century soldiers?")

Distraction is also perceived as disrespect on the part of paranormal researchers, and disrespect is anathema to convincing spirits to communicate. The dead, in the cosmology of American ghost hunting, have plenty to do, and ghost hunters must approach them as they would any busy person from whom they would like a favor. The dead are not sitting around (or lying around in their graves), waiting for researchers to engage with them. They are, rather, going about their personal business—often not realizing that they are dead—which researchers interrupt with their questions, their technological equipment, and even their inappropriate futurity. The least paranormal researchers can do, in that sense, is to give the dead the benefit of their focused attention for the short period the researchers take out of their everyday lives to attempt communication. (This also has to do with a deeply ingrained feeling, expressed by ghost hunters I have spoken to, that the dead deserve respect for having lived their lives and having finished with them. The Africanist in me sees this as a form of ancestor veneration—and no African person in his/her right mind would act bored with his/her ancestors when those ancestors have chosen to give him/her their attention.)

The twist in this tale, of course, is that the cosmology of American ghost hunters suggests that the condition of death can become one of constant waiting: not so much in purgatory or some other, Christian liminality, but in a misguided, stuck sense of waiting. Ghosts are people who have not "moved on," in the parlance of paranormal research. They also stand around in the dark and sometimes try to communicate with the living, who are able to move more freely in time and through space. They use whatever energy sources are available to them to become temporarily more tangible or more audible, sometimes even more visible, to enter again into the world of motion and sensation that draws them back. They can no longer make memories to enjoy in their spare time; they have become memories in a temporality that is endless and in which waiting is endemic because unconscious for them. The dead no longer know what they are waiting for, in short, as they ceaselessly walk up and down the same stairway or seek to touch those bright, ephemeral beings who traverse rooms that are no longer furnished with familiar objects or lit by recognizable light sources.

Paranormal researchers hope that standing around in the dark will enable them to reach across the boundaries between the living and the dead, as they go willingly into the dark and stand there with their dead companions, waiting for a moment of recognition and reaching for a thread of communication. In a sense, therefore, every ghost hunt is a descent into the space of death. Yet that space is a multivalent space, with coexisting temporalities that make the encounter both fraught and sought for. It is not just that the signs of a ghostly presence mean that the past is not at all past. In a more prosaic sense, the wait for immaterial others is a suspension of the everyday present. It is a carefully constructed time-space, with instruments and techniques that help produce the wait. It is also a space where busyness is overlaid with bored stillness and uncertainties about what is and what is not. Far from being a suspension of time, the wait is an overfilled temporality. Paranormal researchers make it clear that boredom is sought rather than dismissed, for it is the price to pay for being contacted by ghosts. In this sense, the waiting is not time to be "suffered" but time to be "made" with the tools, bodily discipline, and patient anticipation one brings to that space.

Whatever suspense and anticipation paranormal researchers experience are directed not at the future but at the past. While researchers wait for the reanimation of the past, they also bring equipment along to record the experience and to keep their fingers firmly on the markers of life (light, sound, movement, will). And this may be one reason why researchers like to end every ghost hunt with an admonition: something along the lines of, "Thank you for speaking with us tonight, but please don't follow us from here. Where we are going isn't your place; it's ours." Paranormal researchers know that the period spent standing in the dark is of a limited duration, and that the world of life is waiting for them to resume their quotidian activities once they close and lock the doors of the haunted house behind them.

Misty L. Bastian is the Lewis Audenreid Professor of History & Archaeology, Emerita at Franklin & Marshall College. She has conducted research in Nigeria and, more recently, on ghost hunting in the United States. Her work in Nigeria is wide-ranging, focused on issues of gender, witchcraft, and the complicated kinships of Mami Wata, as well as the lively Nigerian popular press. She coauthored *The Women's War of 1929: Gender and Violence in Colonial Nigeria* (Palgrave Macmillan, 2012) with Marc Matera and Susan Kingsley Kent and edited *Great Ideas for Teaching about Africa* (Lynne Rienner, 1999) with Jane L. Parpart.

References

Schweizer, Harold. 2008. *On Waiting*. Abingdon: Routledge.

Chapter 3

Raising Consciousness in the Costa Rican Seasonal Low

Sabia McCoy-Torres

Introduction

I chose a seat that allowed me to complete the circular formation of those already sitting and chatting. Christian had stepped away from "Take It Easy," his self-owned and self-operated food stand, and invited me over to where he was sitting with friends. The workday was slow. The calm was characteristic of the low season in Puerto Viejo, a beach town on the Caribbean coast of Costa Rica where the economy depends on tourism. Christian lit a *puro*, a marijuana-filled cigarette most often hand-rolled in hemp paper. Though I was not participating in the smoking session, Christian frequently attempted to pass the *puro* to me in order to include me in the community he was cultivating with those present.

The conversation grew increasingly analytical as the *puro* made its way around the circle. It shifted from the recounting of banal events of the day to the interpreting of the significance of those events to plans people were making for their lives and speculation about their futures. Between pulls of the *puro*, the seated friends commented on the ramifications of a growing tourist industry and swelling numbers of Central Valley Costa Ricans and foreign expatriates living in town. Together, they crafted meaning out of quotidian social and economic dynamics, creating epistemologies of the everyday. In the process, they engaged in a practice I refer to as "raising consciousness," from the Rastafarian maxim that "you hafi [have to] raise up yuh consciousness," an expression that advocates for producing knowledge and participating in social theorization to achieve personal enlightenment. Accordingly, adherents to Rastafarian ("Rasta") thought celebrate being "full up of consciousness" or fully enlightened.

Smoking marijuana, also referred to as ganja, is sometimes used as a ritual aid in opening pathways for raising consciousness. On various occasions during the indeterminate and economically precarious periods of waiting that characterize the low season, I observed people smoking by themselves. Through ganja's psychic stimulation, they embarked on mental sojourns away from the artisan stands where they sat waiting for patrons who rarely came by. While marijuana consumption and the resulting processes of raising consciousness are practices that people partake in all year round, they become more visible and take on a distinct significance during the low season, when ebbs in commerce suddenly create vast pockets of time for social and economic contemplation. The social and economic vulnerabilities of the low season intersect with other temporal challenges and promises that locals are compelled to navigate.

This chapter examines the convergence, divergence, and ultimately the suspension and reframing of temporalities demarcating the lives of residents of Puerto Viejo, a fishing and cacao-farming village that has become a tourist hub in Limón Province. I discuss how raising consciousness enables people of African descent, who make up a large portion of the town's population, to reflect on the forms of agency, economic dispossession, self-avowal, and value(-lessness) that arise from the different temporalities they inhabit. Raising consciousness allows people to assume power by producing knowledge about the contingencies of temporal, social, and economic challenges. It is a practice that reframes the temporalities governing their lives, suspending the specific challenges that arise within them. Raised consciousness is often shared through diverse discursive practices—for example, through song or sharing the outcomes of one's theorizing with engaged listeners. These "outcomes," the "fruits" of one's intellectual labor in these downtimes, reimagine, rearrange, and restructure the position of Afro-descendants in the historical and present imagination in agentive ways.

In what follows, I discuss historical, present, development, seasonal, and Rasta temporalities. Historical temporality refers to the long history of Afro-Caribbean social marginalization and economic exclusion in Costa Rica. It collides with development temporality, the efforts more recently dedicated to the (predominantly touristic) development of Puerto Viejo. In theory, development time is oriented toward the future and ought to connect to it as it promises material and economic transformations in the lives of those most immediately impacted by its unfolding. Yet, development temporality in Puerto Viejo diverges from the promised future as it brings into sharp relief the realization that these promises will not be fulfilled. Development time is therefore time deferred and, as such, it reproduces past structural inequalities that have disproportionately affected Afro-Caribbean people. Development temporality further produces seasonal temporality, the tourism-dependent cycle of high and low seasons that keeps the economic livelihood of residents of Puerto Viejo constantly in flux.

During the low season, Rasta temporality comes into play. Rasta temporality is characterized by a suspension of notions of progressive time, what could be called *chronos*—time measured based on its chronological passing and using a determinate set of units. From this suspension emerges a more peaceful mode of dwelling in the present, through a focus on *kairos*—time measured by its quality. The construction of this temporality, which I call "Rasta temporality," is intimately linked to raising consciousness. Rasta temporality, in many ways, is a suspended timeframe that is disconnected from historical, development, and seasonal temporalities but that attempts to bring them together by theorizing them through raising consciousness. As such, it hangs delicately in the balance. As people raise consciousness and inhabit Rasta temporality, it becomes evident that they do not anticipate any real changes in the future. This perspective reveals the mutual contingencies of Rasta, historical, development, seasonal, and future temporalities.

This chapter explores how people raise consciousness to navigate and attempt to bring into balance the unique challenges of each temporality, attain mental peace, and turn themselves into agentive subjects. There are a number of theoretical inquiries bundled into this examination. It is first an effort to examine how people mobilize spiritual epistemologies for agentive subjectivity formation. Second, it is an elaboration of previous interpretations of the culturally specific ways in which time is negotiated (Munn 1992; Ralph 2008). In other words, I revisit how time is reorganized into "different representations and activity rhythms" (Munn 1992: 95), particularly representations and rhythms that validate one's existence. In the reading of time and value offered here, validation is found in the meaning-making systems of Rasta that reorient how temporarily unemployed or underemployed laborers situate themselves in and against the world around them—specifically, how they do so in such a way that they have dynamic affective experiences that bring forth different valuations of self and time. In turn, I conceptualize how raising consciousness, which is often preceded by smoking marijuana, is a form of "creative action" (Graeber 2001) that critiques representations of value and labor under capitalism (Elson 1979) and gives meaning to the emptiness of free time (Adorno 1991).

My work tracks the experiences of the unemployed or barely employed whose temporalities clash with capitalist orderings of time and value (Cole and Durham 2008; Denning 2010; Ferguson 2015; Jeffrey 2010; Li 2014; Mains 2013; Millar 2014; Stewart 1996; Weiss 2009). Discursive and social ritual practices are invented to manage moments of economic crisis and create value (Jeffrey 2010; Ralph 2008; Willis 1977; Cole and Durham 2008; Comaroff and Comaroff 2001). I show how people in Puerto Viejo adjust their relationship to time and socially constructed conceptions of lack and value by converting them through transformative praxis into time for self-affirmation. Workers there make use of "dead time" by fashioning subjectivities that highlight their participation in the construction of their reality. They do so by reconfiguring their orientation to the various temporalities that inform dead time. It is this process that characterizes Rasta temporality.

In this chapter, I first connect the low season to historical temporality and show how both have given rise to the very purposeful Rasta temporality during which people raise consciousness in response to social and economic discordances arising from the convergence of temporalities. As we will see, raising consciousness aims to manage the different sentiments that these temporalities produce in the present. I also examine discourse that centers subjects as agents in their "overstanding." The conversion of "understanding" into "overstanding" in the Rasta vernacular plays with the geographic metaphor at work in the latter word. "Overstanding" conveys that one is never *beneath* the unequal social, economic, and political dynamics that are Rastafarianism's epistemological focus, collectively referred to as the conditions of "Babylon" imposed by the "Babylon system"—oppressive histories, institutions, political forces, and their agents. Instead, *raising* consciousness fosters a broader, elevated perspective—a meta-level view of the social, cultural, economic, and even political dynamics from which quotidian life emerges, insisting on the possibility of *over*standing them. Overstanding, the outcome of raising consciousness, reclaims the present and one's place within it. It is an intellectual and discursive navigation of historical temporality and place within a global history of disenfranchisement upon which the present is contingent.

I contend that, ultimately, constructing Rasta temporality through raising consciousness to reach overstanding is a process and practice of overcoming aimed at inhabiting a more peaceful, valued, and quality present. But overstanding in the present anticipates the deferment and disappointment of development temporality because a part of what is "overstood" is that changes accompanying development will not result in a transformation of the material reality, the everyday experience, or the social or economic position of the locals themselves. The peace Rasta temporality offers is rooted in the power derived from having control over one's internal and spiritual state despite these circumstances. Here I invoke Audre Lorde's (2012) use of the spiritual to capture a sense of wellbeing that is derived from refusing to be negated, from self-recognition, self-love, and autonomy. Rasta temporality offers a sense of peace through the acceptance that one does not have the power to define the structural and temporal relations to which one is subject, though one does indeed have the agency to define how one will relate spiritually, psychically and emotionally to them—an exercise in autonomy and subjectivity making. Rasta temporality, thus, could be thought of as a form of radical acceptance of what cannot easily be changed while exercising what can be, namely, how one thinks and feels about it. Yet, it is a radical acceptance that evades hopelessness, as accepting what cannot be changed might seem to convey. Hope is alive in Rasta temporality. This hope is underpinned by the belief that if unequal relations can be unmasked and understood, their rearrangement becomes a possibility, even if it does not happen in one's own lifetime. That is what it means to "chant down Babylon"—to call attention to inequality and its origins to facilitate its deconstruction and bring forth new relations and socio-economic conditions.

Reasons and Seasons

During the high season, Puerto Viejo is abuzz with activity. There are shoppers in front of stands and surfers carrying their boards down streets. Traffic stops as motorists and cyclists attempt to navigate past each other and pedestrians walking on the road because the sidewalks, constructed long before such demographic density could be anticipated, cannot accommodate the high-season crowds. Restaurant and bar staff quickly move about their workspaces to attend to the overwhelming flow of patrons. The music from open-air businesses only barely drowns out the loud voices of patrons. All businesses are open. On weekends and most weeknights, locals join the tourists in bars and the town's small open-air nightclubs, especially early in the month after people have been paid. There is money circulating and fun to be had.

In contrast, during the *temporada baja* (low season), activities come to an abrupt stop. In the absence of movement, time also seems to stop. Sound dissipates and absences are cast in high relief—the absence of people, cars, traffic, noise, and movement, all of which reflect an absence of income. A sleepiness inundates Puerto Viejo. This drowsiness is visible on the face of the fruit vendor who sits in his chair, leaning against a tree in slumber. It is illustrated by the teens who sit on the very same wooden tables that, during the high season, are covered with craft items abundantly on display for the bustling flows of passing tourists. Whereas in the high season visitors to the Saturday green market must squeeze their way through a dense sea of tourists to peruse the produce and artisanry displayed on stands, during the low season, the market is nearly empty. Open-air bars and restaurants are also quiet and empty. Their staff look bored, sitting with their elbows perched on countertops. Locals make up most of the clientele. The low season unequivocally means an absence of business. There is no labor to fill people's time and keep them engaged. Employers have two options: they can maintain overstaffed shifts at the end of which workers must split already slim tips between themselves—a course of action few enjoy as the income is generally not worth the boredom that must be endured. The other option is to cut workers' hours. Idle workers thus loiter in the sleepy streets, looking for ways to create value or revel in *Kairos*—time measured by its quality—despite the temporal and economic precarity of the low season.

Locals also look for ways to materially manage the economic limitations and seasonal fluctuations that are a regular part of life in Puerto Viejo. Twenty-three-year-old Firu adjusts to businesses' seasonal closures and constrained schedules by having multiple jobs. He works mornings at a restaurant that is open during those hours and heads to another establishment for the lunch or dinner-time shifts. Bar and restaurants owners often alternate their opening days or hours to reduce competition and spread modest low-season incomes between them. Christian chooses to set up Take It Easy, his roadside Caribbean food operation, only on weekends when nationals from the Central Valley might still choose to vacation in town. On other days, he picks up hours DJing at bar-restaurants or provides informal contract services to businesses, performing miscellaneous tasks and errands for a fee. Others informally supply goods to locals—for instance, selling gasoline out of their homes to save people a trip to the neighboring town, where the only gas station is located. The sale of narcotics is also impacted by the fluctuating numbers of tourists in town. Demand remains relatively consistent among locals, however, making the drug economy an attractive alternative to the formal economy.

To pass time in the *temporada baja*, people sit and chat, young people play soccer on the beach or can be found in the town's basketball court, women sit on porches watching their children play on the roadside. The shift between the low season and the high season signals uneven development that goes beyond the contemporary configurations. Those who navigate the seasonal shift have become vulnerable to time and its fluctuations. Puerto Viejo's susceptibility to the temporal highs and lows of the tourist season is only partially related to the tropical forests and pristine beaches that dot the coastal landscape and now draw tourists. These temporal shifts—and the various economic vulnerabilities they engender—are also the consequence of the contentious history of Afro-Caribbean labor migration to Costa Rica.

This labor migration spanned half a century, beginning with the construction of the Atlantic Railroad in 1871 (to transport coffee from the Central Valley to the port city of Limón and onward toward Europe) and continuing with the establishment of commercial banana cultivation (under the leadership of Minor Keith, an American businessman who founded the United Fruit Company after being granted 800,000 hectares of land in the region). The influx of migrants—upon which banana farming depended—began to slow in the mid-1930s when the United Fruit Company (UFC) left Limón Province and relocated its banana industry to the Pacific coast (Harpelle 1993). Until then, the UFC had imported West Indian, primarily Jamaican, laborers to the previously unsettled province. Afro-Caribbean laborers and their families lived in an isolated political, economic, and social enclave that encompassed the entire province and was under the full jurisdiction of the UFC. The UFC's departure left Afro-Caribbean residents, who had settled in the region more than sixty years previous, without employment, infrastructure, or basic rights. The Costa Rican government did not recognize them as citizens. It made the legal process to prove eligibility for citizenship even for those born in the country so challenging and the criteria for naturalization for those who had emigrated from the West Indies so difficult to meet that the situation amounted to a denial of citizenship (Foote 2004; Harpelle 1993, 2001; Murillo Chaverri 2006). Afro-Caribbean people endured restrictions on their movements outside Limón Province and discriminatory hiring practices, which the government implemented in response to anti-Blackness and concerns over labor competition in the Central Valley and Pacific regions. These measures perpetuated Limón's economic and social isolation from the rest of the country and marked the beginning of its underdevelopment (Chomsky 1996; Harpelle 2000; Purcell 1993; Purcell and Sawyers 1993).

As a consequence of the travel ban, Afro-Caribbean people were left to establish towns on their own on Limón's coast (Murillo Chaverri 2006; Putnam 2006), including Puerto Viejo. They developed subsistence farming, trade and commerce, and a bartering economy that operated outside the purview of the state until well into the 1970s. The state's eventual incorporation of Limón into the national economy was slow and uneven (Chomsky 1996; Harpelle 2001; Murillo Chaverri 1996; Purcell 1993). Electricity did not arrive in Puerto Viejo until the late 1980s. In the 1990s, tourists began to trickle into Puerto Viejo as Costa Rica oriented its economy toward tourism. Today, Puerto Viejo is a thriving tourist destination. Though it holds much appeal for surfers, eco-tourists, and expatriates in search of exoticism, the beauty of the place is entangled in its history of inequity. For instance, Puerto Viejo's dependency on tourism and the lack of economic diversification are evidence of the state's disinterest in the wellbeing of its residents and its economic development beyond tourism. Within this milieu, development temporality and its deferment are brought into focus.

Development temporality is a utopic one in which everyone reaps the rewards of tourism, coastal development, Limón's incorporation into the nation at large, and global capitalism. For the residents of Puerto Viejo, particularly Afro-Caribbeans who lack the extra-national economic ties that expatriates rely on and the generational wealth or middle-class economic status that many Central Valley transplants enjoy, development time is time deferred. It is defined as a moment that has not yet arrived—and may in fact never arrive. The fact that some homes in Puerto Viejo still do not have interior access to running water reflects the limits of development and the lack of improvements with the passing of time.

Puerto Viejo is located in the canton of Talamanca, one of the six cantons that make up Limón Province. According to 2011 census data, 47 percent of Talamanca's residents lived in poverty—a strikingly higher rate of poverty than in the other cantons. Indeed, the poverty rate in Talamanca is more than three times what it is in San José canton and double what it is in Pacific coastal cantons that are themselves home to tourism-dependent beach towns. In 2011, the unemployment rate in Cahuita, Puerto Viejo's district, was 4.7 percent. This figure did not differ greatly to the figures for other districts.[1] The data, however, do not account for seasonal changes, particularly the rising levels of unemployment during the low season. It can be inferred from Talamanca's seasonally fluctuating employment figures that, when it is available, employment frequently fails to sustain a life out of poverty.

What comes into view are incommensurable temporal tales with promises that contradict everyday lives. A history of Afro-Caribbean exclusion has led to a present in which they are still marginalized. A time of development has been entered into, but the material experiences of those who are a part of its passing change minimally. The high season's flourish is offset by the low season's crash. These contradictions underscore that progression is not linear or chronological. To cope with temporal disjuncture and its emotional and material impacts, some explore Rasta cosmology and inhabit its temporality.

Rastafarian Temporality and Consciousness

The history of Rasta in Limón has more depth and complexity than some scholars acknowledge (Anderson 2005) and constitutes the basis from which raising consciousness grows. It is important to distinguish the claim that Rastafarianism is a thriving religion in Puerto Viejo from a recognition that Rasta interpretive communities abound. Paul Gilroy (1991) describes interpretive communities as being formed by diverse people who are connected to one another through their adherence to a popular ideological movement. The boundaries of interpretive communities are amorphous. Their members might also be ambiguously attached to core tenets and practices or show varying levels of commitment to orthodoxy. The Rasta interpretive community in Puerto Viejo is widespread, bridges age groups and brings twenty- and thirty-somethings into ideological and political communion with sixty- and even eighty-year-olds—the age of the oldest person to ever share some aspect of Rasta thought with me.

The history of Rastafarianism in Puerto Viejo is a long one. The early seeds of Rasta thought were part of the cultural information exchanged along the migration routes that connected Costa Rica and Jamaica historically. Indeed, the Jamaican activist Marcus Garvey, whose political ideas influenced Rastafarianism, established the Central American headquarters of the Universal Negro Improvement Association in Puerto Viejo (Harpelle 2000). He founded the association to promote racial pride and economic self-sufficiency. What is more, Joseph Nathaniel Hibbert, who is credited with forming Rastafarianism in collaboration with Leonard Percival Howell and Henry Archibald Dunkley, emigrated from Costa Rica to Jamaica. Dunkley was a sailor with the UFC (Urban 2015). His work likely required him to make regular, perhaps even daily, trips between Costa Rica and Jamaica (Putnam 2013). These historical figures and the migration channels they accessed contributed to the legacy of Rastafarianism in Limón.

Reggae music is another medium through which the political and social seeds of Rastafarianism arrived in Costa Rica. Rasta cosmology communicated in "roots" reggae traveled to Costa Rica in the hands of *cruseros* (ship workers) carrying vinyl records, and later cassette tapes, as early as the 1960s, when the music developed in Jamaica (McCoy-Torres 2016). Roots resonates with both young people and elders who celebrate its themes of Black pride, working-class solidarity, nature, and anti-oppression. In turn, the ontologies and praxis of Rastafarianism articulated in the music are made available to people across generational divides.

Much of Rasta cosmology helps interpretive community members position themselves within, and make agentive claims to, their social, economic, and political worlds. Rasta concepts and taking time to contemplate one's relationships to quotidian life are used as agentive tools for self-avowal and to confront pervasive depression during the low season. Carving out time to employ Rasta concepts and contemplate life in order to fashion agentive subjectivities structures Rasta temporality, during which consciousness is raised. Rasta temporality is an abstracted temporality. It is a temporal experience, suspended from historical, development, and seasonal temporalities, during which temporal disjuncture and its material and affective impacts are analyzed and interpreted through raising consciousness. As such, Rasta temporality allows people to transcend the challenges or boredom of the present, making the meantime between lulls and action more meaningful. Rasta temporality also serves as a bridge between the lulls and action.

Rastafarianism is connected to an epistemology that seeks to invert power and victimhood (Barnett and Onuora 2012; Mazama 2001). In keeping with this epistemological focus of Rastafarianism, raising consciousness during the Rasta temporal frame is a strategy that affords opportunities to create value through myriad techniques, such as presenting alternative conceptualizations of history. As they decipher and emotionally release the challenges of historical, development, and seasonal temporalities, people can affectively relate to them in different ways. Rasta temporality both witnesses and interprets the clash between historical, development, high-season, and low-season time. It seeks to repurpose absent time and turn it into a space of critical reflection that fosters a suspended and more perfect present in which people are empowered.

Rasta temporality is characterized by producing knowledge in order to come to terms with, and find a sense of peace despite, the social, economic, and temporal conditions that define one's life. Constructing an agentive subjectivity through the act of producing knowledge further defines Rasta temporality. Coming to terms with unfavorable social, economic, and temporal conditions and finding reconciliation through agentive subjectivity-making do not indicate that those who are subject to precarious labor rhythms are simply complacent or do nothing to navigate them. Rasta temporality lies between the multiple low-paying jobs people take on during periods of underemployment to make ends meet. Rasta temporality also should not be mistaken as time for inaction, neither in relation to underemployment nor unequal socioeconomic structures. To the contrary, Rasta temporality is defined by active theorizing and subjectivity-making within a context of accepting what is not within one's own power to change, and exercising the agency to relate differently to this. While it may not be within the power of Puerto Viejo locals to change precarious temporal rhythms, it is within their power to use their agency to affectively relate to them in different ways. Locals create new affective relations during Rasta temporality. Producing knowledge, subjectivity-making, and exercising agency are acts that insist on autonomy and the ability to define one's own wellbeing in spite of what is difficult to change on one's own accord. Producing knowledge is significant for structural change as well. Unmasking the relations that underlie socioeconomic conditions through raising consciousness affords broader social and political possibilities to intervene in unequal structural conditions. The experiences of Edwin Patterson, Firu, and Oscar, presented below, illustrate how Rasta temporality is structured. Further, how raising consciousness during Rasta temporality unmasks unequal power relations and is a mode of creating value in the meantime moments that it bridges.

Reenvisioning History

Rasta temporality and its connections to raising consciousness and affirming agency are well reflected in Edwin Patterson's navigation of time, meaning, and power. Patterson is a business owner and former deputy of Costa Rica's Legislative Assembly, the first from Talamanca. He is rarely available to talk during the high season but he was able to share some of his surplus time with me during the low season. We sat in his mostly empty restaurant. Patterson grappled with historical temporality. In recounting his family's history, he described how some people, envious of Afro-Caribbean greatness, had tried to strip the Afro-Caribbean residents of Puerto Viejo of their power. He began by tracing his heritage to the Ashanti and Zulu of Africa's western and southern regions respectively, people who are celebrated for their courage, power, and skill in war. Patterson explained that his Zulu and Ashanti ancestors were brought to Jamaica as enslaved people, later migrated to Panama as free people, and finally settled in Puerto Viejo in the late 1880s. His dive into history carried him to the present and inspired a critique of power: "The enemy always comes where we are and they infiltrate and start to destroy everything. They have the magic gift of destroying all good that exists," he said in Spanish. I asked who the enemy was: "The state. The government. Some countries are crueler than others, but they do exactly the same. The racism is the same. The lack of opportunities for Afro-descendants the same. Envy. Because basically it's envy and an inferiority complex because they feel, they see us as a danger. Always. They know we are a danger because we are the only group that can overcome anything. It's normal. God made us. We're children of the sun. We were born for this." Patterson implicitly made governing powers metonymic of Euro-descendants, who, according to his rendering, exercise racism against, and delimit the opportunities of, Afro-descendants. He correlated the formation of Euro-diasporic nation-states with European colonialism and the enslavement and displacement of indigenous and African people (Gregory and Sanjek 1994; Omi and Winant 1994). Patterson's shift from the singular "enemy" to plural "they" in his statement is analytically meaningful as well. It conceptually shows his movement between referring to different types of agents. Some are singular (the Costa Rican state) and some are plural (agents of colonialism, imperialism or inequality more generally, and powerful nations).

Patterson went on to compare the state and government's (read Euro-descendants') "magic gift for destroying all good that exists" to what he sees as an Afro-Caribbean proclivity toward inclusiveness. In Spanish, he said: "We are an inclusive not exclusive culture . . . So, we can live together with whatever person, understand whatever person, because we have that ability." He then switched to *Patwá* (an Antillean-derived English patois used socially and in familial spaces among Afro-Caribbean people) to express an emotive shift and capture sentiments and thoughts that might otherwise be lost in translation: "We got the gift of knowledge, wisdom, and understanding." Then he switched to Spanish again: "they can't take that away from us." He went on to credit Bob Marley for his observation that *el negro* (the Black man) possesses the gift of knowledge, wisdom, and understanding, which Marley apparently shared in an interview Patterson once saw. Patterson punctuated his oration with assertions that the only way to move beyond war, destruction, and exclusion is forgiveness. He referenced South Africa's historic post-apartheid Truth and Reconciliation Commission as an example.

Patterson was engaged in a number of specific discursive and theorizing practices that are tied to raising consciousness, constructing Rasta temporality, and reenvisioning historical temporality. His reference to Bob Marley, who many see as a prophet of Rasta theology, oriented him to Rasta concepts, which operated as the epistemological backdrop of his theorizations, thus demarcating his habitation of Rasta temporality. There are a few things that happened during Patterson's foray into history that illustrated his navigation of historical temporality's continuity with the present and also his mode of inhabiting the present.

Patterson saw historic violence as resulting from European efforts to fully economically, politically, and socially dominate others. The violent creation of a racial hierarchy could have inspired a sense of inferiority in Afro-descendants and resulted in great trauma. Instead, however, Patterson presents this history of violence as evidence of European desires to extinguish the innate greatness of Afro-descendants. This view assumed the inherent power, if not superiority, of Afro-descendants. Europeans, he said, suffered from "[e]nvy . . . an inferiority complex . . . they see us as a danger . . . because we are the only group that can overcome anything . . . God made us. We're children of the sun." With those words, Patterson assigned divine status to Afro-descendants. In his view, the ability to overcome obstacles, the absence of an inferiority complex, a tendency toward inclusivity, and the gifts of knowledge, wisdom, and understanding were all indications of divine status. In reflecting on Afro-descendant uniqueness, Patterson envisaged a distinct temporality that transcended history by emphasizing that which remained unchanged despite centuries of oppression and marginalization: the innate greatness of Afro-descendant people.

Patterson's ponderings, communicated as he drifted into a realm beyond where we sat, exemplify the affirming reasoning of raising consciousness. He located Afro-descendants' position within a society defined by structural inequality by detaching concepts of power and value from capitalism and the historically contingent power structures with which they are typically associated. The new present was one in which he was an agentive subject who embodied a peaceful presence as a result of having expressed his wisdom and "overstanding." Effectively, his raising consciousness imagined history's exclusions in ways that offered alternative conceptualizations of, and ways to grapple with, the past, the present, and how they shape subjectivity and value.

Deciphering "No Economy" and Releasing the Lows of Seasonal and Development Temporality

The meditative and discursive techniques tied to raising consciousness that Patterson employed are evident also in a group of young men's rhymed ruminations. Firu, Oscar, and their two friends, all in their early twenties, found themselves in a languid low-season moment, freed from the demands of labor and everyday life. The young men stood under the shade of a tree on a beach shore in town. They passed a *puro* around the circle they had formed. Their fashion was an amalgamation of styles associated with global representations of cosmopolitan Blackness (Perry

2015), inflected with local fashion that accommodated heat, humidity, and beach life—short-sleeved button-ups or white t-shirts paired with flip-flops and surf shorts. Firu's hair was in cornrows (braids affixed to the scalp in rows or layered designs). Another wore a fitted sports hat. Oscar wore his *"pelo rasta"* —literally "Rasta hair," the term for dreadlocks—in a loose bun. A wooden beaded necklace, invoking Rasta fashion, adorned his neck. Their look and music exemplified their engagement with global flows of music, fashion, and constructions of Blackness.

Firu, Oscar, and their two friends sang and rapped in Spanish, their bodies swaying to the rhythms of their melodic song. They repeatedly switched between Spanish and *Patwá*. Their lyrics illustrated their frustrations and their modes of coping with economic exclusion. Like Patterson, who found his way across historical time through his contemplations in Rasta temporality, the young men similarly raised consciousness in the Rasta temporal frame they carved out of an indeterminate moment on a sleepy July afternoon. Their contemplations, however, interpreted development time, particularly development's unmet promise of future prosperity.

Oscar began "freestyling" (the English word is also used in Spanish to refer to spontaneously improvising song lyrics). Freestyling is a widely noted component of Afro-diasporic vernacular culture, as well as reggae and hip-hop (Gates 1988; Hope 2006; Perry 2004; Rose 1994; Stanley-Niaah 2010; Stolzoff 2000), the two music forms the young men drew on in their exchange. As in Rasta chants associated with *Nyabinghi* ritual drumming, freestyling unleashes the subconscious, as words and their organization are fluidly expressed. Freestyling brings the content of the subconscious into consciousness and is often used as a means of offering social critique. Freestyling, *Nyabinghi*, and reggae lyricism can all be in service of chanting down Babylon. Accordingly, participants see these chanted political critiques as more than simple personal reflections: they constitute powerful discourse with transformative potential and are important tools for countering unequal social and economic conditions.

Oscar delivered his words by rapping, a form of melodic chanting that is the vocal basis of hip-hop songs. The instrumental part of legendary rapper Nas's song "If I Ruled the World," featuring Lauryn Hill, served as his background music. Oscar's lyrics settled on the challenges he faces. Rapping in Spanish, he said:

> In these months, I'm not feeling good. I try very hard to hide my scars. The pain I feel is deep inside, so deep inside that sometimes I don't feel it. Sometimes I try and run but reality follows me. I asked an old man and he told me, "life is a son of a — — so live" . . . Life gives to you but sometimes it takes away . . . In whatever craziness the Black man has to act . . . Since I was thirteen, surviving

every type of situation. Sitting at the traffic light, trying to kill my hunger, bro. Here outside it's cold . . . But only me, proud wherever I may be, whether it's the same or different in a different environment with the same people trying to survive in order to live a more decent life. Various times I've been in the dumps, but I offer art . . . it's how I continue forward.

Oscar's lyrics thematically fit Nas's original track, which is a testament to the challenges facing African Americans, with links made to the shared suffering of the African diaspora. Similarly, Oscar draws a parallel between his experience and that of "the same people" in a different environment. Nas also fantasizes about how the world would be if it was not in the shadows of the legacies of slavery and colonialism. The most prominent difference Nas notes is that Black people would be free in a much fuller sense, beyond the grip of mass incarceration, and would be equal participants in, and beneficiaries of, global capitalism and wealth.

Oscar's song insists on survival as the means to remain buoyant and flow through historical and seasonal temporal continuums and navigate utopic development's temporal divergences. He sees "art," the lyrical materialization of his raised consciousness, as crucial to his survival—both embodied and psychic. Oscar also incorporated dynamic affirmation through his acknowledgment of generational wisdom (turning to an elder for insight) and stated, "proud wherever I may be," which has both literal and figurative meanings. Oscar, along with his friends, created a temporal and spatial community that was bounded by their rhyme, reasoning, and the ritual exchange of a *puro*. Indeed, *kairos* defined the moment, a moment that presented an opportunity for the kind of critique that characterizes raising consciousness. Rasta temporality thereby emerged as an option that allowed the young men to inhabit a perfect present.

In a later conversation with me about the significance of moments spent freestyling with friends, Firu described them as integral to his survival, particularly when frustration over the temporal "no economy" threatens to consume him. Firu referred to the temporal lack of wages not as a low season (*temporada baja*), but quite literally as a moment of nonexistence and negation—no economy. The low season connotes a temporal economic crisis that necessitates dynamic material and psychic strategies for coping with the loss of value and purpose measured in capitalist terms. Raising consciousness fills the low season's time voids and assuages the anxieties these voids document—the slowing of income, the dwindling of the sense of esteem that acquiring money gives to people, and the lack of movement. "*No hay movimiento*" (there is no movement) is a common colloquial expression that people in Puerto Viejo use to describe the absence of circulating material and immaterial goods, people, and activity. Raising consciousness to redesign the affective relations through which people experience the temporal negation of "no movement" or economy helps shift moments of individual or collective disavowal to avowal. The verbalization of social and economic insight gathered from this new purview, whether it is through song or conversation, becomes an important emotional outlet.

Firu explained:

> Music is a good way to vent, vent to feel free. I feel free when I sing so I do it every day. Then nothing stays inside, instead . . . it's made for ears to listen to . . . That's why it's called relief, because you pull it [hardship] out from inside you. It's not going to stay inside. So, when the song comes out, most likely you will overcome it faster, because you're accepting and singing about it. So, that's why it's easier to accept, because you give your full dedication to that life situation, like daily situations.

Here, Firu makes a number of contributions to the conceptualization of raising consciousness. His words reveal that his lyrics are the product of theorizing or giving "full dedication" to life's "situations" or hardships. Lyrics are the sonic matter of the interpreting process. This sonic matter gives form to the consciousness raised, making it tangible. The melodic chanting in reggae and hip-hop lyricism can, furthermore, offer a therapeutic sensory experience, becoming even hypnotic through the repetitive utterance of certain phrases or when people call and respond to each other. The circularity of musical time, in turn, creates comfort and allows people to affectively relate in a new way to the present, changing how it is felt. Reggae's lyricism is also evocative of Rastafarian *Nyabinghi* drumming ceremonies—the early origins of reggae music—during which recitations are delivered in rhythmic chants. The process of theorizing through music to raise inner sentiments and speculation to overstanding releases psychic toxicity and the heaviness of embodying the hardship of life. This transformation and liberation are important to Rasta belief systems too. In *Nyabinghi* ritual ceremonies, raising consciousness offers healing while stitching the quilt of Rasta cosmology along the way.

As a result of creating music, Firu is able to move beyond the pain, frustration, or anger that might otherwise define the present moment for him. He thereby occupies the plane of self-gratifying Rasta temporality and affectively relates in a different way to time and its chronicling loss by shifting how he feels about it. As Firu indicates, Rasta temporality transforms the present by giving opportunities to overstand its conditions. In a way, it also anticipates that things will remain the same, revealing the fragility of its comforts.

The Fragility of Time

Born in May 1937, Alberto Lewis Fisher is one of Puerto Viejo's oldest residents. His parents were among the earliest Jamaican immigrants to Costa Rica who helped establish the town. His dominant language is still *Patwá*. A grandfather to many, he offers keen insight into the transformations Puerto Viejo has witnessed and all that it has not witnessed. He is an archive of images and enchanting stories that precisely underscore the contradictions and deferments of development time. He has seen firsthand who benefits from development and who it leaves behind. Alberto peacefully inhabits the slower temporal frames of life. He shapes his activity not around the energetic flows of the high and low seasons but around the sun's temporality—times of high or low heat that determine how comfortably he can stroll through Puerto Viejo's streets.

During a moment of high sun, Alberto sat in a rocking chair on his porch as he described to me what Puerto Viejo was like when he was a kid. He remembers a town that was bare, where satisfying most needs was a laborious task, and how, as a kid, he would fetch water for cooking and drinking from a nearby stream that is now polluted with garbage and the town's runoff. For most of his adulthood, buying commercial products was a luxury that was possible only at *el chino*, Puerto Viejo's first and, for many decades, only general store, owned by the descendants of Chinese immigrants—hence the name. Other food items were grown and traded among the residents. In those times, Puerto Viejo was an isolated place. Excluded from both the national imaginary and development processes, it remained insulated until the 1980s.

Alberto pointed down the street to one of Puerto Viejo's most popular and expensive restaurants. It sits on what was once his family's land. Back then, it was an expansive, open space. His family, like many others, sold their land cheaply to foreigners, fearing an uncertain future. Their fears stemmed from the financial pressures and precarity they faced when development shifted from locally sustained commerce, subsistence farming, and trade to an economy based on commercial farming and tourism. What is more, as the state began formalizing land ownership, Afro-Caribbean locals anticipated that, in the absence of formal titles proving that they owned property, they might be dispossessed of the land they had settled on and farmed for decades.

Today, Alberto's home is surrounded by restaurants, pharmacies, supermarkets, a car rental business, and clothing boutiques that accommodate tourists as well as Central Valley transplants who have migrated to the city to enjoy Caribbean culture amid modern infrastructure. In such surroundings, the home feels small and quaint. Though the neighborhood has developed, Alberto and his family have not reaped the benefits of this development. Like many residents of Puerto Viejo, they have witnessed the rapid transformation the town has undergone in recent decades. If their lives are constrained by the material conditions in which they live, the resources available to them remain scarce. They feel that time is suspended between the past, the seasonally contingent present, and a utopic development future, from which benefits are not expected.

Sometimes locals express nostalgia for the unanticipated promises of development positively as a belief, and relief, that the "essence" of the town and the aura of its people remain. Yet, as locals are being pushed to the fringes, where housing is still affordable, I have the haunting feeling that the essence of the town is certainly changing, along with how locals inhabit its spaces. Nonetheless, Afro-Caribbeans see themselves as being in flow with a temporality that is suspended from both development time and historical time—much like how Patterson emphasized the persistence of Afro-descendants' greatness in a way that envisages them occupying a distinct temporality that transcends history. The spirit of the locals consistently endures, suspended as it is from historical, seasonal, and development temporalities. Raising consciousness offers this temporally suspended purview.

What this chapter has revealed of the temporal purviews examined is that the ways in which people relate to time illustrate a collision of social constructs. These constructs imply how people should relate to time and what life in each temporal frame should be like, but also encompass the deconstructed interpretation of these "shoulds." Constructed and deconstructed interpretations of time meet and shape the perception of experience and what people feel in each temporal frame. Navigating diverse (de)constructions offers opportunities for ruminations about time that inform feeling as well. Thus, time creates and is defined by myriad affective relations that shape how people experience and conceptualize its passing. Affect characterizes time, the interpretation of time is affective, and time induces affect as well. Could it be said that time chronologically measures accumulations of affect? The affective dimensions of time offer an explanation of why residents of Puerto Viejo seek to manage it affectively through the affirming process of raising consciousness.

What this exploration has also shown is that creating music offers opportunities to animate the meantime between infrequent low-season activities and synthesize temporal disjuncture. It also potentiates transformation by offering a medium to critique the social and economic conditions to which people are subject. Music is a medium for interpreting, feeling, and finding relief, and a form of temporal transference from one moment to the next that also bridges the way to high season's action. The chanting, singing, and ceremonial exchange of the *puro* among people brings them into an affectively and psychically shared temporal and meditative state in which the contemplation that defines raising consciousness is accessed. Ganja, for many, assuages the anxieties that time provokes, helping those who turn to it as a medicinal instrument to overstand the complexities of temporal relations as they raise consciousness.

It could be argued that raising consciousness is an elevation of the belief that now is all that there is. Such a claim points to the limits of the expanded and affirming view of life that raising consciousness offers and transforms it into an admission of hopelessness. It might further be argued that overstanding seeks to overwrite history, the present, and development time with empowerment, pride, and agency; yet does not actively transform the unequal social, economic, and political conditions that have emerged from these temporal frames. Overstanding, the argument could hold, merely changes how such conditions are experienced. To these critiques, I would respond that raising consciousness and the discursive practices that extend from it are part of myriad adaptive processes people employ to live life in its best forms through temporal transitions and collisions. It is transformative and transgressive even if it does not bring about reform, though it can. Indeed, raising consciousness, I propose, is what Rex M. Nettleford describes as an "authentic expression[] of organic revolt in appropriate if anguished response to some of the deepest social forces that have shaped and still determine the discrepancies of . . . Caribbean society" (1978: 188).

Raising consciousness transforms the meaning and psychosocial impacts of what time documents—stagnating capital flows, temporal waiting, and the deferment of a utopic future, which are indicative of a history of socioeconomic disadvantage. In accordance with Rasta epistemologies, the knowledge produced in the theorizing process serves as a critique of structural dynamics and repositions the theorist as agent rather than subject within various temporal frames. Raising consciousness to overstand suspends and reframes the temporalities governing one's life and the specific challenges arising within them and is a strategy for exploring the spiritual and psychological dimensions of social life and their material outcomes. It is an act that affectively transforms relationships to time and value (*chronos* and *kairos*), shifting how they are measured and, significantly, moving them away from economic achievement, toward spiritual and philosophical gain.

Sabia McCoy-Torres is Assistant Professor of Anthropology and Africana Studies at Tulane University. She earned a PhD in social and cultural anthropology from Cornell University. Her research centers on race, gender, sexuality, transnationalism, and Black popular performance in the English- and Spanish-speaking African diaspora. She initially focused on reggae culture in the context of Afro-Caribbean migration to and between Brooklyn and Costa Rica. Her current research involves a comparison of sex work in Costa Rica and millennial dating culture in the United States. Her articles have appeared in *Transforming Anthropology*, *Black Music Research Journal*, *Popular Music & Society*, and *The Global South*.

Note

1. All data was gathered from Instituto Nacional de Estadística y Censos Costa Rica at https://www.inec.cr/ [last accessed 24 August 2020].

References

Adorno, Theodor. 1991. "Free Time." In *The Culture Industry: Selected Essays on Mass Culture*, ed. J. M. Bernstein, 187–88. London: Routledge.

Anderson, Moji. 2005. "Arguing over the 'Caribbean': Tourism on Costa Rica's Caribbean Coast." *Caribbean Quarterly* 51(2): 31–52.

Barnett, Michael, and Adwoa Ntozake Onuora. 2012. "Rastafari as an Afrocentrically Based Discourse and Spiritual Expression." In *Rastafari in the New Millennium*, ed. Michael Barnett, 159–74. Syracuse, NY: Syracuse University Press.

Chomsky, Aviva. 1996. *West Indian Workers and the United Fruit Company in Costa Rica, 1870–1940*. Baton Rouge: Louisiana State University Press.

Cole, Jennifer, and Deborah Durham, eds. 2008. *Figuring the Future: Globalization and the Temporalities of Children and Youth*. Santa Fe, NM: School for Advanced Research Press.

Comaroff, Jean, and John L. Comaroff. 2001. "Millennial Capitalism: First Thoughts on a Second Coming." In *Millennial Capitalism and the Culture of Neoliberalism*, ed. Jean Comaroff and John L. Comaroff, 1–56. Durham, NC: Duke University Press.

Denning, Michael. 2010. "Wageless Life." *New Left Review* 66: 79–98.

Elson, Diane. 1979. "The Value Theory of Labor." In *Value: The Representation of Labour in Capitalism*, ed. Diane Elson, 115–80. London: CSE.

Ferguson, James. 2015. *Give a Man a Fish: Reflections on the New Politics of Distribution*. Durham, NC: Duke University Press.

Foote, Nicola. 2004. "Rethinking Race, Gender and Citizenship: Black West Indian Women in Costa Rica, c. 1920–1940." *Bulletin of Latin American Research* 23(2): 198–212.

Gates, Henry. 1988. *The Signifying Monkey: A Theory of Afro-American Literary Criticism*. New York: Oxford University Press.

Gilroy, Paul. 1991. *"There Ain't No Black in the Union Jack": The Cultural Politics of Race and Nation*. Chicago: University of Chicago Press.

Graeber, David. 2001. *Toward an Anthropological Theory of Value: The False Coin of Our Own Dreams*. New York: Palgrave.

Gregory, Steven, and Roger Sanjek. 1994. *Race*. New Brunswick, NJ: Rutgers University Press.

Harpelle, Ronald N. 1993. "The Social and Political Integration of West Indians in Costa Rica: 1930–50." *Journal of Latin American Studies* 25(1): 103–20.

———. 2000. "Racism and Nationalism in the Creation of Costa Rica's Pacific Coast Banana Enclave." *The Americas* 56(3): 29–51.

———. 2001. *The West Indians of Costa Rica: Race, Class, and the Integration of an Ethnic Minority*. Montreal: McGill-Queen's Press.

Hope, Donna. 2006. *Inna Di Dancehall: Popular Culture and the Politics of Identity in Jamaica*. Mona, Jamaica: University of the West Indies Press.

Jeffrey, Craig. 2010. "Timepass: Youth, Class, and Time among Unemployed Young Men in India." *American Ethnologist* 37(3): 465–81.

Lorde, Audre. 2012. "The Use of the Erotic: The Erotic as Power." In *The Lesbian and Gay Studies Reader*, ed. Henry Abelove, Michèle Aina Barale, and David M. Halperin, 339–43. New York: Routledge.

Li, Tania. 2014. *Land's End: Capitalist Relations on an Indigenous Frontier*. Durham, NC: Duke University Press.

Mains, Daniel. 2012. *Hope Is Cut: Youth, Unemployment, and the Future in Urban Ethiopia*. Philadelphia, PA: Temple University Press.

Mazama, Ama. 2001. "The Afrocentric Paradigm: Contours and Definitions." *Journal of Black Studies* 31(4): 387–405.

McCoy-Torres, Sabia. 2016. "'Cien Porciento Tico Tico': Reggae, Belonging, and the Afro-Caribbean Ticos of Costa Rica." *Black Music Research Journal* 36(1): 1–29.

Millar, Kathleen M. 2014. "The Precarious Present: Wageless Labor and Disrupted Life in Rio de Janeiro, Brazil." *Cultural Anthropology* 29(1): 32–53.

Munn, Nancy. 1992. "The Cultural Anthropology of Time: A Critical Essay." *Annual Review of Anthropology* 21: 93–123.

Murillo Chaverri, Carmen. 2006. "The Railroad and Afro-Caribbean Migration to Costa Rica, 1872–1940." In *Regional Footprints: The Travels and Travails of Early Caribbean Migrants*, ed. Annette Insanally, Mark Clifford, and Sean Sheriff, 228–47. Kingston, Jamaica: Latin American-Caribbean Centre, University of the West Indies.

Nettleford, Rex M. 1978. *Caribbean Cultural Identity: The Case of Jamaica: An Essay in Cultural Dynamics*. Kingston: Institute of Jamaica.

Omi, Michael, and Howard Winant. 1994. *Racial Formation in the United States: From the 1960s to the 1990s*, 2nd edn. New York: Routledge.

Perry, Imani. 2004. *Prophets of the Hood: Politics and Poetics in Hip Hop*. Durham, NC: Duke University Press.

Perry, Marc D. 2016. *Negro Soy Yo: Hip Hop and Raced Citizenship in Neoliberal Cuba*. Durham, NC: Duke University Press.

Purcell, Trevor W. 1993. *Banana Fallout: Class, Color, and Culture among West Indians in Costa Rica*. Center for Afro-American Studies, University of California, Los Angeles.

Purcell, Trevor W., and Kathleen Sawyers. 1993. "Democracy and Ethnic Conflict: Blacks in Costa Rica." *Ethnic and Racial Studies* 16(2): 298–322.

Putnam, Lara. 2006. "Kinship Relations and Social Networks Among Jamaican Migrants in Costa Rica 1870–1940." In *Regional Footprints: The Travels and Travails of Early Caribbean Migrants*, ed. Annette Insanally, Clifford Mark, and Sean Sheriff, 204–27. Kingston, Jamaica: Latin American-Caribbean Centre, University of the West Indies.

———. 2013. *Radical Moves: Caribbean Migrants and the Politics of Race in the Jazz Age*. Chapel Hill: University of North Carolina Press.

Ralph, Michael. 2008. "Killing Time." *Social Text* 26(4 [97]): 1–29.

Rose, Tricia. 1994. *Black Noise: Rap Music and Black Culture in Contemporary America*. Hanover, NH: University Press of New England.

Stanley-Niaah, Sonjah. 2010. *Dancehall: From Slave Ship to Ghetto*. African and Diasporic Studies. Ottawa: University of Ottawa Press.

Stewart, Kathleen. 1996. *A Space on the Side of the Road: Cultural Poetics in an "Other" America*. Princeton, NJ: Princeton University Press.

Stolzoff, Norman. 2000. *Wake the Town & Tell the People: Dancehall Culture in Jamaica*. Durham, NC: Duke University Press.

Urban, Hugh B. 2015. *New Age, Neopagan, and New Religious Movements: Alternative Spirituality in Contemporary America*. Oakland: University of California Press.

Weiss, Brad. 2009. *Street Dreams and Hip Hop Barbershops: Global Fantasy in Urban Tanzania*. Bloomington: Indiana University Press.

Willis, Paul. 1982. "Cultural Production and Theories of Reproduction." In *Race, Class and Education*, ed. Len Barton and Stephen Walker, 112–42. London: Croom Helm.

Chapter 4

Stranded in Decolonization
The Attritional Temporality of Sahrawi Activism in Moroccan-Occupied Western Sahara

Mark Drury

Life Is Waiting, a recent documentary about the Western Sahara political conflict, a long-standing territorial dispute between Morocco and the Sahrawi Arab Democratic Republic (SADR), opens with scenes from a 2013 street protest in Madrid. The demonstration marks the fortieth anniversary of the founding of the Polisario Front, the anticolonial liberation movement that sought to end Spanish colonialism in Western Sahara. The crowd is mostly made up of members of the Sahrawi diaspora who support the Sahrawi nationalist effort, but also includes a number of Spaniards, reflecting broad support in Spain for the cause of self-determination in the former Spanish colony. Nearly everyone is bedecked in the green, black, white, and red of the SADR flag,[1] infusing the march with the festive energy of a commemorative parade. Sahrawi rappers perform onstage to an ululating and otherwise appreciative crowd of onlookers, amplifying the event's celebratory atmosphere. Released in 2015, the film has been screened internationally at film festivals, on college campuses, and by solidarity groups that support Sahrawi nationalism. I viewed the documentary at two such events in New York City, both of which were sponsored by the Sahrawi Association in the United States. As part of a diplomatic effort to make the Sahrawi nationalist effort visible to a broader public, the film, like the demonstration, addresses its audience with a sense of urgency.

Punctuating scenes of the march and backed by a drumbeat, archival footage is used to introduce the viewer to Western Sahara through a series of the conflict's defining moments. 1973: the Polisario Front is founded by Sahrawi activists to fight for independence from Spanish rule. November 1975: the Madrid Accords transfer power over the territory from Spain to Morocco and Mauritania, preempting decolonization by self-determination.[2] That same month, Morocco invades and annexes much of the territory both militarily and via a state-organized civilian march, an event celebrated in Morocco as the "Green March." Thousands of Sahrawis flee to southwest Algeria, where Polisario establishes the base of the Sahrawi Arab Democratic Republic (or SADR), a state-in-exile that continues to govern the refugee camps today. 1975–91: war between Morocco and the Polisario Front, during which Morocco effectively occupies the majority of Western Sahara, building a 2,700-kilometer earthen wall to separate its territory from that which remains under SADR/Polisario control.[3] 1991: a ceasefire signed between Morocco and Polisario establishes UN oversight of the organization of a referendum to determine the territory's political future. Only, as the documentary notes, the referendum has never been held.

In the course of tacking back and forth between the history of the Western Sahara conflict and the film's present, we hear from a number of Sahrawis participating in the protest, each addressing the camera with the energized tone and elevated pitch that are common in in situ protest reportage. At one point, the camera shows a young man, described in the film as "an activist for armed struggle," named Benda Lebsir. An olive-green *litham* (head covering) matches his loose-fitting, camouflage fatigues, the uniform of SADR/Polisario's military and political leaders. Draped in the SADR flag, Benda addresses his interviewer, exclaiming in Arabic, "It has been forty years of fighting, and this is a key moment to say: enough is enough!" The young man's efforts to make himself heard above the din of the march only heighten the urgency in his voice. Together with his military garb and how he is labeled in the documentary, the implication is clear enough: Sahrawis, many of them living in exile, demand the right to determine the future of Western Sahara—by armed struggle, if necessary.

Life Is Waiting celebrates the political activism that Sahrawis maintain in anticipation of an independence that has yet to arrive. The juxtaposition of contemporary Sahrawi political activism with a narrative history of violence and injustice remains the documentary's focus throughout: from refugee camps in Algeria to Moroccan-occupied territory to a diaspora in Spain, we meet Sahrawi poets, calligraphers, hip-hop artists, and media and human rights activists devoted to the cause of realizing Sahrawi self-determination. Nor is this focus merely a construct of the film: as I found during ethnographic fieldwork in Moroccan-occupied Western Sahara, refugee camps in Algeria, and even northern Mauritania, committed nationalist activism animates the lives of many Sahrawis—often at considerable risk of arrest and physical abuse. Nearly a decade after the making of the film, Sahrawis remain in an anticipatory state, "waiting" to exercise the right to self-determination.

David Scott (2014) uses the phrase "the trace of futures past" to refer to the collapse of a horizon of revolutionary change, which, for broad swaths of the Global South, was subtended by decolonization and anti-imperial struggle. As the drive for revolutionary emancipation and anticolonial liberation has dissipated, largely displaced by a global humanitarian ethic and projects of transitional justice, Scott notes that the very relationship between past, present, and future has been reconfigured. No longer is the past something to be liberated from. Rather, "we are left with . . . *aftermaths* in which the present seems stricken with immobility and pain and ruin; a certain experience of temporal *afterness* prevails in which the trace of futures past hangs like the remnant of a voile curtain over what feels uncannily like an endlessly extending present" (Scott 2014: 6). Scott characterizes this collapse of past political horizons in terms of being "stranded in the present" (67). At first blush, the Sahrawi nationalist cause of self-determination may appear to be one of these traces: an unresolved remainder, the aftermath of a bygone post–World War II period when a relatively open horizon of possibility animated a range of different decolonial political projects and aspirations (Amin 1994; Cooper 2014; Wilder 2015).

For Sahrawi nationalists, the protracted, unresolved condition of the Western Sahara conflict has indeed produced a temporal condition of being stranded: between decolonization and national sovereignty, between the right to self-determination and its enactment, between international law and occupation, between conflict and resolution, between war and peace. Scholars of Western Sahara term this a state of conflict "irresolution" (Zunes and Mundy 2010). For Scott, the postcolonial condition of being "stranded in the present" entails the dissolution of a clear set of stakes around which Third World collective political action might mobilize. Stranded as it may be, the Sahrawi nationalist movement, I argue in this chapter, is facing a very different quandary. The politics of the Western Sahara conflict are such that, far from the collapse of decolonization as a horizon of expectation, Sahrawi nationalists are stranded *in* and *by* the process of decolonization. Though hardly "stricken with immobility," Sahrawis have been waiting for two generations now to decolonize and realize self-determination. As we shall see, Sahrawi activists feel compelled to undertake continuous, ongoing action with the aim of achieving a political future that is both apparently imminent and chronically unattainable. *Life Is Waiting* captures the constant mobilization that reflects how politicized many Sahrawis are, whether they live in Spain, in the refugee camps, or in Moroccan-occupied territory.[4] However, in portraying its subjects as indefatigably committed partisans of a nationalist movement, the film sets aside the ethnographic question of the socially meaningful temporal experience (Munn 1992) engendered by living in a state of political "irresolution." How do political partisans contend with life in a conflict that seems to demand their constant mobilization? What is the social experience of a political future that appears perpetually imminent but remains unattainable? It is this particular mode of "being stranded" that I examine in this chapter.

Transformation and Continuity in a Situation of "No Peace, No War"

Benda Lebsir's call for a return to armed struggle was realized in November 2020 when the Sahrawi Arab Democratic Republic abrogated a 29-year-old UN-brokered ceasefire and began carrying out armed exercises along the berm that separates the Sahrawi government-in-exile from Moroccan-occupied Western Sahara. Yet SADR's military strikes have so far done little to alter the conflict's balance of power (Hilton 2021; Drury 2020b; Wilson 2020; Allan 2020). The conflict remains entangled with regional and international dynamics related to the political recognition of sovereignty. Rather than marking a drastic shift in the mode of political struggle, both the call for a return to armed conflict in 2013 and the return to armed conflict in 2020 can be seen as a continuation of decades of political conflict suspended between war and peace. In this sense, the shifting terrain of conflict between ceasefire, diplomacy, armed struggle, human rights campaigns, and decolonization might be thought of as a space of "no war, no peace" (Lombard 2016; Richards and Helander 2005)—or, perhaps more accurately, as a space of overlapping war *and* peace.

The liminal space of overlapping war and peace that has shaped the last three decades of the Western Sahara conflict has produced a period of restless living in the meantime of waiting for decolonization and conflict resolution. This chapter, based on field research conducted in Moroccan-occupied Western Sahara, explores these developments through the subjective experience of Sahrawi nationalist activists, with particular attention to the experience of Moulay. Moulay, a Sahrawi *munadil* (militant) who lives in Moroccan-occupied territory and supports Sahrawi self-determination, has faced relentless state repression and intimidation. I examine Moulay's commitment to political activism under such adverse conditions through what Sian Lazar (2014) has called "attritional time."

Lazar uses this phrase to conceptualize the repetitiveness of sustained political activism, wherein the experience of time "is one of constant protest or negotiation, the continuance of the day to day of political life when there is no resolution in sight to a particular conflict or problem, coupled occasionally with a dramatization of what can become quite banal over time" (2014: 92). I use Lazar's concept to consider the multifarious temporal experiences of "political life" from the perspective of human rights activists in Moroccan-occupied Western Sahara. But where Lazar uses the concept of "attritional time" as a temporality that sometimes intersects with "historical time" to produce recognition of an event of particular significance, I use it here in relation to a non-event, or, more accurately, an unresolved event: decolonization. In this way, the repetitive experience of constant political struggle can usefully complement Scott's notion of the temporal structure of being stranded. The Western Sahara conflict's temporal structure of strandedness is symptomatic less of a bygone revolutionary era and more of a contemporary crisis in global political authority.

Matchat: Rehearsing and Measuring the Gains of Activism through Time

Since 1991, and especially in the last fifteen years, human rights activism has become increasingly central to the Sahrawi movement for self-determination. Building upon a burgeoning human rights discourse in Morocco during the 1990s (Slyomovics 2005), Sahrawis living under Moroccan control began organizing nonviolent demonstrations in Western Saharan cities such as Laâyoune, Dakhla, and Smara (Asmar 2015). Beginning in 2005, nonviolent protest in Moroccan-occupied Western Sahara took a more organized form through the initiative of a student-led *intifada*, when Sahrawi students demonstrated against the presence of Moroccan security agents in their schools. This massive uprising, coordinated across Moroccan-occupied Western Sahara and including Sahrawis living in parts of southern Morocco adjacent to the disputed territory, initiated a sustained effort to make Moroccan illegitimacy in Western Sahara visible through ongoing, nonviolent protest (Mundy and Stephan 2006). Known as *intifadat al-istiqlal*, or the Independence Intifada, it indoctrinated a new generation of Sahrawi students into political activism. The *intifada* also established nonviolent civil disobedience as the primary political tactic for drawing attention to the illegitimacy of Moroccan rule, which continues to animate a generation of militants, or *munadilin* (sing. *munadil*, f. *munadila*) a decade later.

Establishing research contact with Sahrawi *munadilin* in Morocco was not easy. Unlike researchers and journalists who embedded themselves in the Sahrawi activist network, I registered with Moroccan authorities (cf. Allan 2017). While this approach enabled me to grasp the complex range of political identifications that often defied the polarized terms of nationalist conflict, including a group known as "returnees," which refers to those who have switched sides in the conflict, it also left me subject to intense state surveillance.[5] I quickly learned that the Moroccan state would deploy significant resources to make Sahrawi *munadilin* and *huquqiyyin* (human rights activists; sing. *huquqi/yya*) off limits to researchers and journalists. My interactions with Sahrawi activists required significant planning and generally took place in private residences. The following excerpt is based on an interview I conducted with an activist:

> Munadila: Even with the children who were born after the ceasefire, [the *intifada*] made things clear for them. Then they began asking about this issue that we have—I was born the year of the ceasefire. I also began asking, inquiring, and discovered that I have martyrs [in my family], people who were kidnapped.
>
> M. D.: Meaning, your parents didn't talk about that—
>
> Munadila: I had never asked. I wasn't aware of the issue, didn't know what they said about the war. I hadn't known that half of my family was in refugee camps, that my family had been subject to difficulties [*mudayyiqat*] during that time. And kidnapping.
>
> Even when I became aware of the issue and asked about it, and found books, and researched, and people who provided cassettes and photos: through that, my awareness increased until the beginning of the Independence Intifada in 2005. The 2005 *intifada* was the turning point for changing the direction of the national cause.
>
> M. D.: Could you explain to me how it changed the direction?
>
> Munadila: The world, and all of the international organizations and human rights organizations became open to our issue, in general, and with a clear sense that the Sahrawi people demand self-determination. From 2005, human rights delegations started coming to the region.[6]

Today, the strategy of deploying nonviolent protest to attract the attention of the international community remains foundational to Sahrawi activism in Moroccan-controlled territories.[7] To broaden the movement's impact, media activists often record these protests and disseminate them internationally. Engaging in nonviolent protest requires tremendous commitment on the part of these activists, who must be willing to expose themselves to violence, imprisonment, torture, and intimidation. Those who record and disseminate activists' protests face challenges of their own in the form of the massive military and security presence in the territory, buttressed by a media blackout that often leads to the expulsion of dozens of foreign visitors annually.[8]

In 2013, when I arrived in Laâyoune, the largest city in Moroccan-occupied territory, the context in which nonviolent protest took place was particularly charged, as demonstrators were calling for MINURSO, the UN-run entity overseeing the ceasefire in the territory, to include human rights oversight. However, expanding MINURSO's mandate in this manner requires UN Security Council approval (Morris 2013). The campaign had been building for several years, peaking each spring when the UN Security Council meets to discuss the renewal and terms of MINURSO's mandate. The US Department of State, which had indicated support for MINURSO human rights oversight the previous year, backtracked when Morocco threatened to withdraw from joint military exercises. By April 2014, Laâyoune was enveloped by protest and the possibility of imminent change. That spring, Aminatou Haidar, one of the most prominent Sahrawi *huquqiyyin*, had an audience with the US Congress as part of a movement-based diplomacy effort to build support for expanding MINURSO's mandate. Sahrawis in Laâyoune were celebrating her every move online. They were also preoccupied by the approaching UN Security Council decision and its possible ramifications. But they were not passively waiting for these events to unfold.

Protests seemed to take place daily in Laâyoune. Planned demonstrations organized at *al-Zemla*, the symbolically important site of the first demonstration of Sahrawi nationalism in 1970, had to overcome relentless efforts by Moroccan security forces to prevent the gatherings from taking place. The number of vans containing riot-helmeted police and auxiliary soldiers parked along *al-Zemla*, a central intersection in Laâyoune, served as a barometer of the level of political activity on any given day. Though I was never able to directly observe these more organized protests due to the massive police presence in Laâyoune, I occasionally saw women and children raising the SADR flag and chanting for self-determination outside my apartment window. And, periodically, young people ran past me on the street, rocks and chunks of concrete in hand, fleeing or pursuing a confrontation with the police.

Given the difficulty of meeting with *munadilin*, who were actively involved in these street protests, I was thrilled to get to know Moulay, who had been taking part in the protests calling for an expanded mandate for MINURSO, through a mutual friend. We first met at Moulay's family's apartment in Lahshaysha, a popular quarter that developed rapidly after the government convinced people to resettle in Western Sahara with the promise of housing and land throughout the 1990s and 2000s (Veguilla 2017). Seated on the carpet, buttressed by pillows, and fortified by a continuous supply of tea that steeped over the heat of a charcoal brazier, the three of us talked for hours.

Toward the end of the evening—after many rounds of tea and once it became impossible for them to ignore my fatigue (the two friends likely could have continued talking through the night)—Moulay recalled his participation in a recent protest at *al-Zemla*. With an irrepressible energy that betrayed neither fear nor lingering pain, Moulay described how he and his friends had stood in a busy intersection until the police descended upon them, at which point they had received their expected beating and the protest had ended. Having participated in several protests involving nonviolent civil disobedience, Moulay noted how much he looked forward to them. He felt a nervous anticipation ahead of the confrontations, which he countered by engaging in a preparatory regimen: laying out what he would wear in advance, visualizing how the protest might play out, and so on. These preparations culminated in the protest itself, which, Moulay said, took place in a reassuringly predictable fashion: you show up at the appointed time, take your beating, and come home feeling better for it. With regard to the physical exertion involved, he noted, with a broad smile, that participating in the weekly demonstrations was *"bhal matchat,"* like playing in soccer games.

Lazar describes "attritional time" as "one of constant protest or negotiation, the continuance of the day to day of political life when there is no resolution in sight" (2014: 91–92). This characterization of the temporality of activism implies continuity and repetition, both of which emerge from Moulay's discussion with his friend. In contrast to Lazar's characterization, however, when this conversation took place, resolution was seemingly in sight: the UN Security Council decision promised the possibility of some kind of breakthrough in relation to the demand for human rights oversight in Western Sahara, a step that Sahrawis believed would provide them with an opening to express their dissent from Moroccan rule. This conjuncture only heightened the sense of urgency for a set of activists (*munadilin* and *huquqiyyin*) involved in long-standing and continuous conversations about how to achieve Sahrawi self-determination. With events unfolding at the international, regional, and local levels almost on a daily basis—involving press or diplomatic events abroad, communication with SADR/Polisario in the refugee camps, and the latest news regarding Sahrawi political prisoners across Morocco—the conflict reproduces a political field replete with new developments, pressing demands, and a shifting sense of progress and hope, or setback and retrenchment. Most immediately, in Laâyoune, the efforts to either confront police and security agents, or, in other cases, to outmaneuver them, produce an urban terrain of protest and counterinsurgency that is relentlessly adversarial and continuously shifting.

And yet, as Lazar also notes, the temporal experience of activism is defined less by the exceptional sense of effervescence or communitas and more by an engagement with the repetitive experience of mundane political action:

> Individual demonstrations were an opportunity for the repetition of particular political arguments and the constant rehearsal and refinement of political narratives and understandings, in formal speeches and audience/participant commentary. This repetition is participation in attritional time, the mundane, repetitive, constant struggle that makes up political activism in the everyday. (2014: 101)

When Moulay compares his participation in the protests at *al-Zemla* to "*matchat*," he casts this repetition in both ritualistic and recreational terms. Whereas many political demonstrations in Laâyoune were spontaneous, and their outcome was very much unknown, the relatively high-profile protests in which Moulay was taking part occurred weekly at the same time and place, providing a cyclical sense of temporality like any regularly scheduled appointment. Repetition inscribed Moulay's sense of commitment and involvement in the community of Sahrawi political activism into a temporality of continuous struggle, while also re-instantiating, with every protest, a horizon of expectation for change animating future political action. This is not to say that each protest was predictable, or its outcome preordained: most immediately, excessive violence was never out of the question. Meanwhile, the very purpose of nonviolent disobedience, in this context, is to draw the attention of the "international community," an unpredictable and shifting entity, to Moroccan human rights violations. In other words, uncertainty and danger were not absent from Moulay's description of his participation in these protests and, indeed, Sahrawis have suffered numerous, serious injuries, including broken limbs and the loss of eyes, during protests, and some have been killed.

Yet there was an unmistakable sense of ritual, repetition, and scripted, sacrificial bodily practice in Moulay's account. He seemed particularly pleased by the reference to a soccer match; as with the physical exertion of team sports, one effect of participating in a protest was feeling physically and morally cleansed. While the significance of the protests may have been particularly heightened at the time of Moulay's participation because of the relatively high level of international attention on Western Sahara (due to the pending UN Security Council decision), his account emphasized the satisfaction of political activism in terms of physical involvement, iterative practice, and even ritual purification. Drawing upon Ernst Bloch, Banu Bargu (2014) notes that faith in a political cause and victory imparts transcendent meaning and motivates collective sacrifice in avowedly secular political movements. Rituals give form and expression to this faith that, as techniques of the body, shapes the political subjectivities of those who carry them out. Or, as she notes, "[t]hese rituals are important because they express, in condensed and stylized form, how ideology is actually lived" (Bargu 2014: 241). Bargu's attention to how political ritual generates the mutually constitutive subjectivities of "militant" and "martyr" through active sacrifice resonates with Moulay's account.[9] Moulay's participation in human rights protests entails the possibility of martyrdom, a term used to refer to those who have died for the cause.[10] Repetition, meanwhile, reenacts his political commitment as a *munadil*, or "militant," through physical sacrifice and moral purification. And yet Moulay's analogy of a soccer match, characteristic of his lighthearted conviction, seemed to deliberately downplay the stakes, emphasizing the voluntaristic side of his activism—the banality, in Lazar's framing—rather than the sense of duty or sacrifice. Whether associated with the ethics of human rights discourse or the righteousness of the Sahrawi cause, Moulay's comparison of nonviolent resistance to playing a weekend soccer match suggests that the repetition of activist protest may be both a mundane aspect of attritional time, as Lazar suggests, and constitutive, through ritual and renewal, of his political subjectivity as a *munadil*.

"Politics Ruins the Minds of the Young": The Attritional Effects of Continuous Activism on Activists Themselves

So far, I have examined how political protests in Moroccan-occupied Western Sahara constitute a cyclical experience of renewed commitment through repetitive engagement in political action. According to Lazar, attritional time serves to maintain commitment in a prolonged struggle, often against a more powerful adversary. However, in my ethnographic experience with Sahrawi activists, the attritional dynamics of activism potentially cut both ways.

Despite the fact that there is no neutral ground in the political field of Moroccan-occupied Western Sahara, there are distinct levels of involvement. Pro-Moroccan Sahrawis view their pro-independence brethren with disdain, calling them "separatists" (*infissaliyyin*) and, in keeping with Moroccan nationalist ideology, dismissing their political position as a preference for discord over a willingness to participate in "modern" national processes of economic development and practices of citizenship. Others, for whom a salaried position with the state may be at stake, attempt to remain neutral and to avoid politicized events at all costs. Sahrawis in this position are often co-opted into participating in cultural and political institutions that celebrate tribal identity, still a kinship group with significant affective pull in Saharan (and, to a lesser extent, Maghrebi) society more generally. The generation of students that came of age during *intifadat al-istiqlal* became politicized at a relatively young age and many, including Moulay, remain Sahrawi activists. And for them, the day-to-day developments of the cause of Sahrawi self-determination unfold upon a dense emotional terrain.

The emotional effects of this sustained engagement in political activism were expressed most clearly to me during a late-night dinner at the home of a media activist in Laâyoune. Following the campaign to reform MINURSO that culminated in April 2014, the grim disappointment resulting from the UN Security Council report had given way to a simmering rage. Our meal was taking place amidst a rock-throwing confrontation between children and the police outside of my host's apartment complex. Periodically, when the headlights of a security vehicle turned onto the dirt pathway behind the apartment in which we were dining, conversation would stop as everyone crouched below the window frame. No one in the room was actively participating in the confrontation outside, but the topics we were discussing—compounded by my presence in the room—could draw unwanted attention. This physical response reflected the activists' vigilant sensitivity to the probing eye of the Moroccan state.

During one of these tense moments, when everyone else was lying on the carpeted floor, remaining quiet, the media activist could not contain himself. He began recounting the litany of beatings, arrests, and experiences of torture that different activists had suffered at the hands of the Moroccan security forces over the previous few weeks. Some incidents involved women, whose mistreatment by the police only amplified this activist's moral outrage. Whereas the customary view would be that the holiness and social obligations of Ramadan would trump political activities for a month (the month of fasting, prayer, and reflection was only a few weeks away), the young man claimed that this year would be different. These violations, he warned, portended a month that would be hot with protest and confrontation. This short speech, fiery and intense, conveyed the young man's sense of injustice and, unlike some political scripts that I encountered, left no doubt about the authenticity of his anger and sense of urgency.

Though my interactions with *munadilin* were constrained by the conditions of pervasive surveillance in Moroccan-occupied Western Sahara, these obstacles contributed to my appreciation of the litany of dangers that Sahrawi activists faced in the form of a security state intent upon destroying their political will by any means necessary. This included the potential for physical injuries suffered during protests: I interviewed one man with his arm in a sling as a result of an injury suffered while protesting Morocco's extraction of Western Sahara's natural resources without popular consent. The Sahrawi activist Sultana Khaya famously lost her eye when security forces descended upon her during a protest.[11] Likewise, I heard from young activists who had experienced rape, had their fingernails removed, and suffered other forms of torture and brutality while in Moroccan prisons. On one occasion, when, by chance, I ran into a *munadil* in the open-air market of Laâyoune, his hesitation and the fact that he quickly looked away after our eyes had met indicated that he feared being seen in the act of acknowledging the presence of a foreigner. His overarching sensitivity to the presence of security personnel during our encounter exhibited an embodied disposition of fugitivity (Goffman 2015). Because of the pervasive surveillance and fear that it engendered, interviewing Sahrawi activists often required convoluted arrangements.

On one occasion, I met a young Sahrawi who spoke angrily about the effects of Moroccan rule in Laâyoune. Coming from a prominent family, he projected a confidence in public and a deep concern with political developments. He seemed to know every local member of Sahrawi society who came up in conversation, whether *huquqi*, *munadil*, or otherwise, and repeatedly promised to connect me with some of these figures. Though my encounters with this young man were typically fleeting, one day he invited me, impromptu, to drive around town with him and his friend. At this point, I was not unaccustomed to clandestine arrangements, such as friends and intermediaries arranging for a cab to pick me up without revealing the destination in advance. As the three of us wound our way through the afternoon traffic in Laâyoune, I was surprised to learn that our destination was a Moroccan hashish dealer and not a group of Sahrawi activists. Although widely available thanks to its importation from the north of Morocco, among Sahrawis in Laâyoune hashish was generally stigmatized as an addictive drug. For some of my friends, even cigarettes would be smoked far away from family, so as not to disappoint their elders. Given this context, taking me to a hashish dealer was not in keeping with the young man's stated interest in wanting to introduce me to people in the activist community.[12]

When I recounted this experience to a friend, he shook his head and said, "Politics ruins the minds of the young."[13] My friend was talking about living through the volatile ups and downs, gains and losses, moral outrages and righteous victories, that characterize close engagement with the polarized politics in Moroccan-occupied Western Sahara over months and years. With the shifts from armed conflict to talks of a referendum to human rights discourse and diplomacy, the foot soldiers in this conflict are increasingly young men and women protesting and filming non-violent protests in the streets of their cities. As the Sahrawi *munadila* noted earlier, many young people grew up with limited knowledge of the violent conflict that the previous generation had experienced. As they become more aware of what happened, many of them get involved in the struggle for self-determination. Once involved, the sense of urgency of those young activists who support self-determination never abates, simply because the goal of Sahrawi sovereignty continues to seem both imminent and attainable. Participating in the long-term, attritional time of political activism, *munadilin* are also subject to the effects of this temporality. Lazar notes that the constant, repetitive struggle of political activism can be "extremely draining," but otherwise focuses on the continuity that keeps many activists engaged in the long term. Indeed, many Sahrawis, such as Aminatou Haidar, Sultana Khaya, and Moulay, who joined the cause early on, remain actively involved for decades. From this perspective, "attritional time" can be deployed through activism to sustain a cause through repetition and renewed commitment. The Sahrawi context shows, however, that "attritional time" also unfolds upon a dense emotional terrain of danger and fear, as well as hope, moral outrage, and disillusionment, threatening to wear down activists through the experience of this relentless temporality. Whether in the form of a broken arm or a compromised spirit, which is how my interlocutors interpreted drug use, the varied effects of attritional time can be seen in injured bodies, but also in activities believed to compensate for trauma, injury, torture, or simply deep disillusionment. While many have resolutely continued their activism despite the many dangers, sustained political struggle wore some activists down: activism for Sahrawi self-determination in Western Sahara undoubtedly subjects the mind and body to relentless attacks by the blunt instruments of fear deployed by the Moroccan state.

Muktessabat: Measuring the Gains of Activism over Time

May is usually a tumultuous time in Laâyoune, and May of 2014 was no different. The initiative calling for human rights oversight in Western Sahara had reached a fever pitch that spring, with protests and clashes between riot-helmeted police and Sahrawi protesters taking place daily, supplemented by rock-throwing skirmishes throughout the city at all hours. And after the UN Security Council renewed MINURSO's mandate without adding human rights oversight in late April, the city remained on edge. As an outlet for the annual frustration of unmet expectations in relation to the UN Security Council's meeting, May brings two of the most significant holidays for Sahrawi nationalists: the founding of the Polisario Front on 10 May 1973 and its declaration of an armed struggle for independence ten days later. Supporters of Sahrawi nationalism living in Morocco commemorate these events inside their homes, through private gatherings that often involve consuming SADR television and radio programs broadcast from the refugee camps in Algeria. Both dates are marked by annual public demonstrations, which invariably entail confrontations with the Moroccan security state apparatus. The lingering bitterness of the unresolved campaign for human rights oversight, combined with the Sahrawi nationalist holidays, meant that tensions between Sahrawis and the Moroccan state in 2014, already at boiling point, would remain high through the month of May and beyond.

In this context, I caught up with Moulay at a café near where we both lived. Although the intensity of the protests in which he was participating had begun to taper off—eventually shifting from weekly to monthly demonstrations—the political foment that had animated the spring had not subsided. Besides protests, discussions among Sahrawi activists concerning political organizing and tactics were ongoing. Moulay had recently attended two events, one a memorial service and the other a human rights training session supported by an EU-based organization. Both were held in private and both had attracted a heavy police presence.

Moulay reported that both the service and the training took place undeterred and without major interruption by, or confrontation with, state security forces. Arguing that, in the past, similar events would have been raided, blockaded, or otherwise violently broken up, he claimed that the possibility of holding both events should be considered *muktessabat*, or gains made through political activism and struggle. This statement struck me initially as an overly optimistic view and perhaps a reflection of Moulay's resolutely positive outlook. His view that these events constituted *gains* in the movement's struggle only seemed to underscore the relentless repression and surveillance faced by those struggling to create space for the expression of pro-Sahrawi politics in Morocco. To me, the celebration of an uninterrupted memorial service seemed to emphasize the tight confines of repression within which activists operated more than it signaled new possibilities in the present.

In describing the memorial service and human rights training in terms of *muktessabat*, however, Moulay situated these events in relation to a longer history of activism and struggle. Another activist made a similar reference, emphasizing that the very fact of our meeting (in the secrecy of a home on the outskirts of Laâyoune) was itself the manifestation of certain gains made through a larger struggle:

> The national issue remains larger than any individual . . . Like now, [my friend] might encounter insults, or something, but what's important is that the issue reaches the world so that the world knows about the dispute and that there are real violations with the [Western] Sahara issue. Morocco always knows about the protests and movements/mobilization—and even this meeting now, it is secret. If it weren't, they would have encircled/blockaded this whole place, and no doubt if someone came here, they would arrest them. You understand? Meaning, if they just notice you, they will start wondering. Those [members of the Moroccan security state], I know that they're pragmatic, they want to erase any picture, or anything published on the Sahara issue, or if someone met with you—you understand me? But thank God that, despite this blockade, we have achieved many gains . . .[14]

Unlike the temporality of repetition and renewal expressed through his comparison of political protest to a soccer match, here gatherings of different kinds mark *muktessabat*, or gains, turning political events, however mundane, into measurements of progress or setbacks over time.

Later in the summer of 2014, Moulay and I caught up again over coffee. He had recently returned from a conference at the University of Ibn Zohr in Agadir, where Sahrawi students had gathered to commemorate that it had been over forty years since the founding of the Polisario Front. As in many countries, university campuses in Morocco are nodes of political organizing and, at times, they become political battlefields for opposing student factions. For Moulay, organizing protests years ago at university on behalf of Sahrawi students who had been denied admission had been a formative experience in "practicing politics," even though the months-long campaign was met with hostility and violence, and ultimately won few immediate concessions. In remembering the experience as an epic series of challenges, hardships, and sabotage faced by the protestors, Moulay's narrative had a dual significance. First, he described protest as an act of attrition that strategically deploys time from a position of relative weakness. Second, even when not marking gains, this example shows how, for Moulay (and others who began protesting as youths), the attritional aspect of political activism as a university student created the very foundation for a longer trajectory of becoming and remaining a *munadil*.

Lazar's coinage of "attritional time" emphasizes the banality of political activism. She notes that those who remain committed to this mode of politics do so in part because they recognize that their actions must necessarily be continuous and ongoing. This level of commitment, she suggests, often entails both an awareness of the longer, historical temporality of a given struggle and a recognition that any discrete political action is unlikely to be the one that unlocks revolution or realizes utopian ambitions. These activists, she notes, "seemed on the whole comfortable with the ongoing and attritional nature of their struggle. This was in part because many of them successfully folded it into [historical time], seeing themselves as a small part of a much larger narrative, a longer tradition of struggle" (Lazar 2014: 102). For instance, by appraising the memorial service and human rights training in terms of *muktessabat*, Moulay situated these events within a longer temporality, enabling him to evaluate his activism in attritional terms—of small gains achieved over time. Likewise, situating specific demonstrations and gatherings in what Lazar terms "historical time" marks change in terms of the forms of public collective action in the present that would not have been possible in an even more militarized past. Waiting, in the Western Sahara context, corresponds to the condition of being "stranded" in and by the formal political processes of decolonization, a largely diplomatic process that motivates constant political mobilization. In the meantime, activists mark the relative gains made within this stalled, unresolved temporal condition through the state's shifting responses to their repetitive actions.[15] These gains, or *muktessabat*, situated in relation to the past, can then be attributed to and motivate their ongoing activism.

Conclusion: Repetition, Audience, and the Structure of Sahrawi Strandedness

Danilyn Rutherford (2012) notes that, in the postcolonial era, efforts to establish an independent nation-state depend as much upon international recognition as they do upon relations of force. This tension in sovereignty being split between legal recognition and the brute fact of occupation has been noted by a number of political theorists (Anghie 2004; Schmitt 2006), but the post–World War II process of decolonization, in establishing an international order of expanded legal recognition without the concomitant transfer of power, extended and entrenched this contradiction in the nation-state form. For many anticolonial movements culminating in national independence, this meant acquiring a compromised form of "negative sovereignty" that was supported by international law and also subject to international intervention (Jackson 1990). In writing about a postcolonial temporal condition of being stranded in the present, Scott (1999) refers to the shifting stakes of political movements across the Global South operating "in the aftermaths" of having acquired this compromised sovereignty. Western Saharan self-determination is, in many ways, the inverse of the condition addressed by Scott. Sahrawi nationalists continue to seek this status (however compromised) because they are simultaneously included in and excluded from the process of decolonization. SADR/Polisario remains the UN-recognized representative of the Sahrawi people, able to testify before the UN Special Committee on Decolonization and to receive recognition from other governments.[16] With their right to self-determination validated by the International Court of Justice (Franck 1976; Drew 2007), but operating either in exile or under Moroccan occupation, Sahrawi nationalists operate very much at the nexus of a form of sovereignty that is disaggregated into international recognition and territorial control.

As a result, Sahrawi activists are constantly in search of an audience. Benda Lebsir, from *Life Is Waiting*, wields the threat of a return to war as a means of capturing the attention of the international community and possibly even inviting its intervention. SADR/Polisario's return to armed conflict seven years later reads similarly: far from weakening Morocco's territorial hold on Western Sahara, these military campaigns seek to garner international attention in order to resolve the conflict by other means. Across this political terrain of overlapping war and peace, human rights activism has become the most consistent and direct mode of seeking international recognition in a situation of long-standing, unresolved conflict. As Rutherford (2012: 21) notes, when would-be sovereigns seek an audience for recognition, "it is not just the promise of international intervention but often also the thrilling experience of moving between perspectives that accounts for the longstanding appeal of demonstrations like flag raising." The rehearsal of certain political scripts and signs in the Western Sahara conflict, such as a call to return to armed struggle, the reproduction of the SADR flag, or coordinated nonviolent public demonstrations, indexes a frustration with broader power dynamics (state, regional, international). The repetition of certain political scripts indexes the stranded temporal condition of the Sahrawi nationalist movement. This present, however, is not a time-space of uncertain political stakes: decolonization remains an immediate goal for Sahrawi nationalists in 2022, just as it has been for decades. Their political present is thus shot through with the urgency of a seemingly achievable political goal that is perpetually out of reach. Caught within the tensions of sovereignty between recognition and occupation, a tension that derives from a broader crisis in global political authority, Sahrawi activists remain effectively stranded in decolonization.

Based largely on research conducted in Sahrawi refugee camps in Algeria, scholars of Western Sahara have long described the Sahrawi "citizen-refugees" and their role in "prefiguring" the nation-state (Isidoros

2018; Wilson 2016; Martin 2010; Mundy 2007). Increasingly, however, this literature has attended to the importance of an international audience in motivating Sahrawi political processes, within the camps and beyond (Solana 2019; Allan 2019; Fernández-Molina 2015; Fiddian-Qasmiyeh 2014). Human rights activists in Moroccan-occupied Western Sahara, increasingly pivotal to the political terrain of conflict, bring this element of international audience into high relief. As I have demonstrated in this chapter, Sahrawi political activists are constantly in search of an audience. Their prolonged engagement in modes of political action that demand international recognition reflects the "strandedness" of their cause of self-determination: this temporality has shaped a generation of Sahrawi activists, particularly those who have grown up in Moroccan-occupied Western Sahara. Beginning with *intifadat al-istiqlal* in the 2000s, young Sahrawis became aware of both a history of violence inflicted upon their families, as well as the presence of international organizations responding to their protest. As with Moulay's involvement in protests at university, participation in the *intifada* created the foundation for a generation of *munadilin* whose political subjectivity has been defined by ongoing struggle. At the same time, paying ethnographic attention to the multifarious experience of this struggle shows how repetitive engagement in political activism builds resolve through corporeal experiences of protest-as-ritual, and by marking gains over time. But this continuous involvement in the fraught day-to-day terrain of political conflict can also have devastating effects through sustained exposure to the security state's blunt instruments of fear, intimidation, and torture.

In focusing on the temporal experience of Sahrawi human rights activism, this chapter presented an ethnographic example of strandedness that is defined not by the evacuation of horizons of possibility, but by prolonged engagement in political action for the sake of a goal that continuously appears to be imminent, yet remains unattained. The structure of this strandedness is related not only to the machinations of the United States, Spain, Morocco, Polisario/SADR, and other state actors, but also to sovereignty's disaggregation into territorial occupation and international recognition. By focusing on the temporal experience of this strandedness, I have drawn attention to the complex relationship between temporal experience, political action, and political subjectivity. The conditions of human rights activism in Moroccan-occupied Western Sahara reveal both the temporal structure of being stranded in decolonization, as well as the enduring presence of Sahrawi nationalists living in this particular "meantime."

Coda

Much has taken place in the Western Sahara conflict since the events I recounted in this chapter. The release of the film *Life Is Waiting*, as well as fieldwork for this article, coincided with the height of efforts to obtain UN oversight of human rights violations in Moroccan-occupied Western Sahara. When these efforts were unsuccessful, attention turned to leveraging the United States' erratic foreign policy under former President Trump into diplomatic gains for the Sahrawi cause. Articles asked optimistically "Is One of Africa's Oldest Conflicts Finally Nearing Its End?" (Niarchos 2018). In the fall of 2020, dynamics shifted abruptly when Polisario/SADR abrogated the ceasefire, followed by the United States recognizing Moroccan sovereignty over Western Sahara in exchange for Morocco normalizing relations with Israel. Over the past two years, as Polisario/SADR continues to carry out military campaigns on the margins of the territory, headlines have focused on Morocco's increasingly aggressive foreign policy. This aggression has affected Spain, which, in turn, has developed a more favorable position toward Morocco despite widespread criticism within Spanish civil society, much of which remains supportive of Western Saharan self-determination (Bartolomé 2022). Meanwhile, a contingent of US activists visited Western Sahara in the spring of 2022, drawing attention to ongoing and even increased Moroccan repression in the territory.[17] Yet for foreign activists, too, following the vicissitudes of state realpolitik can be both draining and, in some ways, distracting. As long as enough Sahrawi activists remain engaged in the struggle for self-determination, the conflict over Western Sahara will continue. In this respect, the attritional temporality of their movement politics may still work in their favor.

Mark Drury received his PhD from the Anthropology Program at The Graduate Center, CUNY. He is currently a postdoctoral fellow in the Center for Contemporary Arab Studies at Georgetown University and is working on two projects concerning histories of decolonization in northwest Africa. His research, based on fieldwork conducted in Morocco, Mauritania, Algeria, and the disputed territory of Western Sahara, focuses on sovereignty, human rights, and international law; surveillance, security, and political conflict; and the historiography of decolonization.

Notes

1. The SADR flag closely resembles the Palestinian flag. Palestinian national liberation provides a frame of reference from which Sahrawi nationalist politics seeks to draw. Another example of this can be seen in a recent documentary about Moroccan repression in the disputed territory entitled *3 Stolen Cameras*. The title is patterned after a well-known documentary about Israeli repression in Palestine entitled *5 Broken Cameras*.
2. Mauritania withdrew its claim to Western Sahara in 1979. While the Spanish state attempts to retain a position of official neutrality, in that it recognizes neither SADR nor Moroccan sovereignty over Western Sahara, Spanish civil society supports Sahrawi movements for self-determination in multiple ways, most extensively through a number of humanitarian programs for Sahrawi refugees in the camps (Fiddian-Qasmiyeh 2014).
3. Since the ceasefire between Morocco and Polisario in 1991, Morocco has controlled an estimated 75–80 percent of the territory (Wilson 2016: 6). Polisario Front is technically the liberation movement for Sahrawi nationalism, and the Sahrawi Arab Democratic Republic (SADR) is the state-in-exile that governs the refugee camps in Algeria. As Alice Wilson (2016: 2) notes, however, the two operate in "sometimes indistinguishable fusion." In following Wilson's usage, I will hereafter refer to them in tandem as "Polisario/SADR" unless discussing an activity that solely involves one or the other.
4. Most documentary accounts of Western Sahara focus on Sahrawi activists. See Goodman 2018; RåFilm and Equipe Media 2017. For a contrasting depiction that portrays Sahrawis as a "forgotten" people, see Vandeweerd 2011.
5. The name "returnee," known as *'a'id* (pl. *'a'idin*), refers to the label ascribed by King Hassan II when he called for Sahrawis to leave the refugee camps and "return" to Morocco. The subject position has something in common with both "refugee" and "defector" in the context of the political conflict (Drury 2020; Boulay 2016; Boulay 2014; Hernández Moreno 2001).
6. Interview, 26 December 2014, Laâyoune, Moroccan-occupied Western Sahara.
7. For a recent example, see a campaign in the spring of 2022 in which a United States-based group of human rights activists resided with the prominent Sahrawi activist Sultana Khaya in an effort to end the Moroccan siege on her home and protect her from ongoing violence and abuse: https://justvisitwesternsahara.org/ (MacDonald 2022; Amnesty International 2022).
8. Media activists have been targeted for arrest; the most infamous case involves a group of twenty-five known for the 2010 protest, Gdeim Izik, for which they were arrested and received sentences ranging from twenty-five years to life imprisonment. See Witness Media Labs for archived footage, most of which has been filmed by Sahrawi media activists: https://lab.witness.org/tag/western-sahara/ (accessed 10 October 2022). Eighty-four foreigners were reportedly expelled from the territory in 2016 (Adala 2017).
9. The political rituals Bargu examines among extraparliamentary Marxists in Turkey—fasting to death—have little in common with the nonviolent resistance of Sahrawi *munadilin*. Nonetheless, her broader insight resonates with nonviolent political activism in Western Sahara in part because of the largely secular ideology of Sahrawi nationalism (see Fiddian-Qasmiyeh 2014).
10. Estimates of the numbers of disappeared Sahrawi civilians vary, but Abdesslam Omar, director of AFAPREDESA, the Association of Families of Sahrawi Prisoners and Disappeared based in the refugee camps, claims that there are "over 400" (Interview, 24 January 2016, Rabouni, Sahrawi refugee camps). Omar provided a similar figure to the *New York Times* (Gall 2015).

11. Khaya's experience is frequently featured in journalistic and academic accounts of Moroccan state violence in Western Sahara (Allan 2019; Goodman 2018; Lee 2015).
12. In retrospect, it seems likely that this young man was an informant who was put up to engaging with me by someone in the Moroccan security state apparatus.
13. "Al-siyassa takhareb nafsiyya al-shabab."
14. Interview, 26 December 2014, Laâyoune, Moroccan-occupied Western Sahara.
15. Thank you to the editors of this volume for this insightful observation.
16. Eighty-four UN member states either recognize SADR or have in the past.
17. The following blog chronicles the solidarity activists' efforts in Boujdour, a city in Moroccan-occupied Western Sahara, between March and September 2022: https://www.nonviolenceinternational.net/khaya_siege_updates (accessed 10 October 2022).

References

3 Stolen Cameras. 2017. Documentary. RåFilm and Equipe Media. http://www.3stolencameras.com/ (accessed 10 October 2022).
Adala UK. 2017. "Morocco Continues the Arbitrary Expulsion of International Observers from Western Sahara," January 22, 2017. https://adalauk.org/2017/01/22/morocco-continues-the-arbitrary-expulsion-of-international-observers-from-western-sahara/ (accessed 20 February 2017).
Allan, Joanna. 2017. "Activist Ethics: The Need for a Nuanced Approach to Resistance Studies Field Research." *Journal of Resistance Studies* 3(2): 89–121.
———. 2019. *Silenced Resistance: Women, Dictatorships, and Genderwashing in Western Sahara and Equatorial Guinea*. Madison, WI: University of Wisconsin Press.
———. 2020. "British Corporate Plunder Helped Provoke the War in Western Sahara." *Democracy in Africa* (blog), 25 November. http://democracyinafrica.org/british-corporate-plunder-helped-provoke-the-war-in-western-sahara/ (accessed 10 October 2022).
Amin, Samir. 1994. *Re-Reading the Postwar Period: An Intellectual Itinerary*. New York: Monthly Review Press.
Amnesty International. 2022. "Moroccan Authorities Assault Sahrawi Women Activists." MDE 29/5648/2022. Amnesty International. https://www.amnesty.org/en/latest/news/2022/05/morocco-western-sahara-investigate-targeted-assault-on-sahrawi-women-activists/ (accessed 10 October 2022).
Anghie, Antony. 2004. *Imperialism, Sovereignty, and the Making of International Law*. Cambridge; New York: Cambridge University Press.
Asmar, Khalil. 2015. "The Stages of Peaceful Resistance in the Occupied Western Sahara." *Jadaliyya*, 2 April. http://www.jadaliyya.com/pages/index/21168/the-stages-of-peaceful-resistance-in-the-occupied- (accessed 10 October 2022).
Bargu, Banu. 2014. *Starve and Immolate: The Politics of Human Weapons*. New York: Columbia University Press.
Bartolomé, Marcos. 2022. "Why Is Madrid Pandering to Morocco?" *Foreign Policy* (blog), 13 May. Accessed 19 June 2022. https://foreignpolicy.com/2022/05/13/spain-sanchez-morocco-polisario-western-sahara-algeria/ (accessed 10 October 2022).
Boulay, Sébastien. 2014. "Poétique et politique de la migration au Sahara occidental. Les â'idîn': repentants, migrants ou ralliés?" In *La migration prise

aux mots: Mise en récits et en images des migrations transafricaines [Poetics and politics of migration in Western Sahara. The "â'idîn": repentants, migrants, or rallyists?], ed. Cécile Canut and Catherine Mazauric, 91–110. Paris: Le Cavalier Bleu.

———. 2016. "'Returnees' and Political Poetry in Western Sahara: Defamation, Deterrence and Mobilisation on the Web and Mobile Phones." *The Journal of North African Studies* 21 (4): 667–86.

Cooper, Frederick. 2014. *Citizenship between Empire and Nation: Remaking France and French Africa, 1945–1960*. Princeton, NJ: Princeton University Press.

Drew, Catriona. 2007. "The Meaning of Self-Determination: 'The Stealing of the Sahara' Redux?" In *International Law and the Question of Western Sahara International Law and the Question of Western Sahara*, ed. Karin Arts and Pedro Pinto Leite, 87–105. Leiden: International Platform of Jurists for East Timor.

Drury, Mark. 2018. "Disorderly Histories: An Anthropology of Decolonization in Western Sahara." PhD dissertation. New York: The Graduate Center, CUNY. ProQuest.

———. 2020a. "Disidentification with Nationalist Conflict: Loyalty, Opportunism, and Mobility in Moroccan-Occupied Western Sahara." *Comparative Studies of South Asia, Africa and the Middle East* 40(1): 133–49.

———. 2020b. "Sahrawi Self-Determination, Trump's Tweet and the Politics of Recognition in Western Sahara." *MERIP* (blog), 22 December. https://merip.org/2020/12/sahrawi-self-determination-trumps-tweet-and-the-politics-of-recognition-in-western-sahara/ (accessed 10 October 2022).

Fernández-Molina, Irene. 2015. "Protests under Occupation: The Spring inside Western Sahara." *Mediterranean Politics* 20(2): 235–54.

Fiddian-Qasmiyeh, Elena. 2014. *The Ideal Refugees: Gender, Islam, and the Sahrawi Politics of Survival*. Syracuse, NY: Syracuse University Press.

Franck, Thomas M. 1976. "The Stealing of the Sahara." *American Journal of International Law* 70(4): 694–721.

Gall, Carlotta. 2015. "Fighting Is Long Over, but Western Sahara Still Lacks Peace." *The New York Times*, 22 February. http://www.nytimes.com/2015/02/23/world/fighting-is-long-over-but-western-sahara-still-lacks-peace.html (accessed 10 October 2022).

Goffman, Alice. 2015. *On the Run: Fugitive Life in an American City*. New York: Picador/Farrar, Straus and Giroux.

Goodman, Amy. 2018. "Four Days in Occupied Western Sahara—A Rare Look Inside Africa's Last Colony." *Democracy Now!* https://www.democracynow.org/2018/8/31/four_days_in_occupied_western_sahara (accessed 10 October 2022).

Hernández Moreno, Ángela. 2001. *Sáhara: Otras voces*. Malaga: Editorial Algazara.

Hilton, Daniel. 2021. "Ghost Towns, Rockets and Drones: Polisario's War in Western Sahara." *Middle East Eye*, 9 December. http://www.middleeasteye.net/news/morocco-western-sahara-polisario-war-rockets-drones (accessed 10 October 2022).

Hultman, Tami. 1977. "A Nation of Refugees: Western Sahara." *Response* 9(3): 4–7, 42.

Isidoros, Konstantina. 2018. *Nomads and Nation-Building in the Western Sahara: Gender, Politics and the Sahrawi*. London: I.B. Tauris.

Jackson, Robert H. 1990. *Quasi-States: Sovereignty, International Relations, and the Third World*. New York: Cambridge University Press.

Lazar, Sian. 2014. "Historical Narrative, Mundane Political Time, and Revolutionary Moments: Coexisting Temporalities in the Lived Experience of Social Movements." *Journal of the Royal Anthropological Institute* 20(3): 91–108.

Lee, Iara. 2015. *Life Is Waiting: Referendum and Resistance in Western Sahara*.

Lombard, Louisa. 2016. *State of Rebellion: Violence and Intervention in the Central African Republic*. London: Zed Books.

MacDonald, Alex. 2022. "Sahrawi Activist Enlists Americans to Stop Police Beatings and Sexual Assault." *Middle East Eye*, 5 May. http://www.middleeasteye.net/news/morocco-western-sahara-activist-us-support-prevent-police-sexual-assault (accessed 10 October 2022).

Martin, Pablo San. 2005. "Nationalism, Identity and Citizenship in the Western Sahara." *The Journal of North African Studies* 10(3): 565–92.

———. 2010. *Western Sahara: The Refugee Nation*. Cardiff: University of Wales Press.

Morris, Loveday. 2013. "In Western Sahara, Women Play Large Role in Forgotten Struggle for Independence." *The Washington Post*, 7 July. https://www.washingtonpost.com/world/africa/in-western-sahara-women-play-large-role-in-forgotten-struggle-for-independence/2013/07/07/f46f23ec-dd06-11e2-85de-c03ca84cb4ef_story.html (accessed 10 October 2022).

Mundy, Jacob. 2007. "Performing the Nation, Pre-Figuring the State: The Western Saharan Refugees, Thirty Years Later." *Journal of Modern African Studies* 45(2): 275–98.

———. 2012. "Moroccan Settlers in Western Sahara: Colonists or Fifth Column?" *The Arab World Geographer* 15(2): 95–126.

Mundy, Jacob, and Maria J. Stephan. 2006. "A Battlefield Transformed: From Guerilla Resistance to Mass Nonviolent Struggle in the Western Sahara." *Journal of Military and Strategic Studies* 8(3): 1–32.

Munn, Nancy. 1992. "The Cultural Anthropology of Time: A Critical Essay." *Annual Review of Anthropology* 21(1): 93–123.

Niarchos, Nicolas. 2018. "Is One of Africa's Oldest Conflicts Finally Nearing Its End?" *The New Yorker*, 29 December. https://www.newyorker.com/news/news-desk/is-one-of-africas-oldest-conflicts-finally-nearing-its-end (accessed 10 October 2022).

Richards, Paul, and Bernhard Helander. 2005. *No Peace, No War: An Anthropology of Contemporary Armed Conflicts: In Memoriam Bernhard Helander*. Athens: Ohio University Press.

Rutherford, Danilyn. 2012. *Laughing at Leviathan: Sovereignty and Audience in West Papua*. Chicago: University of Chicago Press.

Schmitt, Carl. 2006. *The Nomos of the Earth: In the International Law of the Jus Publicum Europaeum*. New York: Telos Press.

Scott, David. 1999. *Refashioning Futures: Criticism after Postcoloniality*. Princeton, NJ: Princeton University Press.

———. 2014. *Omens of Adversity: Tragedy, Time, Memory, Justice*. Durham, NC: Duke University Press.

Slyomovics, Susan. 2005. *The Performance of Human Rights in Morocco*. Philadelphia: University of Pennsylvania Press.

Solana, Vivian. 2019. "Hospitality's Prowess: Performing Sahrāwī Sovereignty in Refugee Camps." *PoLAR: Political and Legal Anthropology Review* 42(2): 362–79.

Vandeweerd, Pierre-Yves, and Richard Skelton. 2010. *Territoire perdu/Lost Land*. Paris; Bruxelles: Zeugma Films; Cobra Films.

Veguilla, Victoria. 2017. "Changes in Moroccan Public Policies in the Western Sahara and International Law: Adjustments to a New Social Context in Dakhla." In *Global, Regional and Local Dimensions of Western Sahara's Protracted Decolonization: When a Conflict Gets Old*, ed. Raquel Ojeda-Garcia, Irene Fernández-Molina, and Victoria Veguilla, 235–55. New York: Palgrave Macmillan.

Wilder, Gary. 2015. *Freedom Time: Negritude, Decolonization, and the Future of the World*. Durham, NC: Duke University Press.

Wilson, Alice. 2016. *Sovereignty in Exile: A Saharan Liberation Movement Governs*. Philadelphia: University of Pennsylvania Press.

———. 2020. "Trump Enables Occupation and Threatens Peace Prospects in Western Sahara." *Democracy in Africa* (blog), 22 December. http://democracyinafrica.org/trump-enables-occupation-and-threatens-peace-prospects-in-western-sahara/ (accessed 10 October 2022).

Zunes, Stephen, and Jacob Mundy. 2010. *Western Sahara: War, Nationalism, and Conflict Irresolution*. Syracuse, NY: Syracuse University Press.

Entretemps

Machine-Made Time
Dialysis and the Complexities of Waiting and Planning

Janelle S. Taylor and Ann M. O'Hare

Widespread availability of dialysis treatment in many developed countries has created complexities around time, waiting, and the future for people with kidney failure who have access to this form of treatment. Dialysis machines, originally developed in the early 1940s, filter impurities and excess fluid from the body when the kidneys no longer can. Receiving hemodialysis treatment, or "dialyzing," as it is called, generally requires that a person sit still in a chair, next to a dialysis machine and hooked up to it, with his/her blood running into and out of the machine, for three to four hours at a time, three times a week. Dialysis is widely regarded as a miracle of modern medicine, staving off deaths that would otherwise be inevitable. Since the early 1970s, when it first became reimbursable, dialysis has come to be considered a routine treatment for people with advanced kidney disease in the United States.

The advent of dialysis is part of a broader historical trajectory in which the ultimately finite horizons of a human lifetime have come to seem elastic, on both individual and societal levels. On the level of the individual life, medicine as practiced in well-resourced parts of the world has generated a panoply of new technologies, procedures, and medications that promise to prolong life, while raising the troubling specter of a prolonged death—the dilemma of "where to draw the line" that Sharon Kaufman (2015) identifies as a central feature of "ordinary medicine." The extension of life that dialysis has allowed might seem like an unalloyed good. Our research suggests, however, that the quality of the time gained through dialysis is complex and contradictory, involving much waiting but also many crises and competing incompatible visions of the future.[1]

The three dialysis centers where we conducted interviews are located behind several layers of security in nondescript office buildings in different areas of Seattle, Washington. In all three settings, recliner chairs, each one paired with a dialysis machine approximately the size of a small photocopier, are arrayed around the perimeter of a large room. People sit in the chairs, with what look like red tubes (in fact, they are clear tubes filled with blood) running from their arms into the machines. Some of them sleep, some read, some watch TV on screens suspended from the ceiling, some listen to music or play games. A few are accompanied by a friend or family member who sits next to them. Each machine is topped by a screen with graphic real-time displays of blood pressure, heartbeat, and various other biological measures. Occasionally, when an abnormality in some metric triggers an alarm, a bright light flashes on the screen and a loud piercing alarm sound is emitted. This results in the arrival of a staff member, gowned in white, with latex gloves on their hands, a paper mask over their mouth, and a plastic shield covering their eyes, who looks at the screen, presses buttons, and sometimes talks to the person in the chair.

We began each interview by asking people to tell us how they came to be on dialysis. With striking consistency, they described initiating dialysis as a matter of it having been "time."

> I didn't have much choice, you know? When they said, "You need dialysis," I said, "Okay." Now I'm alive.

For patients with a clearly progressive loss of kidney function, the initiation of dialysis is presented as what "needs" to be done when "the numbers" reach a certain threshold. In this manner, dialysis technology and treatment are framed as a phase or extension of the expected course of the disease itself:

> Well, see, I was under the care of Dr — — way before I ever came here. And he said that with the tests that he'd run and everything, that he did, "You're eventually going to be on dialysis." And I said, "Thanks a lot." [laughs]. So anyway that's how it started, and he eventually put me on dialysis. I knew it was coming. It just started. I mean, I had no choice, if I wanted to live . . . I knew it was coming and then it came.

There is, in such stories, a sense of inevitability. At the same time, however, the open-ended time horizon of what clinicians call "maintenance dialysis," dialysis that will continue until one dies, can also afford glimpses of hope in the form of the possibility of a transplant, even if this will not materialize for the majority of people on dialysis:

> They did more and more testing, and testing my blood or something, I'm not sure, but they said my numbers were dropping . . . I thought my time was up. And I asked the doctor, "How much longer do I have, to be around?" So he says, "Well, you can be around for a long time, as long as you stay on dialysis. And when you can get a transplant, then be around a while longer."

In dialysis, the inexorability of the "time to start" opens out into the unbounded openness of "a long time," with the end time of a transplant shimmering like a mirage on the horizon.

When it is "time to start" dialysis, what starts is a lot of waiting. The usual regimen for hemodialysis typically involves three four-hour sessions per week. For twelve hours each week, in other words, a person who is on dialysis will sit hooked up to the machine, waiting for it to filter their blood and remove excess fluid. How people experience this time varies. Some are bothered by physical symptoms such as painful leg cramps, itchiness, or nausea, and some feel exhausted and sleep.

For those who do not suffer such symptoms, time on the machine may be, in the words of one retired doctor receiving this treatment, "very boring." This boredom was one of the reasons that the people we spoke with were willing to take part in our research. One man, when we approached him to ask about interviewing him, responded "I've got *nothing* but time!" More than an hour later, when our interview ended and we thanked him, he jokingly scolded us, "Oh, you're going to leave me now, huh?" He still had two more hours of dialysis to go.

Some people, however, found positive benefits in the time they spent dialyzing. One woman described dialysis as a sort of test that had forced her to confront and overcome some of her own shortcomings, and that had provided a structure that imposed a beneficial order on her days:

> It's taught me patience. That was my worst trait. I've had no patience. And it teaches humility, totally . . . Dialysis makes you focus on, for me, stuff in your life that you didn't . . . you weren't necessarily aware of or . . . you know, you thought you were managing them, but you're not. You have to deal with those things now. And so, for me, that was a good thing. Accountability for my health. Setting me on this set schedule. I like the routine. The routine helps me, having this specific routine is like having a job . . . I'm getting up earlier. I'm eating better because I have to. It keeps me in check with things.

Another man described the time he spent on dialysis as the catalyst for a transformation in his relationship to his religion:

> When I had my dialysis, I was out of work, I had all the time to read. So I went back to reading the Bible. And then when I was reading, reading, reading, reading, my eyes got opened. I don't know, somehow I started to ask questions. I said, "If God is a God of love, how come He kills us at the same time?" ... And then I challenged my pastor ... I asked him a million questions. He said, "Please don't come back here anymore." So ... it's kind of like I was exiled or something, just because I was asking questions ... only because of my dialysis. ... So I was, I kind of like, woke up. For forty-three years, I've been a Christian, now I've kind of like rejected Christianity, all baloney. "Why, why I have dialysis? Why give me this condition?" You know, I used to be a devout Christian, but now I'm agnostic. I can't believe it.

The dialysis schedule of four-hour sessions three times a week appears to be quite standardized, notwithstanding the considerable biological and health variations among patients. We suspect that the reasons for this lie not only in biology and medicine but also in bureaucracy and finances; patients' dialysis schedules need to accommodate one another and intersect with the work schedules of the nurses and technicians who staff the center.

Whatever the reasons behind it, the fixity of the dialysis schedule has the additional effect of producing conditions of possibility for social relations to form among the people who regularly encounter one another in the space of the dialysis center.

> We've gotten to know quite a few of them, yeah. Maybe not real well, but we try and be friendly with everybody because it makes the day go better, you know?

Some form friendships with fellow patients and exchange information, including warnings and recommendations about individual technicians, nurses, and nephrologists, and advice on how to handle symptoms or how to negotiate treatments. One man told us:

> It's a pretty close-knit community. You know, we all have the same problem, so they talk about it. That's how I found out that they have itch problems, like I do, because I thought that it was unique only to me ... I have cramps sometimes and they, these people all have cramps.

He went on to explain to us how, through experimentation and close observation, he had learned that he could control his cramping symptoms by instructing the dialysis technicians to adjust the amount of fluid removed from his blood during dialysis. He then shared this with other patients who attended dialysis with him:

> Sometimes when I come a little early, I sit in the waiting room and they come in and we all, you know, "How you doin'? How you doin'?" "Oh, I had some

cramps." So, I just tell them. I said, "This is what I do for myself. I can't say it will work for you, but this is what I do for myself."

Forming such friendships, however, also opens people up to pain and fear when a fellow patient dies, an experience described by several people we interviewed. As one said,

> Y-y-yeah . . . I've got to know a couple of [the other patients] and they winded up passing away. I got to the point where, "Do I really want to get to know somebody if they're going to wind up passing away?" And I got enough problems of my own that I don't need that to happen.

Continuing on, this man described how policies designed to protect patient privacy ran counter to acknowledgment of the human bonds forged in the bureaucratic space and time of dialysis:

> There was one guy that all of a sudden he just . . . stopped. All of a sudden he just wasn't coming around anymore, and it was like, I finally asked, and "Oh, I'm not supposed to say anything, but he passed away."

Some felt similarly hurt by policies that seemed to discount the relationships that they forged with staff:

> You know, this was really hard: my nurse, — —, died of lupus. There's someone *taking care of me* and she passes. And you know, I didn't get to find out until a *week* later. And they told me when they were putting me on [the machine] and I mean, I burst out . . . I was bawling. I went to school with her and all her cousins and it was like, "You didn't *tell* us?" And then there was like no social worker, counselor, you know? They didn't honor her or anything and she's been with the company for over twenty years.

Many people who receive dialysis for kidney failure are older, and many also have other chronic conditions and disabilities, and may need assistance (with transportation, shopping, cleaning, laundry, etc.). Travel to and from dialysis centers can be time-consuming, especially if it involves long waits for a bus. Some people feel very weak and exhausted after dialysis; for them, each session is followed by a long recovery period afterward. Wishing to remain at home and independent, but needing assistance, they describe the help they receive in ways that make it clear how keenly conscious they are of others' time as a limited and valuable resource, not to be tapped carelessly or too often:

> The daughter that lives on Bainbridge [Island] helps as much as she can. But she's a very involved, busy person. But she helps when she has the time to do it. She's very *willing* to help, but she's got so many other things going on that she . . . she doesn't have the time.

Some who were on dialysis also hoped to receive a kidney transplant and were waiting for an organ to become available. For them, time spent on dialysis could feel like a wait on a bridge to a healthier future. Here, too, however, caregivers' time enters the picture as a scarce and precious resource. One of the requirements for being "listed" for transplant is that one must have someone who can be available to provide full-time care at home for thirty days. One man who was otherwise eligible for a transplant had been unable to proceed with one because he had no caregiver. Estranged from his ex-wife and two children, he lived with his elderly and disabled father and a brother with substance abuse issues, and had a sister who was cognitively disabled. An aunt who had agreed to take care of him was diagnosed with cancer shortly before the transplant was to take place and died soon afterward. He said,

> there are some things that I need to do that I can't do. Mostly because I need somebody to be with me for thirty days. And I have nobody.

Dialysis also interferes with work schedules; some do continue to work, but many cannot. Beginning dialysis thus often means abruptly entering into a kind of forced "retirement," a new and ill-defined phase of life.

Many of the people we spoke with expressed a sense that their lives were divided into a "before" and an "after" dialysis. They struggled to make sense of what had happened to them, often looking back regretfully and with self-reproach upon their "before" self, chiding themselves for not having known and/or their providers for not having explained what they believed they should have done or not done to avoid kidney disease:

> It was my fault because I was not able to control my diabetes. Because my kidneys started stage one, which is the healthy one, until it went up, went up, went up, went up. Plus, I'm a pastry cook. So, you know? All the sweets. I just wasn't able to resist the temptation. I love chocolate, especially with nuts.

Others, however, framed their kidney disease as the outcome of structural linkages in the United States between employment and health insurance that rendered preventive care unattainable and dialysis inevitable. One 61-year-old man said:

> They only let you, you know, so much off the job and stuff like that, so I tried to come back after three months, but I just couldn't do the job. So it ended up I couldn't work anymore and I was off about a year, a year and a half, and I tried to get back to work, which I couldn't. Which meant my insurance was starting to lapse and stuff like that, so . . . I mean, I had to make a choice that I either had the insurance, but at the same time trying to keep my medical . . . or eating and so on, you know? Because my insurance would just skyrocket after

> I got out of the job. And which meant, you know, I didn't take no medication . . . and three or four years afterwards, I went to the doctor and he says, "Well, you know, your kidneys are failing."

The fact that Medicare covers dialysis for people who are too disabled to work means that for this man, as for many others, the catastrophic decline of his health and finances ironically afforded him, for the first time, access to the comprehensive medical care that, if he had been able to receive it earlier, might have made a difference in the course of his kidney disease:

> So I'm on disability and stuff like that, and which pretty much took care of my insurance and stuff, and then I get great help from the staff up here, social worker and dietician, everybody, you know. [But] I think I'm . . . I'm not going to get better. Do you know what I mean? There's so much damage and stuff like that and also, you know, it caused [all this] . . .

For the clinicians who care for people with kidney disease, dialysis entails quite different temporalities and futures. They work on tight schedules, characterized by much rushing and punctuated by moments of activity motivated by crises. Moreover, in contrast to some patients, they understand kidney failure as an "end stage" of a long-standing progressive disease process, characterized by high rates of burdensome symptoms and a limited life expectancy. Many therefore consider it important to encourage people on dialysis to engage in advance care planning (ACP), that is, considering, discussing, and documenting in advance what their wishes would be if they became incapacitated. ACP is implicitly premised on waiting for various expected health crises to happen and, in fact, it requires engaging patients and their families in a process of imagining and acting upon versions of the future that they are actively trying to avoid.

Many of the people we spoke with asserted that they had indeed "filled out the papers" and indicated their wishes to their families. Their wishes, however, were usually quite vague and phrased in ways that would be very difficult to translate into any actionable instructions in practice. One man, who indicated that he had in fact taken part in a lengthy course about ACP, said:

> pretty much I would like to be revived, but at the same time . . . I figure, I mean if I'm going to become like a vegetable or whatever, then . . . my point of view is, what the heck you're going to waste it on somebody, you know, that ain't gonna get any better.

Asked if he had ever thought about, or talked to anyone about, the possibility of someday stopping dialysis, he replied:

> Um, not as far as stopping. I mean, you know, I'm grateful enough to come in here because I figure going through dialysis, it's another day of living. I mean, that's my attitude.

Others expressed similar views. One woman said:

> I have the medical directive, and I of course talked with my son about what I want and what I don't want. And it's all written in those directives. Mostly, you know, it's about resuscitation, it always is. And I said, "If there's any hope of my recovering, then let me do it. But if the doctors say there really isn't and if I may recover somewhat but I have no quality of life left, then let me go."

As another man said:

> I told them, I says, "If I'm a vegetable, you know, if I can't function the way I'd like to, just let me go." See, if that's going to happen, I don't want to be around. I don't want to be stuck in a chair all day long, or a bed, or whatever.

Statements such as these both capture, and dance around, the central difficulty of machine-made time: dialysis, which is often begun without much discussion or deliberation "when it is time," cannot answer the question of whether or not there is hope—but unless an active decision is taken to discontinue dialysis, it also does not readily allow for "letting someone go."

Coda

This essay was written just weeks before the outbreak of the Covid-19 pandemic. In March 2020, when the pandemic began, most anthropological fieldwork came to a screeching halt; the prospect of spending an hour or more sitting close to a stranger, interviewing them face to face, without masks on, suddenly seemed reckless. People with advanced kidney disease, however, had little ability to self-isolate at home. Medically vulnerable, often elderly and poor, disproportionately Black, they were "the pandemic's perfect victims" (Eldeib 2021). Some contracted Covid-19 in the congregate setting of the dialysis unit, while some died of complications resulting from missing their regular dialysis appointments. The death rate among dialysis patients in the United States jumped by nearly 20 percent in 2020, compared with the year before. The temporalities and futures of machine-made time described here have thus been altered, and for many people foreshortened, with consequences that we do not yet fully understand.

Janelle S. Taylor is a medical anthropologist and professor in the Department of Anthropology at the University of Toronto. She is coeditor of *Consuming Motherhood* (Rutgers University Press, 2004), author of *The Public Life of the Fetal Sonogram: Technology, Consumption, and the Politics of Reproduction* (Rutgers University Press, 2008), and has published widely on topics including medical education, care planning and decision-making in end-of-life medicine, and dementia.

Ann M. O'Hare is a professor in the Division of Nephrology at the University of Washington School of Medicine, and practices at the Veterans Administration of Puget Sound Health Care System in Seattle. Her primary clinical, teaching, and research interest is in the optimal care of older adults with chronic kidney disease, and she has published widely on this topic in the medical literature.

Note

1. Funding for this study came from the National Institute of Diabetes Digestive and Kidney Diseases (NIDDK; U01DK102150). The funding source had no role in study design or the interpretation of study results and the opinions expressed in this manuscript are solely those of the authors and do not represent the opinion of NIDDK or the United States Renal Data System (USRDS).

References

Eldeib, Duaa. 2021. "They Were the Pandemic's Perfect Victims." *ProPublica*, 28 December. Accessed 4 January 2022. https://www.propublica.org/article/they-were-the-pandemics-perfect-victims.

Kaufman, Sharon. 2015. *Ordinary Medicine: Extraordinary Treatments, Longer Lives, and the Dilemma of Where to Draw the Line*. Durham, NC: Duke University Press.

Chapter 5

Waiting for Thieves
Nighttime Capital and the Labor of Sitting in Niger

Adeline Masquelier

Eight-thirty in the evening. Save for the mosque, two small shops, and a handful of houses hooked to the electrical grid, the rest of this poor and crowded Niamey neighborhood—a tangle of mud-walled alleys linking secluded courtyards and threading through bumpy, uneven terrain—is pitch-black. The only glimpses of street life that I catch in what feels like an ocean of darkness are isolated pools of light, created by oil lamps and, here and there, a wandering flashlight. Occasionally a passing car rumbling down a bumpy dirt path pierces the blackness with its headlights. Though I know the way, having walked in this neighborhood many times, I hesitate as the lane suddenly curves to the right—should I be heading straight instead? At night, the townscape looks and feels different: if darkness flattens depth, paradoxically the silhouettes of certain trees and buildings appear ominously large. Meanwhile, other shapes are softened, as if swallowed by their obscure surroundings. As I make my way along a narrow, winding alley, I hear the young men before I can see them. In the dark, stillness grows and sounds acquire a distinct quality; their origin is harder to trace. Having just returned from *isha*, the last Muslim prayer of the day, the *samari* (unmarried young men) are assembling at the *fada*, the conversation group or "tea circle" they join every evening to socialize, pass time, drink tea, and play cards. As we exchange greetings, a young man makes space for me on the bench on which he is sitting. The *fadantchés* (*fada* members) are planning to host a dance party in a few weeks and there are details to attend to, such as the design and printing of tickets (male guests are charged an entrance fee), the event promotion, the catering, and so on.

Someone lights an oil lamp and I notice things—the boom box set on a mat and, next to it, the utensils used for tea preparation—that were previously hidden in the darkness. Within minutes, a young girl appears, carrying a large dish of rice with sauce; she lays it at the feet of the assembled *fadantchés*. The young men huddle around the dish and dip into the pile of sticky rice with their right hands. I imitate them. We eat in silence, quickly. Once the dish is emptied, a plastic jug filled with water—which *fadantchés* use for their pre-worship ablutions—is passed around so everyone can rinse their hands. Tahirou, the "tea-man" (or tea-maker), is lighting coals in a small funnel-shaped brazier. As the coals start to turn red, he shuffles them a bit before fanning them gently with a small piece of cardboard he just tore from the empty packet of tea. He then sets a tiny kettle on the glowing embers and waits for the water to boil. Next to him, a couple of young men have started a game of checkers, while the rest of the men return to their discussion of who will do what in preparation for the upcoming party.

In Niger, *samari*, whose economic futures are overshadowed by uncertainty, meet every evening at the *fada* to pass time and partake in ordinary pleasures: playing backgammon, circulating jokes, sharing cigarettes, and enjoying each other's company. The *fada* provides a refuge from the harsh world out there. As a place of friendship and conviviality, it comes alive in the early evening when young men huddle around bubbling teapots, waiting for what will be the first of several rounds of tea-drinking. *Samari* often say that tea is the main reason for having a *fada*: without tea, they point out, there can be no *fada*. As we shall see, waiting for the tea to brew at the *fada* is not only an important mode of sociality, it is also a form of time management, central to the way that young men, many of whom are un(der)employed, transform insecure presents into purposeful temporalities. Waiting happens in time, yet it also makes time. When marginalized *samari* colonize the streets as others sleep, obscurity turns out to be less a feature of the nighttime (though it is that too) than it is a characteristic of young men's futures. How young men, by repurposing the nighttime, carve out places of relevance for themselves through tea-making and other practices is what this chapter is about.[1]

Ayouba, a gangly economics student with a proclivity for quoting Marx, is explaining to me how Galaxy, his *fada*, came to be: what brought the original members together, how the *fada* acquired its name, and so on. When I ask him whether he and his friends ever got into a clash with a rival *fada*, he laughs before recounting an encounter he had with some other *samari* that almost led to a fight:

There was a *fada* named Death Row in Yantala [a Niamey neighborhood]. The leader was called Talls le Guerrier [the warrior]—his father worked at the US embassy. Those guys were mean, they threatened everyone. If you walked with a girl, they would kidnap her and rape her in their *ghettos* [sleeping quarters for unmarried young men]. They terrorized everyone . . . Talls was known throughout Niamey. Even little kids knew him—they admired him. He had a territory. His name appeared on the walls of the city . . . One day we were walking in Talls's neighborhood to go to a dance organized by some girls. We walked past the place where Talls was sitting with his lieutenants. He hailed us; he was angry: "What are you doing here? Do you know where you are?" He insisted that we had provoked him, he wanted to fight. We had to deflate the situation—quickly, calmly. It turns out he was upset that girls who belonged to his *fada* had invited us. He felt that we had stolen "his" girls. He wanted to knock us down. That was a long time ago.

Even longer ago, when young men's *fadas* were first created, they became part of an emerging security landscape that often operated in the twilight zone between the legal and the illegal.[2] According to a well-rehearsed narrative, when international lenders pressured the Nigerien government to trim its security budget in the late 1980s as part of a global trend of deregulations and privatizations, law enforcement agencies were gutted, crime rose in urban areas, and ordinary citizens feared for their safety. The large-scale layoffs and reduced recruitment in the police initiated under the new regimen of structural adjustments signaled the retreat of the state as enforcer of law and order. In emerging contexts of austerity compounded by rising unemployment, new forms of urban violence emerged, triggered by the quest for survival. These perceived threats, in turn, prompted the creation of an array of non-state policing organizations, such as private security guard companies and vigilante groups, that operated largely beyond the reach of the state in the 1990s. In Niamey, the vigilante groups, known as *'yan banga*, were composed of marginalized, unemployed youth. Financed by local political leaders and businessmen, the *'yan banga* scoured neighborhoods after dark when ordinary residents slept. They largely operated with impunity and with the support of a political leadership concerned that rising crime could affect its popularity. Taking advantage of the night's potential for blurring legality and illegality, they routinely preyed on the individuals they caught, assaulting them and robbing them. Rumor has it that a number of thieves were killed by *'yan banga*. The young vigilantes' brand of swift justice was initially approved of by a populace eager for the restoration of a sense of safety. With time, and as details of their exactions came to light, they became something of a liability, and many local residents and business owners withdrew their patronage.

Searching for alternative ways to protect their homes and businesses, urban residents and shop owners turned to the jobless young men who had taken to drinking tea in the street late into the night. In the 1970s, under the military regime of Seyni Kountché, a curfew was instituted in urban areas that prevented any type of gathering in the street at night—urban youth represented a threat that needed to be contained. After Kountché's death, the curfew was lifted as part of the wider liberalization process that affected markets, media, policing, and politics. Unemployed young men, who did not have to get up in the morning, sat together outside their homes after nightfall. They became a trusted resource that people came to rely on in the absence of organized modes of policing, even though some of them were suspected of using predatory methods.

For a number of urban residents, including civil servants and Muslim religious leaders, the *fada* symptomatizes youthful indulgence and laziness. These critics derogatorily refer to young men sitting in *fadas* as *'yan zaman gari banza* (the good-for-nothing town residents) to stress their worthlessness. "They would rather drink tea by the side of the road than pick up a hoe, these youths of today. No wonder the country is in trouble," a retired science teacher told me. Rather than seeing *fadas* as an offshoot of precarity—a means of confronting social immobility—the former teacher blamed them for feeding young men's addiction to tea. By joining a *fada*, he implied, *samari* compromised not only their future but also their country's future. Fending off criticisms that *fadas* promote idleness and substance addiction, many *samari* strive to present themselves as virtuous, productive citizens. They point to their civic-minded forms of engagement, including security work.

As people turned to the *fadas* for security, they plied the more dependable ones with tea, cigarettes, and beans, and tasked them with guarding their *quartiers* at night. Many *fadas* earned reputations as gatekeepers of their neighborhoods and were progressively incorporated into an informal security system that filled the gap left by the retreating state. Years later, some *fadas* have disbanded, their members dispersed across the country in the search for livelihoods. Others live on but no longer have crime-fighting ambitions: when members meet, it is largely to unwind in the company of friends. Meanwhile, new *fadas* have emerged, fueled by chronic joblessness and a recognition that sociality is the best remedy for idleness, despair, and frustration. Many of them watch for thieves. After sunset, the streets of Niamey and other Nigerien towns are filled with tea-sipping young men, prompting anthropologist Mirco Göpfert (2012: 63) to observe that the nighttime urban landscape is "dominated by *fadas*."

People commonly say that by standing watch while other residents sleep, *fadas* ensure the safety of their neighborhoods. There is less crime, I was often told, because young men sit in the street for much of the night, deterring burglars from breaking into people's homes. Friends and neighbors have shared harrowing stories of nocturnal intruders caught by *fadantchés* and carted off to jail. Yet not everyone is convinced that *fadas* enhance nighttime security.

The line between protection and predation can be rather porous, and it is not unheard of for *fadantchés* to be accused of engaging in the same scare tactics the *'yan banga* drew on to maintain order in their neighborhoods.[3] More often than not, it is the potential for violence between *fadas* that has people worried. Members of Death Row were known to keep a tight watch on the patch of streets they policed—so tight that they would deny members of rival *fadas* entry into "their" territory. The very act of walking in front of them was perceived as a provocation. As Ayouba makes clear, nevertheless, Talls's claim that the members of Galaxy were trespassing had more to do with control over the "social capital" girls represented for Death Row than with the safety of the neighborhood. At another level, the claim bolstered Talls's projection of tough masculinity and Death Row's uncontested dominance over the district.[4]

"Young boys wrote Talls's name on all the [street] walls.[5] They wanted to be like him. But he scared people. Talls's guys, if they liked your clothes, they would steal them. A bunch of ruffians, I tell you, they even intimidated the military," Ayouba explained. Beyond the question of whether *fadas* such as Death Row operated as gangs, Ayouba's testimony points to the role of violence in young men's quest for self-realization. In landscapes of diminished opportunities, the reputation *fadas* built by engaging in street brawls fed into a "culture of compensation" (Gilroy 1993: 85) built around gritty masculinity. Central to this boastful masculine culture and serving as a counterweight to deprivation was bodybuilding. Bodybuilding produced "champions," strong, muscular, belligerent individuals who avenged the *fada*'s honor when it was threatened. Many *fadantchés* developed an obsession with muscularity—a trend some observers found worrisome. By using their bulky, burly physiques as "means of intimidation and serviceable hardware" (Wacquant 1998: 334), Death Row members promoted their thuggish image. Paradoxically, such schemes increased the young men's employability. Several Death Row members landed permanent jobs as watchmen or bouncers by capitalizing on the security industry's growing need for manly, martial bodies.

In this chapter, I consider the *fada* through the lens of the nocturnal to examine how idle, mostly unemployed young men reclaim a place in society by sitting nightly in the street while others sleep. Specifically,

I examine how some *samari* have inserted themselves into the shifting landscape of crime prevention by deploying their social immobility—and the temporal freedom that comes with it—as an asset. In branding themselves as nighttime sentinels, alert to potential threats, *samari* convert the act of sitting—denounced by some as an expression of slothfulness—into a form of labor. How does the *fada*'s engagement in community policing exploit the "meantime" in which unemployed *samari* find themselves? What productive temporalities do night watches yield for young men faced with compromised futures? How do these temporalities shape the *fada* itself as a structure created specifically for managing time in the absence of routine occupations? As an organizing principle, David Pratten (2008: 11) writes, providing security can become a central locus of creativity and improvisation. In what follows, I discuss how the experience of waiting for elusive futures is redefined through the cultivation of nighttime vigilance. As a distinctive temporality located between sunset and sunrise, nighttime is often reduced to a negative space in which darkness is synonymous with stillness and slumber. Yet, for *samari* who are excluded from the arena of stable wages, the night offers the chance to appear to be "doing something"—something useful. Put very simply, the night is the time for catching thieves. Through a critical focus on the nocturnality of *fadas*, this chapter unsettles the notion that nighttime is reducible to a suspension of activities while shedding light on ways in which youths at the margins survive by making the most of nighttime's interstitiality.

Youths at the Margins

In Hausa, Niger's lingua franca, the term *"fada"* conventionally designates the chief's or the emir's court, a masculine place of public audience and deliberation. Thirty or so years ago, young male urbanites recuperated the concept of the *fada* as a customary form of assembly to designate their own social gatherings. In the process, the *fada* of *samari* became a nighttime congregation—a place of nocturnal encounters for young men who had nowhere to go.

It is often said that young men's *fadas* (or tea circles) first appeared in Niamey in 1990, when university students went on strike to pressure the government to institute a multiparty democracy. Against the backdrop of political instability and economic insecurity, the *fadas* constituted a forum where striking students could pass time and debate the fate of their country. The *fadas* became privileged sites for the performance of citizenship (Masquelier 2019). Today, these *fadas* are nostalgically remembered by some as incubators of political careers—"chronotopes" (Bakhtin 1981) bridging personal histories and collective experience. It was allegedly in such *fadas* during that period that *samari* who later made a career in politics articulated their vision of democratic futures.

An alternative narrative situates the birth of *fadas* in Zinder, Niger's second-largest city, in tandem with the emergence of private radios (Lund 2009). In recent years, some of these youth groups, locally referred to as *palais* (French for "palace"), have become synonymous with gangs. Like the *fadas*, *palais* are a product of chronic poverty and disaffection. Yet they often elicit fear and suspicion in the citizenry, who hold them responsible for robberies and general insecurity (Schritt 2015). In 2011, a civil protest turned into a violent riot after being infiltrated by members of *palais*, summoned by agenda-driven politicians. The incident, which caused widespread terror and significant material damage, consolidated in the public eye the close kinship between *palais* and criminality.

Although some *fadas* have a history of vigilantism, it is problematic to reduce them systematically to gangs. There is a great deal of diversity between *fadas*. While some operate as non-governmental organizations in which young men hone their activism, many serve as training platforms where *samari* acquire professional skills, develop musical talents, and learn the ABCs of courting girls. During elections, a number of *fadas* become campaign headquarters for political parties. Although membership generally transcends ethnic affiliations, educational levels, and religious orientations, some *fadas* are more homogeneous. Most unite young men of the same age with shared musical interests or religious commitments. "I live in a *fada* where people have a more or less identical conception of the world despite the differences that occasionally arise," nineteen-year-old Boubacar, a recent high-school graduate, told me. "Most of us are high-school or university students but some never attended school. I am not close to everyone, but still, the *fada* is a good place for friendship."

Not all *fadas* are structured around the same notions of sociality and citizenship. Some are informal conversation spots lacking a specific agenda.[6] A significant number of them, however, are formal organizations, supervised by an executive team and animated by a spirit of competition. Among other things, *fadantchés* give names to their *fadas* and adorn the walls against which they sit with loud, occasionally sophisticated, designs, enhancing their prominence in a landscape saturated by youthful signs of ingenuity in the midst of want. These creative endeavors are a reminder that rivalry often plays a part in the making of empowered selves. Through dress and bodybuilding, musical shows and masterful expressions of hospitality, romantic conquests but also violent confrontations, *fadantchés* experiment with, and compete through, various configurations of manhood. Diverse as *samari*'s pastimes and preoccupations may be, one cannot grasp their significance without acknowledging the context of precarity and scarcity that paved the way for the emergence of *fadas* (Masquelier 2019).

After independence in 1960, education was the springboard for social mobility. Schooled Nigeriens automatically entered the civil service and enjoyed financial stability, as well as the awe and respect they commanded as members of a learned elite. Three decades or so later, the policies of structural adjustment that sought to open up Niger's economy to the world would radically constrict the labor market, eroding formal paths to social mobility for succeeding generations of job seekers. Educational credentials no longer translated into job security, and precarity replaced the promise of upward mobility. Unless someone "with connections" intervened on their behalf, *jeunes diplômés* (young graduates) rarely obtained the well-remunerated, permanent positions that they assumed their education, command of French, and professional competence entitled them to. While some refused to take low-skilled jobs that they viewed as degrading, many were trapped in temporary, low-level, white-collar jobs. Their less educated peers who navigated

Figure 5.1. A wall adorned with the name of the *fada* that meets there. Niamey, Niger, 2018. © Adeline Masquelier.

the informal economy struggled too. The incomes they earned as petty vendors, laborers, motorcycle taxi drivers, or street hustlers were rarely enough to sustain households.

Denied a sustainable pathway to decent livelihoods, many young men repaired to the *fadas*. As places for waiting out the "crisis," the *fadas* became critical spaces of hope and experimentation for bored *samari* struggling to make their lives matter. At the *fada*, young men drank green tea—which they brewed, Tuareg-style, in small kettles on coal-filled braziers. They played games, listened to the radio, and discursively remade the world. *Fadas* provided a refuge from formal social constraints—a kind of "heterotopia" that lay beyond the grasp of dominant social institutions and had its own temporalities, ethical codes, and definitions of success. In the company of their similarly impecunious peers, *samari* momentarily bracketed the indignities wrought by economic marginalization and the anxieties that arose in the absence of predictable social trajectories. "At the *fada*, everyone is treated equally. It doesn't matter if you make no money, we're brothers," I was told.

Infrastructures and Practices of Anticipation

In Niger, much of the labor force works in the so-called informal economy. The retreat of the state implemented through successive waves of structural adjustments has resulted in inadequate salaries, volatile employment conditions, and fewer job prospects for many workers in the formal economy. The private sector, insufficiently developed, could not compensate for the loss of jobs in the public sector. As widespread unemployment turned into a permanent condition, defying predictions that the hurt inflicted by donor-mandated fiscal reforms would be temporary, *fadas* became an enduring fixture of the urban landscape. In the absence of other modes of self-affirmation, young men displaced by the workings of capital turn *fadas* into outlets for the boastful performance of masculinity. Yet, *fadas* do more than host "tournaments of value" (Appadurai 1986). Through daily (or rather nightly) forms of training, routines, and regimens, *samari* cultivate loyalty to the *fada*, as well as patience (*han'kuri*)—a durational ethic that reframes hope as a collective resource and involves "waiting while working to make something happen" (Procupez 2015: 564). The weight work, teatime, and watchful sitting they engage in produce stability and continuity—something like permanence in the face of persistent uncertainty.

The *fada* is a masculine space, designed to address young men's needs and aspirations. Given the gendered division of labor and pastimes operating in Nigerien society, few *fadas* have female members.[7] The presence of women disrupts the *fada*'s homosocial intimacy. Moreover, young women must not appear to loiter in the street, lest they incite gossip. They can ill afford to sit at the *fada* in plain view of passersby. In this overwhelmingly Muslim society, in which women's access to public spaces is regulated, *'yammata* (young unmarried females) do not openly socialize with *samari*. Once darkness has fallen, however, they are less hampered by daytime conventions and strictures. At night, *fadas* provide meeting places for lovers.[8] Insofar as *'yammata* can be said to inhabit the masculine space of the *fada* "in the negative" (Masquelier 2019: 101), that is, confined to the shadows, they help sustain young men's enactment of masculinity, orienting their desires and aspirations in specific directions.

Unemployed or barely employed young men forced to navigate volatile economic contexts often mention the emotional cost of waiting for things to pick up. The wait is a source of anxiety largely because it is open-ended. Until the job market expands, young men face considerable uncertainty. Some of them are hopeful that their situations will improve—in the meantime they must arm themselves with *han'kuri*, patience—while others live with a gnawing sense that the future they yearn for may never come to pass. For yet others, hope alternates with disillusion when attempts to position themselves in the path of opportunity meet with failure. No matter where they stand, they feel dispossessed of the predictable futures they were promised by politicians seeking the support of young voters and by development organizations advocating education as a solution to poverty and underdevelopment.[9] Trapped in the imposed presentism of destitution, many postpone marriage and parenthood.

For *samari* unable to fulfill social expectations associated with adulthood, time is often experienced as a burden. Some fret that the search for employment gets harder with each passing year because, even if they can claim additional professional experience, they also have to compete with new cohorts of job seekers. I met *samari* who, when seeking admission to training programs, discovered that they were "too old" to qualify for them. While they were stuck in time, the clock kept on ticking, adding to their sense of "stuckness." As a form of anticipatory infrastructure, the *fada* helps transform the anxious wait of *samari* forced to put their lives on hold into a meaningful set of temporalities. Specifically, it offers mechanisms for punctuating the dead stretches of experience we call boredom.

When people are bored, time lengthens. The Germans have a term that captures the excruciating sense of time's stillness: *langeweile*, which literally means "a long whiling away of time." Rather than being a source of enjoyment, the elongation of now-time is felt as a dulling of experience:

the world turns grey, uniform, senseless (Anderson 2004; Benjamin 2003; Goodstein 2005). At the *fada*, the activities in which *samari* engage "customize" (Flaherty 2003) temporal experience. They restore temporally adrift *samari* to a sense of lived time and in the process alleviate their sense of "stuckness" (Masquelier 2020).

Take the preparation and drinking of tea, which I call "teatime" (Masquelier 2013). Once the water and, later, the tea are boiling, and the sugar has been added, the contents of the kettle must boil for a long while before the tea is ready. There are three rounds to each tea session. Since the same clump of tea leaves is used throughout, the first round of tea is the strongest (and bitterest) while the last one is the weakest. Teatime cannot be hurried as the duration of each step of the process is critical not only to the quality of the tea produced but also to the pleasures of anticipation felt by participants. One might say that waiting for the tea to brew is inseparable from the experience of drinking it.[10] Teatime takes time in the sense that it absorbs time while also giving participants a heightened awareness of duration. As a collective form of waiting, it creates a timespace for catching up with friends, strengthening social connections, and brainstorming about new projects. Time, which *samari* living with an unclear temporal horizon experience as stagnation, flows again. Rather than being endured, teatime is a form of durational enjoyment.

Teatime is a time filled with rhythms, durations, routines, and events; it is a time that allows for both stability (through repetition) and forwardness (through novelty). While *samari* often stress the addictive qualities of tea, noting that they become dependent on the rush it causes to function normally, they also allude to its soothing properties. In sum, tea is an effective remedy for boredom. As we shall see, so are the night watches in which many *fadas* engage.

Nighttime and Its Labors

In the writings of poets, philosophers, and historians, the night has often been constructed as a space of license, lawlessness, and volatility where the rules regulating daytime activities do not apply. Nighttime "heightens fears," Yasmine Musharbash (2013: 56) notes. The Greek tragedian Euripides wrote that "the day is for honest men, the night for thieves." Until the advent of the Industrial Revolution, evening hours escaped legal oversight in both urban and rural Europe. The conviction that "nighttime fostered duplicity" led many localities to forbid transactions of various kinds after dark (Ekirch 2005: 84). Meanwhile, constables and watchmen in England enjoyed considerable latitude when dealing with suspected criminals at night (Ekirch 2005). In Venice and Florence, summary courts arose in the late Middle Ages for the prosecution of nighttime offenses. In Denmark, citizens were sometimes granted permission to convene nightly courts for trying offenders (Ekirch 2005). Across Europe, magistrates exacted more severe punishments for nighttime offenses. To this day, breaking and entering at nighttime is more harshly punished in many jurisdictions than similar daytime offenses. In sum, the night has its "own space" (Certeau 1984) and, as such, it escapes the normalizing temporal order and its moral, social, and legal dictates.

Remarkably, despite the rich repertoire of images, narratives, and activities the night has produced, nocturnity has, until recently, prompted only limited anthropological interest. A general assumption guiding anthropological analyses has been that, due to sleep's psychophysiological constraints, nighttime corresponds to a "collective 'parenthesization' of society's activities in daytime" (Galinier et al 2010: 820). To be sure, anthropologists noted early on that the night is often experienced as a "time of insecurity" (Radcliffe-Brown 1922: 333), during which all sorts of mysterious and menacing creatures, unbeknownst to the slumbering masses, go about their nefarious business. Witches are frequently portrayed as nocturnal agents, as are vampires and ghouls of various kinds. Anthropological accounts also mention the night in combination with unusual, marginal, or liminoid activities. For instance, certain rituals are held after dark to capitalize on the power of "the between"—that space between sunset and sunrise that is associated with normative laxness. The all-night performances held in Sri Lanka to exorcize demons and restore to health the people they harm have been well documented (Kapferer 1983). In Niger, secluded Muslim wives, confined to their homes during the day, enjoy freedom of movement at night (Masquelier 2009). However, the night is not perceived as a legitimate anthropological object in these accounts. It is merely the backdrop against which human activities, or the lack thereof, unfold.

Recently, scholars have come to recognize that the night deserves its own analyses (Hornberger 2008). They have urged us to take a closer look at the nighttime, the infrastructures it depends on, the social dynamics it shapes, and the knowledges it produces. Robert Blunt (2017) focuses on things nocturnal in Western Kenya to analyze how a form of "night-running" practiced by individuals alleged to be sterile depends for its efficacy on the anonymity of darkness. In Rijk van Dijk's (2007) discussion of Ghanaian Pentecostal churches in The Hague, the night emerges as a treacherous domain where evil powers that cannot bear the light of day reside. By holding nighttime vigils, church members not only defy these nocturnal powers but also put their own faith to the test (van

Dijk 2007). Beatrix Hauser (2005) considers how the night is produced by Indian worshipers during a Hindu festival for the goddess Buddhi Thakurani. Night, she notes, is associated with a particular quality of time that matches the character of Thakurani, who "travels through the night" (Hauser 2005: 221) and is therefore more accessible to her devotees at that time. Nighttime, in these works, typically figures as anti-structure—a space that comes with its own rules and rhythms.

Rather than treating nighttime as rupture, other scholars have analyzed it as an extension of daytime through a critical focus on nightwork. Their discussions of the "nocturnalization" of professional activities in late capitalist society has thoroughly unsettled the notion that nighttime signals the suspension of social life. With the spread of flexible, intermittent, and temporary forms of employment, the night, far from being the exclusive domain of thieves, constables, and night soil men, is filled with people working night shifts. Nightwork turns workers into disposable units of the post-industrial age while guaranteeing the round-the-clock production—and consumption—demanded by capitalism (Crary 2014). Rather than disrupting the architecture of time maintenance, night workers consolidate it even as their own lives become marked by "social asynchrony" (Lallement 2003).

The forms of informal surveillance in which *fadas* engage after dark signal that the unemployed also seek to insert themselves in the nighttime economy. In the poor urban neighborhoods lacking police patrols, *fadas* remain associated with crime prevention. At night, the streets of Niamey, Maradi, Dosso, and other urban centers are filled with clusters of idle young men who monitor the comings and goings of passersby, ready to pounce on suspected thieves. "We are the ears and eyes of the *quartier*," I was told by a young man, who sat with friends for much of the night in front of his father's compound. "If someone looks suspicious, we don't let him go through. I can assure you no crime gets committed on our watch." For keeping watch over their neighborhoods, *fadantchés* are sometimes referred to as *'yan sa ido* (literally "those who keep their eyes out"), that is, those who remain alert—the observers.

Fadantchés have been given a variety of nicknames referencing idleness that constitute an expression of laziness and vice. As a form of passive inactivity that leaves one vulnerable to the devil's snares, idleness leads to delinquency. Some *fadas* are suspected of harboring criminals; others are criticized for fostering moral decay and substance addiction. *Sumuri* anxious to discredit these narratives have capitalized on the urgent need for security to demonstrate their worth. Mounkaila, a young man from the town of Dogondoutchi, told me that people in his neighborhood were initially suspicious of his *fada*: "Some elders insulted us, they thought we were delinquents." After Mounkaila and another *fadantché* caught a thief absconding with his loot one night, the neighbors' attitude toward their *fada* changed. "People even brought us tea and sugar."

Mounkaila's testimony provides something of a model for how some *fadas* have become integrated into the landscape of security. By catching a thief and handing him, unharmed, to the police, the two *samari* demonstrated that they were honest, responsible. The *fada*, their feat suggested, served a purpose in the community. Jobless *fadantchés*, who stay up late at night because they have no reason to rise early, can watch over the street while others sleep. Their watchful presence deters would-be burglars. Once synonymous with impotence and irrelevance, the sitting of *samari* is here redemptively classified as useful occupation. Note that the kind of labor that "sitting at the *fada*" encompasses varies from *fada* to *fada*. Beyond security work, *fadantchés* open and close gates for cars, unload packages from trucks, and perform a variety of other tasks for neighbors and patrons. Now that it has been relocated in the "chief's court," the low-pay, manual work many young men would otherwise reject becomes a form of honorable labor.

Fadantchés delight in narrating their exploits as crime fighters. They cite the numerous thieves they have caught as proof of their indispensability to the neighborhood. They recall (with great accuracy) the circumstances that led to the capture of intruders and other "criminals." Their feats occasionally acquire a mythical dimension. Talls, the leader of Death Row who guaranteed Yantala's security, became a role model for many young men: "Many *samari* left school to join Talls's *fada*. They wanted to be *considérés*—you know, be like him," Ayouba told me. As Talls's story suggests, however, the distinction between perpetrators and law enforcers can be fuzzy. Mindful that the days of the *'yan banga* and their summary brand of justice are over, *fadantchés* stress that they do not inflict violence on their "prisoners" and simply hand them to the police. Boubacar, who had apprenticed to become a carpenter but was jobless, told me about a thief he and his friends caught one night. It was the week before Tabaski, during which Nigeriens slaughter sheep in commemoration of the sacrifice of Abraham. The man was stealing a ram in a neighbor's compound (the price of rams rises sharply before the holiday). The young men knew better than to beat him up. After brutalizing an individual he suspected of carrying stolen goods, Boubacar's older brother had received a jail sentence. There had been hospital bills to pay. "My brother, you see, he thought he could punish the guy. But it was he who ended up behind bars," Boubacar noted.

Interstitiality: The Work of Time

Recent scholarship has shed light on the temporalities of precarity, pointing to the ways in which the experience of time is mediated by impoverishment and economic dislocation. Bruce O'Neill (2017) writes of how life for homeless people in Bucharest loses its pulsing quality, ultimately slowing down to a crawl. Martin Frederiksen (2013: 11) describes how, in Georgia, young men for whom life has been emptied of its forwardness exist in a state of "temporal marginality." Other anthropologists have noted how a characteristic of precarious time is the fusion of work and leisure, to the extent that the search for money absorbs every moment. In the process, time loses its rhythms, its eventfulness, its texture; it is experienced as a dull, suffusive, and endless "now." Meanwhile, scholars of securitization in uncertain times argue that security, given its future-oriented nature (that is, its reliance on the temporality of threats, dangers, and fears to formulate risk-free futures or, conversely, eschatological futures), must be considered in relation to time and temporality (Holbraad and Pedersen 2013; Konopinski 2014). How, they ask, is security invested in forging particular kinds of futures and who exactly is included in this vision? Grasping *fadantchés'* experience as gatekeepers of the neighborhood, I argue, requires attending to both the enforced presentism of economic privation and the forward-looking stance of security work. It calls for an exploration of the temporal regimes followed by *fadantchés* that transform the *fada* into a kind of anticipatory infrastructure—a place of and for watchful waiting.

Waiting at the *fada* (whether one waits for a job or for a thief) is both an experiential condition and a calculated posture for seizing opportunities as they arise. Consider this testimony from a sociology student for what it suggests about the *fadas'* mobilization against threats of any kind:

> We ensure the security of the *quartier*. No theft takes place on our watch. Since we're here until *vingt-trois heures* [11 PM] or even *zéro heure* [midnight], we keep watch on the *quartier* and people feel safe. A few days ago, a car caught fire. The owner wasn't around. We were at the *fada,* so we saw it; we immediately mobilized ourselves and brought sand to quench the fire . . . If we hadn't been there, who knows what would have happened.

For young men faced with an abundance of time but limited prospects, sitting is part of a repertoire of deliberate moves through which to carve out spaces of relevance in a landscape of uneven access to work and wealth. By attending to the ruses and maneuvers that form what he calls a network of antidiscipline, Michel de Certeau illuminates the less visible forms of agency in which ordinary people engage. He calls these practices,

Figure 5.2. "Couloir Danger" (Corridor Danger) is the name some *fadantchés* gave to a *fada* to keep away potential trespassers and thieves. Niamey, Niger, 2015. © Adeline Masquelier.

which the apparatus of power tries to repress, tactics. Determined by the absence of power, tactics seize opportunities on the sly. They are the "clever tricks of the 'weak' within the order established by the 'strong'" (Certeau 1984: 40).

Samari, who describe themselves as the eyes and ears of the neighborhood when other modes of surveillance are lacking, demonstrate the flexibility, cunning, and surreptitiousness that are the hallmarks of the tactic. Indeed, it is by "vigilantly mak[ing] use of the cracks that particular conjunctions open in the surveillance of the proprietary powers" (Certeau 1984: 37) that their nocturnal watchfulness has gained some measure of legitimacy. By naming their *fada* "Rien À Signaler" (All Is Clear) or RAS, a group of young men formalized their roles as guardians of the stretch of street they occupied at night. In the fashion of Couloir Danger (Corridor Danger), a *fada* that functioned as a roadblock, forcing cars and motorbikes to slow down and occasionally shaking the drivers down, RAS was said to be constantly on the watch, with members waiting and watching, ready to tackle intruders at a moment's notice. "We once woke up the *quartier* trying to catch an intruder. We were like a patrol. Always sitting. Thieves cannot pass through," a *fadantché* turned schoolteacher recalled, implying that immobility was its own form of action.

Figure 5.3. The *fada*'s name, "22H00," is painted on the wall against which members gather in Dogondoutchi, Niger, 2015. © Adeline Masquelier.

Jamilou, a member of Guerriers du 3ème Millénaire (Warriors of the Third Millennium), conflated waiting with watchfulness: "We are at the *fada* from 9 PM until 5 AM . . . We are watching, we see everything. One night a thief came running down the street. We pulled up a chair, and he tripped over it. Then we delivered him to the police." Rather than being made to wait (Auyero 2012), Jamilou and his friends turned waiting into watchfulness—a critical mode of tuning in to the darkness. By inserting themselves into a specific temporality, a "dead" time that they animated with their intentionality, their orientations to others, and their powers of scrutiny, they made sitting tactical: "We keep watch while others sleep," Jamilou said. At night, linear time is suspended for those who sleep; for *fadantchés* on nocturnal watches, on the other hand, it is precisely at night that linear time is lived. Put differently, the watchful waiting of *fadantchés* is purposive, relational, engaged. As an instance of what Peter Dwyer (2009: 18) calls "situational" waiting, it is eminently preferable to the dull, oppressive wait—the "existential" wait (Dwyer 2009: 18)—experienced by those who lack temporal agency.

In the way it exploits interstitial opportunities, the attentive vigilance of *fadantchés* exemplifies how tactics, unable as they are to control time, can only seize propitious moments. Tactics, Certeau (1984: 39) argues, pin their hopes "on the clever utilization of time." The notion is not lost on certain *fadantchés*. "We called our *fada* '0 Heure' [Zero Hour] because we meet at night. And we're happy. It's the time when everyone is sleeping and we're here," explained a young man nicknamed Lama, after a former goalie of Guyanese origin on the French national soccer team. Aside from suggesting that tactical moves earn validation in relation to "the pertinence they lend to time" (Certeau 1984: 38), the name "0 Heure" signals that the *fada*'s nocturnity is not an instance of temporal insurgency. Granted, as the moment when day-night folds into night-day (Handelman 2005: 248), midnight is liminality par excellence. Nevertheless, the time spent at the *fada* after dark calibrates—and fits into—a larger temporal order: far from disrupting the productivity of others, members of 0 Heure protect it by ensuring that their time of rest is not interrupted.[11]

Lama's testimony is also a reminder that, in contrast to the day, which people typically experience as a period of rules and restrictions, the night comes with freedom (De Boeck and Plissart 2004: 157). At night, visibility is restricted. Darkness is sticky; it clings to matter, blurring the outlines of things. As such, it "protects secrets, private and public ones" (Van der Geest 2007: 24). During that time, *samari* meet with girlfriends without having to fear the disapproving stares of elders. Darkness empowers them in other ways. After nightfall, young men rendered irrelevant by the workings of daytime capital become watchmen to whom local residents entrust their property. Freed from the conventions of the daytime, they "own" the street.

Tea and the Production of Nocturnal Bodies

As compensation for ensuring the safety of the *quartiers*, business owners ply *fadantchés* with tea and sugar. Tea and sugar—so often derided by elders for their corrupting effect on youth—keep *fadantchés* awake and attentive to their surroundings. Students told me that drinking tea enabled them to cram for exams: "Tea helps you to concentrate. It gives you time, you don't need to sleep anymore." Besides signaling how surveillance is entangled with sociality (tea is always consumed in the company of others), the nighttime consumption of tea contributes to the fabrication of "nocturnal bodies," impervious to the soporific effect of darkness and alert to potential happenings. Rather than constituting a waste of time (*bata lokaci*), as critics of *fada* culture argue, tea drinking here is about *making* time by helping tea drinkers overcome drowsiness and extend their waketime.

By provoking forced wakefulness, the multiple servings of sweet tea ingested by *samari* enable the diurnization of the night. The night watch makes you hungry, *samari* say. Long after their neighbors have gone to bed, *fadantchés* cook a pot of beans—their favorite food—to calm the rumblings of their stomachs. Not only are beans (with rice) the best remedy for hunger, but they also absorb the acidity that tea may cause on an empty stomach. Rather than marking the cessation of civil society, nighttime at the *fada* is filled with cooking, card games, and conversations. As such, it differs from the repetitive tedium of security work performed by guards at roadblocks, buffer zones, and border checkpoints (Konopinski 2014).

The tea *fadantchés* drink is sometimes laced with tramadol (opioid pain medication). In fact, some not only consume the beverage to stay awake but also, by supplying it to other *fadas*, draw revenues from it. Some *fadas* are allegedly embedded in networks of cocaine consumption and distribution. Substance use is a coping strategy for dealing with stress and uncertainty. A young man told me he sniffed glue to forget his problems: "Sniffing glue makes me feel strong." Other *samari* are regular consumers of amphetamines, which are available through informal networks of pill sellers. Amphetamines are stimulants. Their consumption provokes an increase in brain activity, resulting in a sense of greater energy, focus, and confidence and possibly euphoria. In *Hausa*, they are called *hana kwana* (literally, "prevent sleep"). Tea and other stimulants thus become part of a technology of alertness, helping craft wakeful bodies through the alteration of brain chemistries. Eyal Ben-Ari (2005) writes of the "pharmorgs," a hybridization of pharmaceuticals and organisms that can fight day and night without falling prey to circadian rhythms. For this custom-designed soldier, the night's veil of darkness is no impediment to action. By "medicating" to stay awake and chase away fatigue while on night duty, *fadantchés* function like pharmorgs, though, unlike them, they sleep during the day. Tea, often synonymous with apathy and indulgence, has become part of a new repertoire of tools and practices forged by *fadantchés* to test the limits of the nocturnal.

Conclusion

In this chapter, I examined how the *fadas*' involvement in community policing in Niger has transformed the "negative social value" (Radcliffe-Brown 1922: 333) of nighttime into a space of productivity and civic engagement. As contingent projects temporarily stabilized by the aesthetic, discursive, and domestic practices that flourish in their midst, the *fadas* reveal how a sense of belonging can emerge out of the very vulnerability of urban existence. As sites of experimentation, *fadas* make young men forget the world out there while paradoxically readying them for it. They form an infrastructure of anticipation—what Florence Boyer (2014: 12) calls a "*salon temporaire,*" a temporary sitting room—that buffers un(der)employed *samari* from harsh realities while providing tactical means of confronting social immobility. At the *fada*, I have argued, idleness contains space for action. It is around teatime, a practice that splinters the temporality of aimless deferral by endowing waiting with a purposeful, yet pleasurable dimension, that an informal system of surveillance has emerged through which *samari* regain a semblance of temporal agency.

A stone's throw from the River Niger, in a densely populated Niamey district, some friends created a *fada* they called CIA to signal that the security of the neighborhood was their priority. "Ours is a useful *fada*," they told me. "We serve a purpose in the *quartier*." CIA was an unusual name. *Fadas* don't typically borrow from the language of statecraft, looking instead to hip-hop, action cinema, and religion for inspiration. Many nevertheless enjoy the support of shopkeepers, who find that their presence deters crime. By harnessing the discourse of insecurity, idle *samari* rehabilitate the *fada* while tactically inserting themselves into the landscape of crime prevention. Half salons, half checkpoints, their *fadas* constitute a diffuse, informal apparatus of nighttime surveillance, instantiating how social immobility can be deployed as a civic resource.

Promises should not be confused with achievements, however. Sitting at the *fada* does not inevitably lead to the capture of thieves and even when it does, the prospects of the *fadantchés* rarely improve overnight, as was the case for some members of Death Row. In this chapter, I highlighted how, pace Javier Auyero (2012), those who wait may reclaim some control over the modalities of waiting, transforming the meantime into a site of potentiality. At the *fada*, not only is the wait (the interval) transformed into a purposeful temporality, but the waiting (the modality) turns into a navigational capacity. For those who wait, Valeria Procupez (2025: S56) has argued, patience becomes a "new experience of inhabiting time [that] combines both urgency and restraint." It is a critical disposition for negotiating the temporalities of the present while adjusting to the prospects of future change. For *fadantchés*, patience is about engaging with the "now" through daily activities (including sitting at the *fada*) while keeping an eye on the distant time horizon. It implies waiting in the dark for the tea to "cook" (and enjoying the moment) while also being in a state of brisk readiness in case a thief tries to sneak by. In sum, patience may require that one surrender to one's circumstances (for instance, during teatime) but it just as often demands a more active form of endurance, the kind of unflappable resilience that *samari* demonstrate when they sit all night, night after night, while others sleep.

Adeline Masquelier is Professor of Anthropology at Tulane University. She has conducted extensive research on gender, religion, and health in Niger. She has authored three books, including *Women and Islamic Revival in a West African Town* (Indiana University Press, 2009), which received the 2010 Herskovits Award and the 2012 Aidoo-Snyder prize, both from the African Studies Association. Her latest book *Fada: Boredom and Belonging in Niger* (University of Chicago Press, 2019) was a finalist for the Best Book Prize from the African Studies Association. She has edited three books, including *Critical Terms for the Study of Africa* (University of Chicago Press, 2019). She is coeditor of *HAU: Journal of Ethnographic Theory*.

Notes

1. I am indebted to the many young men who generously shared their time, their space, and their stories with me over the years I have pursued this project. Research was supported by Tulane University's Newcomb Foundation, Tulane University's Research Enhancement Fund, and the Glick Fellowship of the School of Liberal Arts. Write-up was supported by a fellowship from the Aarhus Institute of Higher Studies. I thank Deborah Durham and the reviewers for their valuable editorial suggestions.
2. The plural of *fada*, a Hausa term, is *fadodi*. In the media, the term is often frenchified as *fadas*. It is this form I employ here to stress the cosmopolitan character of these social gatherings.
3. The ways in which people on the margins try to earn money and access resources often confound licit and illicit distinctions (Newell 2012). Meanwhile, even banditry has its own intricate forms of moral order (Roitman 2005; Scheele 2014).
4. If physical confrontations between *fadas* are largely a thing of the past, teasing, pretend fights, and competitive performances based on sartorial elegance and other material signs of success remain an important dimension of *fada* sociality (see Masquelier 2019).
5. To mark their presence in a neighborhood, young men etch the name of their *fada* (together with other decorative motifs) on the walls against which they sit. The trend has given rise to a scriptural economy in urban Niger, which *samari* regulate themselves.
6. Stably employed men also have their *fadas*, to which they repair in the early evening, after work, and at the weekend.
7. The very few *fadas* that include girls are generally composed of classmates. Their members have been sitting on the same class benches and are comfortable in each other's company.
8. Reports of '*yammata*'s nocturnal visits to *fadantchés* fuel virulent criticisms of the *fadas*,

adding to the list of vices for which *fadas* are allegedly the breeding ground. Besides encouraging young men to defer responsibilities (jobs, marriage, and so on), *fadas* are blamed for fostering sexual promiscuity.
9. During the 2011 presidential campaign, posters urging Nigeriens to vote for Mahamadou Issoufou, the former president, read: "Vote for Mahamadou Issoufou! To ensure your children's future."
10. It may take as long as forty-five minutes for the tea to brew, but it often takes *samari* less than five seconds to swallow the shot of tea they are handed.
11. The Ancient Jews, like the Greeks and Romans, divided the night into military watches instead of hours, with each watch representing the period of time during which sentinels remained on duty.

References

Anderson, Ben. 2004. "Time-Stilled Space-Slowed: How Boredom Matters." *Geoforum* 35(6): 739–54.
Appadurai, Arjun. 1986. *The Social Life of Things: Commodities in Cultural Perspective*. Cambridge, UK: Cambridge University Press.
Auyero, Javier. 2012. *Patients of the State: The Politics of Waiting in Argentina*. Durham, NC: Duke University Press.
Bakhtin, Mikhail M. 1981. *The Dialogic Imagination: Four Essays*, trans. Caryl Emerson and Michael Holquist. Austin: University of Texas Press.
Ben-Ari, Eyal. 2005. "Docile Bodies, Pharmorgs and Military Knowledge: The Regulation of Sleep and Night-Time Combat in the American Army." *Paideuma* 51: 165–79.
Benjamin, Walter. 2003. *Selected Writings: 1938–1940*. Cambridge, MA: Harvard University Press.
Blunt, Robert. 2020. "Anthropology After Dark: Nocturnal Life and the Anthropology of the Good-Enough in Western Kenya." *Journal of Religion and Violence* 8(1): 35–57.
Boyer, Florence. 2014. "'Faire fada' à Niamey (Niger): Un espace de transgression silencieuse" ['Doing *fada*' in Niamey (Niger): A space of silent transgression]. *Carnets de Géographes* 7: 1–17.
Certeau, Michel de. 1984. *The Practice of Everyday Life*, trans. Steven F. Randall. Berkeley: University of California Press.
Crary, Jonathan. 2014. *24/7: Late Capitalism and the End of Sleep*. New York: Verso.
De Boeck, Filip, and Marie-Françoise Plissart. 2004. *Kinshasa: Tales of the Invisible City*. Ghent: Ludion Press.
Dwyer, Peter D. 2009. "Worlds of Waiting." In *Waiting*, ed. Ghassan Hage, 15–26. Melbourne: University of Melbourne Press.
Ekirch, A. Roger. 2005. *At Day's Close: Night in Past Times*. New York: W. W. Norton & Company.
Flaherty, Michael G. 2003. "Time Work: Customizing Temporal Experience." *Social Psychology Quarterly* 66(1): 17–33.
Frederiksen, Martin Demant. 2013. *Young Men, Time, and Boredom in the Republic of Georgia*. Philadelphia, PA: Temple University Press.

Galinier, Jacques, et al. 2010. "Anthropology of the Night: Cross-Disciplinary Investigations." *Current Anthropology* 51(6): 819–47.

Gilroy, Paul. 1993. *The Black Atlantic: Modernity and Double Consciousness*. London: Verso.

Goodstein, Elizabeth. 2005. *Experience without Qualities: Boredom and Modernity*. Stanford, CA: Stanford University Press.

Göpfert, Mirco. 2012. "Security in Niamey: An Anthropological Perspective on Policing and an Act of Terrorism in Niger." *Journal of Modern African Studies* 50(1): 53–74.

Handelman, Don. 2005. "Epilogue: Dark Soundings –Towards a Phenomenology of the Night." *Paideuma* 51: 247–61.

Hauser, Beatrix. 2005. "Travelling through the Night: Living Mothers and Divine Daughters at an Orissan Goddess Festival." *Paideuma* 51: 221–33.

Hornberger, Julia. 2008. "Nocturnal Johannesburg." In *Johannesburg: Elusive Metropolis*, ed. Sarah Nuttall and Achille Mbembe, 285–96. Durham, NC: Duke University Press.

Holbraad, Martin, and Morten Axel Pedersen, eds. 2013. *Times of Security: Ethnographies of Fear, Protest, and the Future*. New York: Routledge.

Kapferer, Bruce. 1983. *A Celebration of Demons: Exorcism and the Aesthetics of Healing in Shri Lanka*. Bloomington: Indiana University Press.

Konopinski, Natalie. 2014. "Borderline Temporalities and Security Anticipations: Standing Guard in Tel Aviv." *Etnofoor* 26(1): 59–80.

Lallement, Michel. 2003. *Temps, travail et modes de vie*. Paris: Presses Universitaires de France.

Lund, Christian. 2009. "Les dynamiques politiques locales face à une démocratie fragile." In *Les pouvoirs locaux au Niger*, ed. Jean-Pierre Olivier de Sardan and Mahaman Tidjani Alou, 89–111. Paris: Karthala.

Masquelier, Adeline. 2009. *Women and Islamic Revival in a West African Town*. Bloomington: Indiana University Press.

———. 2013. "Teatime: Boredom and the Temporalities of Young Men in Niger." *Africa* 83(3): 470–91.

———. 2019. *Fada: Boredom and Belonging in Niger*. Chicago: University of Chicago Press.

———. 2020. "The Work of Waiting: Boredom, Teatime, and Future-Making in Niger." In *Time Work: Ethnographic Studies of Temporal Agency*, ed. Michael Flaherty, Lotte Meinert, and Anne Line Dalsgärd, 175–92. New York: Berghahn Books.

Musharbash, Yasmine. 2013. "Night, Sight, and Feeling Safe: An Exploration of Aspects of Walpiri and Western Sleep." *The Australian Journal of Anthropology* 24(1): 48–63.

Newell, Sasha. 2012. *The Modernity Bluff: Crime, Consumption, and Citizenship*. Chicago: University of Chicago Press.

O'Neill, Bruce. 2017. *The Space of Boredom: Homelessness in the Slowing Global Order*. Durham, NC: Duke University Press.

Pratten, David. 2008. "Introduction: The Politics of Protection: Perspectives on Vigilantism in Nigeria." *Africa* 78(1): 1–15.

Procupez, Valeria. 2015. "The Need for Patience: The Politics of Housing Emergency in Buenos Aires." *Current Anthropology* 56(11): S55–S65.

Radcliffe-Brown, A. R. 1922. *The Andaman Islanders: A Study in Social Anthropology*. Cambridge, UK: Cambridge University Press.
Roitman, Janet. 2005. *Fiscal Disobedience: An Anthropology of Economic Regulation in Central Africa*. Princeton, NJ: Princeton University Press.
Scheele, Judith. 2012. *Smugglers and Saints of the Sahara: Regional Connectivity in the Twentieth Century*. Cambridge, UK: Cambridge University Press.
Schritt, Jannik. 2015. "The 'Protest against Charlie Hebdo' in Niger: A Background Analysis." *Africa Spectrum* 1: 49–64.
Van der Geest, Sjaak. 2007. "Life after Dark in Kwahu Tafo." *Etnofoor* 20(2): 23–39.
Van Dijk, Rijk. 2007. "Testing Nightscapes: Ghanaian Pentecostal Politics of the Nocturnal." *Etnofoor* 20(2): 41–57.
Wacquant, Loïc. 1998. "The Prizefighter's Three Bodies." *Ethnos* 63(3): 325–52.

Chapter 6

Waiting to Heal in "Crip Time"
Temporalities of Chronic Skin Wounds among Gunshot Survivors in New Orleans

Daniella Santoro

In his quiet room in New Orleans's Kindred Hospital, Francis waits for many things to happen. He lies in bed and waits for the nurse to come in and carefully clean, drain, and re-dress his wounds, check his blood pressure, change the IV bag for his next dose of antibiotics. He waits for help to turn over onto his side to relieve pressure on his wounds, to drain his urine bag, to shave. He waits, perhaps more eagerly, for the physician to determine when he will be allowed back in his wheelchair so he can sit outside for part of the day. In the meantime, the days are measured by the IV treatments of the antibiotic vancomycin that he receives on a daily basis. For two hours at a time, Francis waits each day while the antibiotic steadily drains, drop by drop, into the peripherally inserted central catheter (or PICC line) in his right arm. He may be waiting for the promised effects of the vancomycin on his infection, but he is not really waiting for a cure. Francis lives in "crip time," where the challenge of waiting is a matter of patience, disturbing the temporalities of curative medicines, holding the everyday now of necessary routines in tension with normative temporalities marked by transformative futures.

Francis was recently admitted for the fourth time in two years for recurring osteomyelitis, a chronic infection in his pelvic bone that originated in a pressure skin ulcer he developed as result of a gunshot wound sustained ten years earlier. The infection is known as MRSA, methicillin-resistant *Staphylococcus aureus*, a strain of the common staph bacterium that has grown resistant to most available antibiotics and is the harbinger of superbug apocalyptic anxieties. Antibiotic treatments are known for effecting dramatic cures, but that is not perceptible here in Francis's room. Rather, healing this wound is a slow process, remarkable not for its speed but for daily acts of waiting that produce small accomplishments. The wound is starting to look less inflamed, the nurse may tell him, but Francis generally takes mental notes of each IV treatment, each day, as he passes the time—a six-week hospital stay and antibiotic regimen that he has come to know well.

Francis is in his mid-forties, an African American man with a deep and gravelly voice that belies his soft features. Born and raised in the Gentilly neighborhood of New Orleans in the 1980s, Francis clarifies, "but all my people from the Ninth Ward," referencing the working-class African American neighborhood that became known to the world ten years earlier when the levees broke after Hurricane Katrina, causing devastating floods. Francis has an organized mind and a preference for order. Especially when he is in the hospital, where he may have to wait for a nurse to come in and help him find something, all his personal items must be neatly organized in the right places. Francis explains this concern for order as part of "wheelchair life," which forces one to always "come clean," a concept that refers both to how one presents oneself in the social world to earn respect and to the necessity of maintaining one's personal hygiene to help stave off infections. Francis does come clean, but even so he is caught wrestling with these wounds, in small but highly significant ways in what he calls "wheelchair life" and some call "crip time"; many a soldierly battle is fought in defiance, patience, and steadfast, small acts of waiting.

As I learned during my ethnographic research on the everyday lives of New Orleans residents paralyzed as a result of gun violence, one of the common features of what Francis and others like him call "wheelchair life" is the ongoing prevention and treatment of pressure ulcers and chronic skin wounds. Many wheelchair users develop these infections at some point and thereafter acquire the knowledge and experience necessary to manage them. Chronic wounds and their complications are one of the most common and urgent topics of conversation among gunshot-paralyzed residents, who must devote energy, attention, and vigilance to preventing such wounds from developing.

What does it mean to be waiting to heal from chronic wounds? The term "chronic" suggests that the wounds are time itself, that is, they are "of time," but also that they make time in the sense that they shape the patient's experience of time. How do these chronic wounds fashion the personal, social, and temporal subjectivities of wheelchair users? Lastly, in what ways do patients construct meaning around the work of waiting? Scholars have observed how people in situations of vulnerability are often made to wait for the state-funded support resources on which they depend (Auyero 2012). Yet, more than an expression of disempowerment, waiting in such contexts may lead to forms of engagement and mobilization centered on the "work" of patience. Patience, Valeria Procupez (2015) suggests in her study of how poor families negotiate permanent housing in Buenos Aires, must be understood as a political stance based on a vision of the future. The sick, too, inhabit a temporality shaped by a sense of hope. As Richard Jenkins, Hanne Jessen, and Vibeke Steffen (2005) have noted, medical treatments are guided as much by rational choice as by a hopeful sense that one's health will improve. From this perspective, waiting for chronic wounds to heal entails navigating a landscape of uncertainty that, while it precludes certitude and control, leaves the door to the future open when one's prospects are grim. It also means arming oneself with patience.

In this chapter, I explore the illness narratives of two men suffering chronic wounds, *waiting to heal*, for whom such waiting is experienced as active engagement with disability identity, challenging social relations, and concerns about their futures. The subjectivities and strategies involved in *waiting to heal* become the new "battlefield" upon which many gunshot survivors must contend with life's adversities, including ordinary challenges. I draw on the concept of "crip time," an alternative to the dominant forms of agency and temporality that shape able-bodied experience, to offer insight into how wheelchair users deal with chronic wounds as part of the ongoing work of inhabiting time after gunshot injury.

Living in "Crip Time"

Rather than rejecting the derogatory qualifier "crippled," disability activist-scholars have embraced and repurposed "crip" as a political and social identity. Robert McRuer (2006), a queer and crip theorist, argues that crip theory troubles the claims of normative embodiments and sexualities in a regime of compulsory able-bodiedness. Under cultural systems based on compulsory able-bodiedness, disability is seen only as a pitiable tragedy that disabled people want to escape or overcome. Crip theory thus unsettles the notion of disability as tied only to "defective" bodies or as the product of specific impairments. As disability scholar Carrie Sandahl (2003: 37) explains, "cripping spins mainstream representations or practices to reveal able-bodied assumptions and exclusionary effects ... [to] expose the arbitrary delineation between (the) normal and defective." "Coming out crip" is claiming a new social identity at the intersections of multiple marginalities where these identities are potentially generative and liberatory sites of embodied wisdom and know-how.

In our contemporary world, time is a critical dimension of how we assess people, and by extension their worth, on the basis of their productivity. The more people do, the more contributions they make, the more valuable they are deemed. Recognizing that individuals with disabilities who live life "slower" or at a different pace are misfits in a society that takes able-bodiedness for granted, disability theorists have pointed to a new understanding of temporality, mobility, and futurity that a critical focus on the disabled subject brings. In Alison Kafer's (2013) and Ellen Samuels's (2017) work, "crip time" describes the particular embodied temporalities that are experienced through non-able-bodied, non-normative experience of being-in-the-world. To "crip" time, Kafer argues, is to view time with flexibility and in terms governed by lived experience with disability or illness, and thus to resist normative expectations of the pace of everyday life based on the rhythms and expectations of "normal," healthy bodies.

"Normal" bodies, when ailing, progress toward reversing that ailment and returning to able-bodiedness, cured by medical intervention or their own healing. "Curative time" orients citizens toward an imagined redressive future, erasing and delegitimizing the somatic realities of living with disability or illness. Disabled bodies and embodiments then become valuable in the context of rehabilitation and the temporalities of cure. "Futurity has been framed in curative terms," Kafer explains in relation to disability, so "the only appropriate disabled mind/body is one cured or moving toward cure" (2013: 28). In contrast to "curative time," an understanding of time as always heading toward a desired cure, "crip time" embraces disabled bodies in the here and now, resisting notions that disability needs to be fixed, repaired, or improved.

In her research on disability and state narratives in South Korea, Eunjung Kim (2017) explores how the state's fetishization of the need to cure, correct, or improve disabled bodies creates conditions of symbolic (and sometimes physical) violence for people with disabilities and chronic conditions: those, that is, outside the nation-state's vision of progress. When bodies are pronounced "incurable," Kim (2017: 18) adds, "they are read as being in a condition of a 'nonlife' — without a future and denied meaning in the present." Understanding the conceptualization of curative time sheds light on how living in "crip time" is about existing in bodies that are marked as not having a future. Yet these bodies live in time built of past, present, and future, if not progressive curative time. For many who live in the crises of ongoing chronic gun violence and insecurity in their neighborhoods, personal time lines have been disrupted and futures thrown into doubt and conjecture, even before their bodies situate them in crip time. Young teenage boys fear that they will not make it to adulthood, and one who survives into his forties can already be considered an elder.[1] Furthermore, within systems of state violence, structural racism, and ableism, poor men of color, often an assumed criminal underclass, are perceived as expected losses in the state's projected future. Disability theorists David T. Mitchell and Sharon L. Snyder (2001) describe something they call "able-nationalism," recognizing the practices of the nation-state that valorize some forms of disability and exclude others. Between structural racism and able-nationalism, we begin to see the interlocking forms of social exclusion embodied by the gunshot survivors I worked with in New Orleans.

In 2019, while involved in a class action lawsuit about the lack of wheelchair access on public transit, Francis reflected on how his survival as a Black man with a disability was an unexpected and undesirable outcome for the state: "The government wished I had died. I'm just being real with you. It would be better off for them if I had died, cause now I have perspective and I am making them pay for things." Francis's survival challenges the curative time of the state and the productive time of normative able-bodiedness. As Kafer (2017: 27) explains, crip time is "flex time not just expanded but exploded; it requires reimagining our notions of what can and should happen in time . . . rather than bend disabled bodies and minds to meet the clock, crip time bends the clock to meet disabled bodies and minds." Ultimately, "crip time" signifies a liberatory politics, in which people like Francis gain (and give) "perspective" on how bodies marked as disabled, ill, or otherwise expendable occupy space and time and move through the world.

Waiting to heal in "crip time," I suggest, is about how disabled gunshot survivors cultivate a response to this chronic suspended state of disability, while navigating the recurrent wounds that give new temporalities to their lives. It not only becomes part of what defines wheelchair life but also shapes the raced, gendered, and disabled subjectivities following the unexpected trauma of gun violence.

Chronic Wounds

"I been dealing with these wounds since the accident," Francis reminds me as he carefully organizes his side table, which is crowded with bottles of Ensure and Styrofoam cups of ice water. "Since being in that nursing home in those Pampers, that's what did it—I deal with one side and then the other—they close, they re-break, they close, they re-break."

In 2004, Francis was walking on the Almonaster Bridge toward the Ninth Ward when he was shot in the head, thrown on the train tracks below, and left for dead. He may never know for sure who tried to kill him, but he says he knows he made some enemies through "life in the [drug] game." Days after the attack, Francis woke up in Charity Hospital, where a doctor explained that he would never walk again. As a result of that fall onto the train tracks, his spinal cord had been severed and his right arm had to be amputated below the elbow. Francis's miraculous survival and recovery from the gunshot and the fall were accompanied by a series of daily challenges that created cascading complications, manifested in chronic wounds.

Among the first skills spinal cord injury patients learn during rehabilitation are "pressure reliefs." New wheelchair users are taught to lift themselves up from their seat cushions to relieve pressure and increase circulation. Because wheelchair users sit in the same position for so many hours each day, they are particularly vulnerable to skin ulcers. With only one arm, Francis cannot lift himself up properly, making him especially vulnerable to developing these pressure ulcers. Francis's complications also resulted from spending several years in various state institutions with minimal and non-preventative care. After being discharged from Charity Hospital, Francis lived in a long-term nursing home, where he first developed the wounds on his coccyx bone. Nearly seven years later, Medicaid approved an electric wheelchair and cushion accessories that would help his mobility and maintain skin integrity, but by then he was already engaged in the lengthy ongoing battle managing his wounds.

In contrast to the nearly instantaneous penetrative trauma of the gunshot wound—and the remarkable recoveries that occasionally follow—pressure ulcer wounds are stealthy and silent and recurrent. They begin with a small, often imperceptible abrasion on the skin's surface and then grow deeper into the body as bacteria steadily digest tissue, sometimes (as in Francis's case) down to and into the bone. New strains of *Staphylococcus* bacteria that are resistant to our arsenal of antibiotics can enter these porous sites on the flesh and cause the ongoing cycle of closing and (re)opening of the wound that Francis described above.

These wounds, also referred to as pressure ulcers, decubitus ulcers, or, in more common lay terms, bedsores, are part of the broader medical category of "chronic wounds." Calling them bedsores obscures the medical complexities and personal intimacies of living with open wounds. The term also suggests that they are mere side effects, complications experienced by patients with more "highly branded" diseases (Sen et al. 2009: 763), such as diabetes, obesity, or debility due to old age. Furthermore, identifying the wounds of wheelchair users as bedsores puts wheelchair users into the category of institutionalized or already debilitated patient populations, locating these types of wounds in sites already marked as zones of exclusion (Biehl 2005). "Bedsores," most people assume, happen to the homeless and the indigent, to patients with immunosuppression and comorbidities, and to aging residents of nursing homes, those seemingly waiting, or already marked, for a "slow death" (Berlant 2007).

Chronic wounds are wounds that move from having an "acute" status—a wound that can be cured and will heal—to having a "chronic" status—wounds that do not heal within a normal, expected time frame. In biomedical literature, wounds are apprehended through temporal logics; they are described as "delayed," "interrupted," or not healing in "proper time." Their progress is slow and dubious; it may stall, reverse, or, most frustratingly, stay unnervingly still, neither moving toward healing nor requiring surgical intervention. Because these wounds do not exist within normative time frames of healing, many patients wait several months, or even years, for their wounds to completely heal, if they ever do. In their refusal to heal, these stubborn sites of open flesh must be negotiated with, managed, and strategized against, requiring extra reserves of personal discipline, patience, and medical and therapeutic resources.

A cohort of biologists and physicians have called attention to pressure ulcers, referring to them as a "major and snowballing threat to public health and the economy" (Sen et al. 2009) and "a neglected disease of the developed world" (Bodavula et al. 2015). Like pressure ulcers, chronic wounds might challenge normative temporalities of healing and curing, but they echo the rise of other chronic conditions. These conditions, such as obesity, diabetes, and diseases accompanying immunosuppression, are often associated with poverty, race, and deviance. They challenge medical histories of progress and healing. At the same time, some have noticed a distressing overlap with a new chronicity in late capitalism, where the future becomes unreachable or unimaginable, except as an ending. Hastened by the beginning of an "antibiotic apocalypse" (McKie 2017), chronic wounds, coupled with the rise of chronic conditions, signal a new normal that reveals the vulnerability of the chronic state of unhealth in which many people increasingly find themselves.

Chronic wounds are thus symbolic of a contemporary temporality of late capitalism, a state that Eric Cazdyn (2012) calls "the new chronic," where previously fatal illnesses without cures are now managed in an unsettled "undying present," embedded in the work of everyday life. Similarly, Zoe Wool and Julie Livingston (2017) explore this notion of the chronic as a particular mode of life lived after trauma, loss, and disaster, when life cannot return to normal, but must be lived in the "temporality of the afterworld." They explain: "The fact is that many people live not in spaces of vitality or in the face of imminent death but in lasting zones of precariousness, temporalities of impasse or slow death or within the continuous present tense" (Wool and Livingston 2017).

Gunshot survivors embody one example of the tensions in the new chronic mode: state-of-the-art emergency medical care and technologies can help gunshot victims survive damage done by the bullet but leave the survivor without ongoing care to manage everyday obstacles and sustain health and wellbeing. The health-care establishment succeeds at "curing" within a specific temporal frame—the immediate crisis of gunshot trauma—but relinquishes any future responsibility for the ongoing quality of life of those patients they just (miraculously) saved. While anyone is susceptible to chronic wounds, the reality of chronicity is especially acute for the population I am familiar with. Being a poor, disabled, person of color in New Orleans often means facing structural racism and ableism, along with housing insecurity, inaccessibility issues, limited employment, and over-reliance on state support for health needs, as well as meager monthly social security payouts, all of which increase the risk of chronic wounds.

The Agency of the Wound

The wound is familiar and often ignored. Acquiring and recovering from wounds is a taken-for-granted aspect of life, where the wound is easily forgotten and the process of healing moves us steadily forward in time. Wounds substantiate the experience of suffering within a distinct temporality because, for most people, the expectation is that wounds will heal. It is just a matter of time, we say. Yet, the unhealing or open wound embodies life's precarity and vulnerability, signaling a disruption of normal time and social life.

Anthropological scholarship has focused on wounds and states of woundedness to explore the tensions of ongoing social suffering and injury. In his ethnography of the intergenerational trauma of the Harkis, Algerians who fought for the French in the Algerian War of Independence, Vincent Crapanzano (2011) observes that psychological wounds of betrayal are those "wounds that never heal." Similarly, writing about Iraqi war refugees seeking asylum in Lebanon, Omar Dewachi (2015: 64) uses the wound to interpret the "multifaceted consequences of war as a process of physical and social injury." Dewachi illustrates how torture scars become "social wounds" in the context of different histories of violence. Yet beyond considerations of how social contexts shape the meaning and significance of bodily wounds, how does the wound figure as its own ethnographic subject? How does the open wound as a material site on the body have agency and act on the social world?

In the biomedical literature mentioned above, for instance, just as wounds are described as having a specific temporality—as chronic and out of proper time—they are also described as "stubborn" and "recalcitrant." In the following examples, open, unhealing wounds emerge as more than mere material sites. Wounds have agency as they reveal, enable, signify, and testify to social realities.

In their photo-ethnography of homeless heroin users in San Francisco, *Righteous Dopefiend* (2009), Philippe Bourgois and Jeff Schonberg explore skin abscesses in their ethnographic context as an important vantage point from which to understand the health risks of drug-addicted homeless people in the United States. Caused by injection-related practices, these abscesses are exacerbated by the conditions of homelessness and by the neoliberal logics of a medical infrastructure that keeps many homeless people locked in a state of chronic unhealth. The photographs embedded within the narrative showcase bodies pieced together in a patchwork of flesh after skin grafts, or bodies with wounds caused by surgical debridement, resulting in gaping holes in which tendons and internal muscular structures are visible to the naked eye. The focus on the materiality of these wounds and how the homeless must manage them highlights their chronic temporality as an embodiment of the ongoing suffering and desperate selfcare practices of managing the addicted body (Bourgois and Schonberg 2009).

In another example of how material wounds have ethnographic significance, Julie Livingston (2013, 2014) examines patient care in an oncology ward in Botswana by focusing specifically on the management of necrotic tumor wounds. Such unsightly wounds, which protrude from the body and form unhealing weeping sores, push the cancer patient out of normal social life and time even as, in Botswana at that time, most were thrust back into their communities and families for daily care because of limited hospital space. Unlike in the West, where technology that can peer into the body can identify tumors in their early stages, Livingston explains that what is revealed in the wound in Botswana is the "florid rotting agonizing obscene cancers of an oncological past, an era before oncology learned how to push cancer below the surface of the body" (2013: 3720). Livingston examines how the objectification and normalization of the tumor wound by nurses during cleaning helps patients sustain their personhood as they manage advancing cancer.

Livingston argues that the wound is a nexus where the moral intimacies and socialities of care manifest themselves and the place from which one must understand the effects of the cancer epidemic. In Livingston's ethnographic accounts, the late-stage tumor wound emerges alongside the cancer patients as an ethnographic subject unto itself—a constellation of affects and actions. The wounds burst through the skin's surface and emit a strong odor. The dying flesh is active as it shapes how patients relate to their own bodies and engage in social interactions. Through a focus on the wound, both Bourgois and Livingston demonstrate the intimacies and socialities at work, as well as the networks of care surrounding wound treatment.

Looking specifically at gunshot wounds, both Jooyoung Lee (2012) and Laurence Ralph (2012, 2014) highlight the importance of flesh wounds as part of the emerging post-trauma identities of gunshot survivors. Lee (2012: 246) focuses on social experiences after injury and how the materiality and severity of wounds contribute to the "sensual scaffolding" of one's sense of self and identity. For those whose gunshot injuries produced stomach and intestinal wounds, for instance, Lee points out how such wounds are often the hardest to adapt to: because of the complications relating to waste management, sharing meals and other such social acts become laden with shame and embarrassment.

Just as wounds can interrupt and impede social life, the state of woundedness can also signify a social status and identity category after war or other traumas. After US Veterans returned from Iraq and Afghanistan with disabilities and complicated injuries, a national discourse emerged, aimed at transforming the bodies of disabled military veterans into "wounded warriors." As Wool explores in her book, *After War* (2015), the wounds of veterans—frequently caused by roadside bombs that necessitate amputations—are interpreted by nationalist narratives that bestow meaning upon their physicality. Wounds, in this iteration, are thus situated close to prefabricated ideas of heroism, patriotism, and service. As such, these narratives may create a crisis for the recovering veteran whose own wounded body does not fit into those frames. For many returning soldiers injured by explosives, the sites of damaged tissue wounds continue to influence and shape their social worlds in the afterlife of the war. In the lives of surviving veterans, these wounds do not heal and close as neatly as national discourse might suggest. Instead, they remain open, testifying to the "limbo of life blown apart and not yet pieced together, not yet sedimented into life stories of before and after . . . full of visceral intensity and uncertainty" (Wool 2015: 3).

Finally, in his work on gang violence and injury in Chicago, Ralph (2012) explores how disabled ex-gang members use their gunshot wounds as signs of broader social disruption, much as Crapanzano and Dewachi did for their respective subjects. In Ralph's study, disabled ex-gang members, contending with injury, make claims through their wounds about the consequences of violence in their communities. In the context of chronic gang violence, Ralph argues, wounds can "enable" social and political commentary. For instance, Ralph sits in on educational programming at Chicago schools for which disabled ex-gang members talk about the risks of gang violence by calling attention to the materiality of their injuries, the ongoing work to prevent pressure sores, and the structural pressures of managing such wounds with limited resources. Ralph (2012) concludes that these men turn to the materiality of their wounds and "employ their defective bodies as testimony to the chronic violence in their communities."

Like the necrotic tumor wounds that signaled the extent to which cancer had gone untreated in Botswana, the chronic pressure ulcer represents one visible manifestation of an often-ignored epidemic of gun violence in US communities of color. In this sense, the wound testifies to the ongoing realities of racial inequity in the afterlife of violence. Bringing together Livingston's quest to examine what is "revealed in the wound" (2013) and Ralph's inquiry into what and how wounds can "enable" (2012) helps us appreciate the wound's potential to shape social life and subjectivities. In these ethnographic accounts, waiting can be understood implicitly as an aspect of the subjective experiences of managing open chronic wounds on the body. How, then, do experiences of waiting to heal emerge in the lives of gunshot survivors as a distinct space of meaning and action? In the following accounts, I consider how gunshot-injured wheelchair users cultivate responses to these wounds and build meaning around the work of waiting.

Crip Futures and the Work of Waiting

"You gotta talk to Kevin," Francis urges, "he going through the same shit, like all of us wheelchairs." Kevin, now in his mid-fifties, grew up in the 1970s and 1980s in the Desire projects in the Ninth Ward. The public housing developments had been a site of Black organizing and civil rights activism in the 1970s. By the early 1990s, it had some of the largest concentrations of open-air drug markets and violent crime in the city.[2] In 1993, a car drove past a block party Kevin was attending in the Seventh Ward. From the car, someone shot Kevin and three other men. Kevin lay on top of one of the injured men to help him stay quiet in the hope that the shooters would not return, but they came back anyway and shot Kevin in the back. He was paralyzed immediately.

The story of Kevin's wound began a decade after that, while he hunkered down as Hurricane Katrina pummeled New Orleans on 29 August

2005. During the hurricane, Kevin was forced to lift himself upstairs and into the attic of his cousin's home, where he waited for help with his cousin in the humid air of the hurricane's wake. Kevin recalls: "I never even needed a nurse until after Katrina. My skin broke down after being on that rooftop for twenty hours; once you get it, it's hard to shake, and now I've had these wounds going on ten years." When Kevin and his cousin were finally rescued by Wildlife Rangers, they were sent to the Convention Center with thousands of other stranded residents.[3] Sitting in a borrowed wheelchair day and night in an overcrowded makeshift care center, without access to clean bathrooms, Kevin tried to get on the helicopter evacuating those who were medically neediest first. But the guardsman monitoring access to the helicopter accused him of stealing the wheelchair and faking his disability. He told Kevin he looked "too healthy" and needed to get to the back of line and wait.

Over a decade later, Kevin manages ongoing issues with two separate wounds, one on his lower hipbone and one on his ankle. The wounds occasionally heal and close up, but then reoccur several months later.

> And, you know how many times since then they've tried to take my feet and my legs? They wanted to amputate a bunch of times. One time I'm sitting in Ochsner [Hospital] and the doctor comes in with the students, "Today we are gonna view Kevin Bush—he's a candidate for amputation." No, Kevin Bush ain't! My bell went to ringing! That's how I come to know it! I say you'll never learn how to amputate a leg if you gotta amputate mine. Go on and amputate a dummy leg . . . Another time, doctor says to me, "What's the problem, they don't work anyway, you don't need them." Now you know me, you can imagine what I told that doctor. I don't even need to tell you. Man, I told him, "You don't know where these legs have been!"

Kevin's resistance to amputation, while he navigates betrayal by and distrust of the state and medical establishment, relies on crip time. Crip time, as discussed above, involves issues of stigma and exclusion, a challenge to the notions of cure and curative temporalities, and, as Kevin's response here makes so clear, ideas about the useful, productive, and valued body. Crip time is a flexible time—a slower time—that resists the linear, normative, and finite temporalities of illness. Kevin demands his right to allow his body to heal in his own time, in his own way. Waiting to heal, in this instance, becomes an active space of resistance to institutional pressures (including hospital care) that appear to take advantage of Kevin's vulnerability as a chronic wound sufferer.

The raced and gendered dimensions of the various exchanges Kevin engaged in during Katrina and thereafter are beyond the scope of this chapter, but it is nevertheless important to acknowledge the ironies associated with inhabiting a youthful, male black body that hides its weaknesses and disabilities. On the one hand, Kevin appeared too healthy to deserve a doctor's care in the immediate aftermath of Katrina. He did not fit the stereotypical profile of an elderly or infirm wheelchair user and was forced to wait. On the other hand, after he acquired chronic wounds, his right to heal more slowly was easily dismissed. His leg refused to heal so it would have to be amputated. These two experiences make plain how illegible the bodies of Black disabled men are and testify to their social invisibility. Victims of gun violence who are assumed to be gang members are only legible as what one survivor calls "the criminal element." They are perceived to be complicit in their injuries and (whether through conscious or unconscious bias) less deserving of care.

The nurse is already in the room adjusting the IV when I come to visit Francis again. "The nurse tells me my levels are low," Francis announces. She turns to me to clarify but offers a further abstraction: "His levels are at a 4 and therapeutic is at 10." Francis interjects, ready to be the expert in his own condition: "Bingo, see the vanco [vancomycin] got to be at the right level to work, or else its gonna blow out my kidneys. Every time I had stage four to the bone . . . I already done six weeks, four different times . . . and I'm resistant to everything except the vancomycin. What that tell you?" Francis often speaks in these rhetoricals, ushering me into his world and challenging me to think through his embodied experience. Amidst the unknown of how well the antibiotics can treat his wounds during this round, and as Francis is told he must simply wait, he practices shaping narrative time: how many more hospital admittances will there be? How many more times will he (and the vancomycin) manage to push the wound back and keep it at bay before it reopens again? Somewhere between hope and doubt, as Francis waits, he must actively engage with managing the uncertainty that the chronic wound manifests.

Susan Whyte (2002) has written about how, in the midst of health crises in Eastern Uganda, people practice health care in the "subjunctive mood": when the success of medical care remains uncertain, and various different regimes of care are available, there is a space for hope, negotiation, and speculation. Even when medical laboratory results return with a specific objective diagnosis, Whyte observes how the subjunctive relational mood shapes the way patients and their social networks interpret the illness and situate it in a social context. In the context of uncertainty, meaningful spaces open up where people engage in the full spectrum of emotional responses and practical actions to manage misfortune and influence outcomes.

For Francis, the wound is always uncertain. Doctors offer interventions that may or may not produce results. The wound may or may not close;

the antibiotic may or may not be effective. Waiting to heal in crip time is thus subjunctive time, a space of practical engagement with uncertainty, of creative (re)imaginings, and of hope. The experience that dominates living with chronic wounds is one of the day-to-day practical and difficult work of waiting, which requires the cultivation of patience and the managing of expectations. In this context, waiting is a specific space not only in time, but also in one's spiritual and psychological worldview. As the body must remain inert, resting and waiting to heal, the emotional and mental self must remain active.

The "Battlefield" of Waiting

Two years after I first met Francis in Kindred Hospital, it was bought out by Cura Health, a multinational corporation that did not accept Medicaid patients. Like Kindred, Cura Health is considered a long-term acute care hospital (LTACH), the kind of medical facility that takes patients after they are discharged from more intensive urgent care in centralized hospitals.[4] LTACH facilities, which are profit-driven, can deny Medicaid patients in favor of more lucrative patients on Medicare. Francis, whose medical bills had been paid by Medicaid, could no longer seek long-term treatment at the same hospital when infection flared up again. I visited Francis soon after he was readmitted to the ER at Touro Infirmary, across the street from the acute care hospital, for an ulcer wound that had reopened. Francis needed six more weeks of antibiotic therapy but, now that Kindred could no longer take him in, he was faced with a limited choice of venues at which he could receive treatment. He was told he would be sent to either a nursing home in New Orleans East, which is difficult to get to by public transit, or an acute care center as far away as Baton Rouge. While waiting to be transferred, Francis reflected on his condition:

> I'm already resistant to vancomycin. I been beat that shit down. Now they got me on daptomycin and I know it's serious, but people, they not taking it serious, they talk to me like it's gonna be alright. I know what's up. If this next antibiotic don't work, I'm gonna wind up a hospice patient, and they just make me comfortable 'til the end. This what killed Corey [a friend of Francis who sustained gunshot-induced spinal cord injuries and later died after an infection set in], bro. I been to every damn hospital in New Orleans dealing with these wounds. It's real out here in the battlefield.

During my doctoral fieldwork, I heard gunshot survivors use military metaphors to describe the city streets as an ongoing war zone.[5] A longtime friend of Francis articulated it best when he said that the street violence is like a war but worse because it is everywhere and never-ending; there is no safe home base to which one can escape.

For many disabled gunshot survivors, surviving on the "battlefield" is not just about finding safety in a violent urban environment or learning to maintain emotional stability and a sense of pride and self-image in an able-bodied and racist world. This "battlefield"—or "the trenches," as Kevin calls it—is also simultaneously a soldiering on in the steady, vigilant, and seemingly unending maintenance of the body in order to survive. For those who manage chronic wounds, like Francis and Kevin, waiting to heal is a battle that requires a soldier's skillset—fortitude, vigilance, and mental discipline. Francis and Kevin's conception of waiting as a battlefield highlights some central aspects of the work of waiting, and the state of waiting as a central aspect of the experience of having a disability as a result of gunshot injury. In this conceptualization, waiting is not just a necessary path toward the goal of the cure when waiting goes on for years and even decades. Waiting and the experience and skillset acquired through waiting become a defining feature of what makes up the "wheelchair life."

The work of waiting is focused on personal and mental discipline and the cultivation of the patience one must acquire to "do" waiting well. This includes managing the psychological trials of waiting for one's wounds to heal, as well as one's interactions with the medical establishment. For Francis, having chronic osteomyelitis means managing repeated surgical interventions, bureaucratic shuffling, and isolation, as he is sent to different care facilities, whereas Kevin (whose sister is a nurse) can secure extra help and independence at home outside of the limitations (and waiting time) of Medicaid approvals. Kevin, who is more outwardly skeptical about the intentions of his doctors, does not rely solely on their diagnoses but instead learns to clean his wounds himself, often waiting longer to seek medical intervention.[6]

When their wounds reach a critical stage and they are forced to retreat from normal life and wait for them to heal, both Francis and Kevin cultivate specific forms of patience by drawing on their past experiences as inmates in the Louisiana State Penitentiary.[7] For Francis, being patient is part of being a good or easy subject of an institution, so he can better pass the time. He tells me he has learned not to ask for things out of turn and that it is best to follow what the doctors say. Francis does not openly distrust his doctors, but he does recognize his vulnerability as a disabled Medicaid patient with few options for care. Patience is thus conceived in this way, as a mental practice that enables him to keep moving ahead in time, and hopefully with healing.

While Francis refers to patient socialities of institutional life, Kevin refers to confinement in prison in order to explain how the period of waiting to heal from a chronic wound is an isolating experience and distinct from everyday life: "When I have a wound I need to take care of, I tell everyone I'm in solitary confinement, just like at Angola when you got in trouble they send you to 'camp J.' I'm in Camp K—Kevin's house, in lockdown. I can't be messing with nobody." The parallels between being an inmate and being a (wound) patient crystallize around the state of waiting and the learned experiences of how to "do" waiting. "Doing time" in Angola requires reserves of patience, endurance, and discipline that can be utilized in the context of wound healing. At the same time, waiting to heal from chronic wounds can limit one's freedom and feel like an isolating, incarcerative space, where one must also "do time" and learn to do it well. Kevin explains further about the importance of maintaining a strong mind in relation to his body: "I need to stay spiritually and mentally tight. 'Cause if not, by the time the wound heals, my mind will be all messed up."

Taking Francis's and Kevin's experiences as a guide, waiting to heal in crip time is not so much a place one moves through toward something else as it is a place one exists and survives in. In crip time, the experience of managing chronic wounds and waiting for them to heal fundamentally shapes the reality of being disabled after gunshot trauma. While pressure ulcers and chronic wounds are a reality for many wheelchair users, the incessant waiting that the wounds require shape the particular "crip" subjectivities that gunshot-injured men present to the world. In this conceptualization, waiting is not just a necessary path toward the goal of the cure when waiting goes on for years and even decades, waiting itself, and the experience and skillset acquired through waiting, becomes an integral part of the texture and testimony of wheelchair life. Ultimately, as an embodied and mindful practice, the labor of waiting to heal produces a new patient subjectivity, which requires active emotional management of ongoing uncertainty about one's state of chronic illness, and the cultivation of a disciplined mental state in relation to one's physical condition.

Within the dominant framework of "curative time," the management of chronic wounds situates waiting as a passive space that the chronic wound patient must tolerate or endure to achieve the next stage of healing or a cure that returns them to the normal temporality of everyday (able-bodied) life. Yet patience is not passive. Patience requires work and commitment. Waiting is a stage of the continued shaping of their identity as disabled gunshot survivors, and disabled men of color, and ensures their value in a world in which value is so often measured on the basis of productive time. In a world in which their survival was not expected, the experience of "waiting to heal" becomes a testimony to the everyday trials that survival requires for managing the chronic state of both skin wounds and the effects of chronic violence in their communities.

Still Waiting

As I write these words in early 2020, Francis waits in a specialty wound care center in Baton Rouge, being treated with another dose of antibiotics in the hope that he will be cleared for a surgical skin-graft operation. After a period of relative stability in Francis's life, during which he found an accessible apartment and moved out on his own, the osteomyelitis that he and his doctors had thought (hoped) had been cured reappeared. During surgery at University Hospital to do a skin graft on an adjacent wound, the surgeons discovered that the MRSA infection had once again dangerously settled in his coccyx bone. Francis explained what happened over the phone, after wishing me a Happy New Year: "I had my surgery scheduled for November 13, but my surgery failed—see the *osteo* never really goes away—it's always there. Now I been laying here in Baton Rouge since December the 9th."

I also spoke with Kevin in mid-January, to check in and share my news about this upcoming publication. He tells me about a wound on his lower back, which he acquired when he bumped against the steering shift in his car while he was pulling himself into the car seat. What began as a small bruise became aggravated by the bullet that has been lodged near his lower spinal cord for twenty-six years and that created a complicated deep wound that grew infected before he even had a chance to care for it. Kevin, a recently diagnosed diabetic, now has his doctor-ordered eight-week home stay interrupted by necessary dialysis treatments twice a week. Sitting in the dialysis chair, he says, aggravates his wound.

Daniella Santoro holds a PhD in Anthropology from Tulane University. Her dissertation "Wheelchair Life" chronicles the lives of disabled gunshot survivors in New Orleans as they vie for public accessibility and social visibility. She is interested in how ethnographic methods can inform gun violence prevention measures and in documenting local disability cultures. She currently teaches anthropology as part of Tulane's College-in Prison Program, and leads seminars on gun violence with medical students.

Notes

1. In an article about PTSD as a result of gun violence among youth in New Orleans, the young man interviewed explains his perception that old age begins at twenty-five (Briggs 2018).
2. For a more detailed history of the Ninth Ward, see Breunlin and Regis (2006).
3. Media coverage and testimonials in the aftermath of the storm report squalid conditions as twenty-five thousand people took refuge at the convention center. Evacuation was not completed until nearly one week after Katrina made landfall. A civil action case filed in response to the death of a New Orleans senior resident Ethel Freeman accuses the city of not having adequate triage services at the Convention Center (see Nicholson 2012: 104).
4. Long-term (post-acute) care hospitals (LTACHs) are relative newcomers to the healthcare landscape, specializing in patients with chronic conditions. They became profitable enterprises in response to changes to Medicare insurance payouts in 1999. The Medicare payouts to LTACH facilities are nearly twice those to nursing homes and more than ten times those to home health care nurses. Wounds and wound care are big business. See: https://www.nber.org/papers/w24946.pdf.
5. The analogy of "inner-city" neighborhoods as warzones is not new, nor is it only metaphorical. Research has indicated that PTSD rates among urban residents in high-crime/violent areas are comparable to, if not higher than, those among military veterans (see Donley et al. 2012).
6. Relying on wound care he learned from his grandmother as a child, Kevin applies a mixture of betadine, sugar, and honey to "eat up the old flesh" of the wound.
7. Known colloquially as Angola, the penitentiary was built on an old slave plantation of the same name.

References

Auyero, Javier. 2011. "Patients of the State: An Ethnographic Account of Poor People's Waiting." *Latin American Research Review* 46(1): 5–29.

Berlant, Lauren. 2007. "Slow Death (Sovereignty, Obesity, Lateral Agency)." *Critical Inquiry* 33(4): 754–80.

Biehl, João. 2005. *Vita: Life in a Zone of Social Abandonment*. Berkeley: University of California Press.

Bodavula, Phani, et al. 2015. "Pressure Ulcer-Related Pelvic Osteomyelitis: A Neglected Disease?" *Open Forum Infectious Diseases* 2(3)

Bourgois, Philippe, and Jeff Schonberg. 2009. *Righteous Dopefiend*. Berkeley: University of California Press.

Breunlin, Rachel, and Helen Regis. 2006. "Putting the Ninth Ward on the Map: Race, Place and Transformation in Desire, New Orleans." *American Anthropologist* 108(4): 744–64.

Briggs, Jimmie. 2018. "The Trauma of Everyday Violence in New Orleans" *Vice* (blog), 4 April. https://www.vice.com/en_us/article/evqvn7/the-trauma-of-everyday-gun-violence-in-new-orleans-v25n1 (accessed 6 April 2018).

Cazdyn, Eric. 2012. *The Already Dead: The New Time of Politics, Culture, and Illness*. Durham, NC: Duke University Press.

Crapanzano, Vincent. 2011. *The Harkis: The Wound that Never Heals*. Chicago: University of Chicago Press.

Dewachi, Omar. 2015. "When Wounds Travel." *Medicine Anthropology Theory* 2(3): 61. https://doi.org/10.17157/mat.2.3.182 (accessed 21 October 2019).

Donley, Sachiko, et al. 2012. "Civilian PTSD Symptoms and Risk for Involvement in the Criminal Justice System." *Journal of the American Academy of Psychiatry and the Law* 40(4): 522–29.

Groah, Suzanne L., et al. 2015. "Prevention of Pressure Ulcers Among People with Spinal Cord Injury: A Systematic Review." *PM & R: The Journal of Injury, Function, and Rehabilitation* 7(6): 613–36. https://doi.org/10.1016/j.pmrj.2014.11.014.

Janeja, Manpreet K., and Andreas Bandak, eds. 2018. *Ethnographies of Waiting: Doubt, Hope and Uncertainty*. New York: Bloomsbury Academic.

Jenkins, Richard, Hanne Jessen, and Vibeke Steffen. 2005. *Managing Uncertainty: Ethnographic Studies of Illness, Risk and the Struggle for Control*. Copenhagen: Museum Tusculanum Press.

Kafer, Alison. 2013. *Feminist, Queer, Crip*. Bloomington: Indiana University Press.

Kim, Eunjung. 2017. *Curative Violence: Rehabilitating Disability, Gender, and Sexuality in Modern Korea*. Durham, NC: Duke University Press.

Lee, Jooyoung. 2012. "Wounded: Life after the Shooting." *The ANNALS of the American Academy of Political and Social Science* 642(1): 244–57.

Livingston, Julie. 2012. *Improvising Medicine: An African Oncology Ward in an Emerging Cancer Epidemic*. Durham, NC: Duke University Press.

———. 2013. "Revealed in the Wound." *Journal of Clinical Oncology* 31(29): 3719–20.

———. 2014. "Figuring the Tumor in Botswana." *Raritan* 34(1): 10–24.

McKie, Robin. 2017. "'Antibiotic Apocalypse': Doctors Sound Alarm over Drug Resistance." *The Guardian*, 8 October. https://www.theguardian.com/society/2017/oct/08/world-faces-antibiotic-apocalypse-says-chief-medical-officer (accessed 4 March 2019).

McRuer, Robert. 2006. *Crip Theory: Cultural Signs of Queerness and Disability*. New York: New York University Press.

Mitchell, David T., and Sharon L. Snyder. 2001. *Narrative Prosthesis: Disability and the Dependencies of Discourse*. Ann Arbor: University of Michigan Press.

Nicholson, William C. 2012. *Emergency Response and Emergency Management Law: Cases and Materials*. Springfield, IL: Charles C. Thomas Publisher, Ltd.

Procupez, Valeria. 2015. "The Need for Patience: The Politics of Housing Emergency in Buenos Aires." *Current Anthropology* 56(S11): S55–65.

Ralph, Laurence. 2012. "What Wounds Enable: The Politics of Disability and Violence in Chicago." *Disability Studies Quarterly* 32(3). http://dsq-sds.org/article/view/3270 (accessed 17 June 2018).

———. 2014. *Renegade Dreams: Living Through Injury in Gangland Chicago*. Chicago: University of Chicago Press.

Samuels, Ellen. 2017. "Six Ways of Looking at Crip Time." *Disability Studies Quarterly* 37(3). https://dsq-sds.org/article/view/5824/4684 (accessed 9 June 2018).

Sandahl, Carrie. 2003. "Queering the Crip or Cripping the Queer?: Intersections of Queer and Crip Identities in Solo Autobiographical Performance." *Journal of Gay and Lesbian Studies* 9(1–2): 25–56.

Sen, Chandan K., et al. 2009. "Human Skin Wounds: A Major and Snowballing Threat to Public Health and the Economy." *Wound Repair and Regeneration: The International Journal of Tissue Repair and Regeneration* 17(6): 763–71.

Thomas, D. R. 2001. "Prevention and Treatment of Pressure Ulcers: What Works? What Doesn't?" *Cleveland Clinic Journal of Medicine* 68(8): 704–7, 710–14, 717–22.

Whyte, Susan Reynolds. 2002. "Subjectivity and Subjunctivity: Hoping for Health in Eastern Uganda." In *Postcolonial Subjectivities in Africa*, ed. Richard Werbner, 171–90. London: Zed Books.

Wool, Zoe. 2015. *After War: The Weight of Life at Walter Reed*. Durham, NC: Duke University Press.

Wool, Zoe, and Julie Livingston. 2017. "Collateral Afterworlds: An Introduction." *Social Text* 35(130): 1–15.

Entretemps

Urgency, Boredom, and Pandemic Mean/Time(s)

Martin Demant Frederiksen

On that particular Thursday morning in March 2020, I relied on a school bus to get me to the train station, from where I would make my way to the department of anthropology in Aarhus, Denmark. All this to teach the final class of a course on fieldwork and methodology, after which my plan was to fly back to Oslo, Norway, where my family and I were living at the time.

But the night before I was due to set off, the Danish prime minister Mette Frederiksen appeared on TV to shut down the country in response to the coronavirus pandemic.

This resulted in a series of hectic phone calls immediately after her TV appearance, both with family and colleagues. With the latter, it was arranged that my co-teacher Nanna and I would be allowed to go to the department the following day in order to pick up our things and hold an impromptu online session with the students instead of the prepared class, essentially to tell them that their upcoming fieldwork around the world, fieldwork they had spent the previous months carefully planning, would now have to be cancelled, or at least postponed indefinitely.

Despite the fact that school in Denmark was also being cancelled, the school bus was there on Thursday morning. The bus driver greeted me as I entered. "I knew there probably wouldn't be any kids today, but no one called me to say whether the bus should do its round or not," he said. "And I figured that I'd try to do something instead of just staying home, in case anyone showed up." He drove me to the train station, which was void of passengers, as was the train when it arrived. This eerie, empty, uncertain atmosphere also prevailed at the anthropology department, where only a handful of staff members had been allowed to show up to close everything down.

Nanna and I packed up the books that we thought we might need during a lockdown, whatever a "lockdown" was. We ensured that all the doors at the department were locked and we set up a room for the online meeting with the students, while trying to figure out exactly how far apart we were supposed to sit to comply with the new distance rules we had heard about the night before.

During all this, it dawned on both of us that there was something familiar about this situation and the sensation it had very suddenly caused.

It felt like fieldwork.

Or, more specifically, it felt like specific times during fieldwork that we had both experienced. This was partly the result of the general experience of immersing oneself in a different temporality, of being in an unfamiliar context, of figuring out what to do on the spur of a moment in a temporary situation of complete disorientation. And it was partly the result of both having been fieldworkers in places of crisis. For me, this connected to the 2008 Russo–Georgian War, which had erupted only days after I had arrived in the Georgian coastal city of Batumi in order to carry out fieldwork for my PhD.

Russian army planes circled above the city, but the Russian army did not enter Batumi during that period. Yet, although one could not see it, the war was there and its consequences were palpable. Hence, in the uncertain atmosphere shrouding the city, there was a distinct sensation that *while this was going on, something else had to be done*. Decisions about what to do had to be taken. Quickly. Should one leave the city and take shelter in the mountains? Should one try to make it across the border to Turkey? Should one stay put, stock up on food supplies, and wait it out?

During that first day of lockdown in the spring of 2020, although you could not really see it, the virus was there and its consequences were palpable. And *while this was going on, something had to be done*. Decisions had to be made. Quickly. A school bus taken for a final round, a department to be closed down, a period of staying put at home arranged. Those first days of lockdown combined a strange mixture of urgency, apprehension, fear, wonder, and a readiness to act—even if acting might be a matter of staying put and waiting it out.

. . .

Cut to a year later.

. . .

And cut the word in two.

. . .

Mean Time.
...

The second lockdown is dragging on. The end of the first one did not signify that the worst was over, but that it had yet to come. And it just continues to stretch on. Urgency has given way to other temporalities. Inertia, boredom, resignation. My family and I moved back to Denmark in order to be closer to friends and family. But now we cannot visit them anyway. All that can happen does so within the walls of the house: ad-hoc home office, kids dragging their feet to attend online classes in their bedrooms, parents dragging their feet to attend yet another Zoom meeting, dead eyes all around, another press conference on TV at which it is announced that this might take a bit longer, stay put, stay safe. We know that the lockdown keeps us healthy, that Denmark is not the worst place to be during a pandemic, but that does not brighten up homeschooling. The house is the world. Why shower in the morning? We are not going anywhere. Feet dragging, see you all on Zoom, repeat.

This shouldn't have come as a surprise. The field taught me this as well.

During the second lockdown, Roman writes me from somewhere on the Indian Ocean. He asks me to send him the transcript of an interview I conducted with him thirteen years ago. He has been at sea for four months now, unable to disembark, and he's bored. He and I first met in Batumi, not long after the war in 2008. He was bored then as well; that was what the interview had been about.

In it, Roman compared life at sea with life ashore. "When you're on a ship," he said, "you often think 'I just want to go home, this work is shit.' But then you arrive in a new port and you forget about your work and you return to the ship refreshed. But it only lasts a few weeks, after that you hate your work again." And currently, there are no ports to enter. The same, he continued, was often the case once he was back in Batumi. At first, it was great to see his friends, but as weeks and months passed, that sense of excitement gave way to boredom, repetitive activities, and "replaying the same conversation every day."

With the urgency of war over, he and the other young men that my research had come to focus on had faced a period of stalemate and resignation. It was near impossible for them to find jobs and although the then government made grand promises about the future of the country, the young men had a distinct feeling that this future would either never come to pass, or that there would be no place for them in it even if it did. Their days were often marked by a sense that there was nothing to do or to be done. Days marked by heavy drinking, depression, drugs. Time spent wandering around in a circle, a giant one; the city was the circle.

Hours, days, weeks spent waiting for a change. *While this is going on, there is barely anything to do.*

The longer the meantime, the meaner the time.

The second lockdown did not come as a shock. We had an idea that it might be coming and we had been through it before. But it was still much different, for exactly those reasons. It was no longer a matter of urgency, but of withdrawal and disengagement. Boredom, inertia, longing, apathy. Mean time, both because of what it was like to be in it and because its eventual end point seemed to constantly recede out of sight. Vaccines are coming, we hear politicians happily exclaim. But then they are delayed. Again. We drag ourselves to another Zoom meeting. Circle around at home. Hours, days, weeks spent waiting for a change. *While this is going on, there is barely anything to do.*

Roman is on a ship, I am in lockdown. "Routines, every day the same," he writes. I agree. There are no harbors in sight. No cures. Neither an entry nor an exit. We both just stay put. And in doing so, in both experiences, there are traces of the time we spent together in Batumi after the war. We stayed put. Bored. Unnerved by the knowledge of endings out of sight. In the meantime, stuck. Mean time. Who even bothers to act?

. . .

The temporalities of the pandemic mean/time might seem new or particular to the situation. But for many, this is only so because the experience itself was foreign. Urgency and boredom in the wake of crisis are experiences that millions of people around the world lived in, with, and through long before the pandemic started.

We made it through that time in Batumi, Roman, an expert on mean/time, lets me know while this is going on. *Perhaps, later, there will be things to do.*

Martin Demant Frederiksen is Associate Professor in Anthropology at the Department of Culture and Society, Aarhus University. He works at the interface of anthropology and contemporary archeology, and his current research focuses on emptiness, temporality, and coastal infrastructures in Croatia and Denmark, and on subcultures and abandoned industrial towns in Georgia. He is the author of *Young Men, Time, and Boredom in the Republic of Georgia* (Temple University Press, 2011), *Georgian Portraits: Essays on the Afterlives of a Revolution* (with Katrine B. Gotfredsen; Zero Books, 2017), and *An Anthropology of Nothing in Particular* (Zero Books, 2018).

Chapter 7

African Time, Waiting, and Deadlines in Botswana

Deborah Durham

It's not certain. It's inevitable.
—Samuel Beckett, *Waiting for Godot*

I have spent a lot of time waiting in Botswana, sitting around the *kgotla* (chief's court) for hours waiting for community meetings to begin, watching a clock waiting for government officers to show up for arranged interviews, patiently waiting for the offered cup of tea or share of a meal to appear. I have stood for over an hour in a short line in a bank while the cashier drew out a cob of cooked corn and slowly, determinedly, munched on it mid-afternoon, and I have spent long days with other impatient applicants, over a period of several months, waiting for someone to find and then process paperwork for a residence permit that is finally issued on the last possible day. People who noticed my frustration would tell me—using the English phrase—that this was "African time," by which they meant that Africans are indifferent to clock and calendar time, and do not rush from task to task. While the term was first used by White visitors to the continent, and gained strength as it was employed by frustrated colonizers and aid workers, it has been seized and mobilized, often with humor, sometimes as an excuse, and occasionally with irritated condemnation, by the citizens of Botswana.

Batswana (people of Botswana) were waiting, too, of course, sometimes rather grumpily, sometimes with uncertain but hopeful anticipation, and sometimes expecting disappointment but willing to wait nonetheless. Sometimes the waiting was fun, or a break from work, or a time to do other things while waiting. While we often say that waiting is the human condition—it is, after all, part of a chronology of past, present, and future—there were a wide variety of forms of waiting, all quite different. Anthropology has too often cast waiting in terms of thwarted plans, frustration, crippling uncertainty. But waiting is not, in Botswana or anywhere, a single modality.

Waiting is such a complex activity, both socially and temporally—no wonder there is so much being written about it in anthropology today, a time of global social anxiety and complex temporal dynamics. It is often associated with the "precarious," suggesting a wait for a feared future, tempered by hope for survival or materializing opportunity. For some, waiting implies a kind of inactivity or wasted time, but here I explore waiting itself as a valued form of activity, in at least some of its diverse forms. To do so, I examine waiting in a variety of situations over the past twenty-five years in Botswana, where I have conducted long-term fieldwork.

Waiting is often seen not only as a suspension of activity, but also a suspension of time, a period of "stuckness" in a present that is disarticulated from both a past hopefulness and a hoped-for but unrealizable future, an empty time of wheel-spinning, the barren plain of Estragon and Vladimir. And that may be the case for some: waiting may be experienced as a time in which past and future are both missing. Other accounts of waiting emphasize its relationship to the future: a future full of hopes, anxieties, or dread. Here, I discuss the time of waiting as deeply connected with—and connecting—past, present, and future, following the lead of Nancy Munn's studies of temporality, and the narratological phenomenology of Paul Ricoeur's attempt to redeem the past through memory. In doing so, I hope to redeem the bleak emptiness of waiting for Godot, and to fill it with past and future, organized through projects of waiting that do what betweens do—connect.

Focusing on youth, and then on a set of anecdotes involving people of all ages, which together convey the rich and diverse temporalities of meantimes, I argue that, for people in Botswana, the future opens up through waiting—waiting is *effective*—and that the future's arrival can be an ending or a reward, but as people organize various waits, ends and rewards overlap. At the same time, waiting takes place with respect to a past, now past, and a present with relationship to that past and to a future: one aspect of its effectiveness is how it is constitutive of these temporalities. Waiting is rich with complex emotional dispositions and enriches affective sociality; its *affectivity* goes beyond hope and anxiety, both of which are individualizing orientations. Let us start with the context: Botswana.

Botswana has been, since it became independent in 1966, a classic "developmental state,"[1] where the role of the state has been to foster development, typically envisioned in the form of improved incomes and material conditions of living. Developmentalism as state policy is, of course, a particular temporality, one that looks to the future, considers its present, and often creates a notion of an undeveloped past. Botswana's schoolbook histories and the National Development Plans from the very early days emphasize continuity with the past, reaching into the nineteenth century, and not a sharp break with either colonialism (Botswana was a protectorate, not a colony) or independence. This continuity is often framed as growth and includes novelty (new veterinary techniques; advanced education; computer-based investment opportunity), amidst continuities (the importance of people's voices in politics, for one; the continued importance of livestock as well as arable husbandry). While, objectively, most development has been accomplished through government projects funded by Botswana's diamond revenues, from constructing infrastructure to funding agriculture, providing jobs in general, and more recently funding entrepreneurship, the government's mantra has long been "*Batswana ba tshwanetse go itlhabolola*" (Batswana must develop themselves).[2] The material/economic side of this developmentalism is embraced by almost everyone I knew or talked to; it is also somewhat consistent and intertwined with projects of developing oneself in a more social manner, extending one's emotional intercorporeality[3] with others in ways that promote one's own and their wellbeing—or that cause illness and harm. While emotional intercorporeality grows with age and demands management, it is not disconnected from developing income, houses, belongings, and the like (see Durham n.d.). The intertwining of the two forms of development means that ideas of growth, development, and time diverge from the ideas of liberal capitalism in places like the United States.

Development, and its planning, takes time in Botswana—for people with their own projects (as I discuss further below) and for the government. A National Youth Policy approved by Parliament in 1996 was the outcome of ten years of planning, consulting with the public, preparing, and reconsulting with the public. And most policies like that, such as arable farming development policies, commercial ranching policies, and educational changes, are the product of many years of work—unreasonably slow work, to the outside observer. In the 1990s, the government began putting together "Visions," beginning with Vision 2016, announcing aspirations for education, security, democracy, and compassion; in 2016, Vision 2036 was released, with a much sharper eye on economic resources and development.[4] And such slowness pervades the country's bureaucracy: applications for land from district Land Boards can take up to ten years to be processed and approved, and not only because there is a shortage of land available for houses; applications for passports go unprocessed and planned travel must be canceled; applications for internships in the programs addressing youth unemployment languish for a year or two. Outcomes in government policy circles and in bureaucratic offices are rarely expected in short order, although being put off in government offices can generate angry complaint.

Botswana's governmentality, since the country achieved its independence but increasingly over the years, is mapped with fixed times, hours, dates, and years. And these very often measure what one does, what one did, and what one can do; this measured, punctual time is now associated, in rhetoric at least, with economic productivity and wasted time (not surprisingly; see Thompson 1967, Weber [1905] 2009). Some Batswana complain vociferously about African time (or Tswana time), saying that failures of punctuality and the lack of any time-measured work ethic have impeded the country's development (see, e.g., Makgala and Thebe 2015).

The Meantime of Youth

Dates and even hours can be used to measure developmental progress, especially in a developmental state—government officials (among others) frequently note how few kilometers of paved road there were in Botswana when it achieved independence, in 1966, and how many there are now; the number of "modern" houses built each year or connected to an expanding electrical grid; and plans for X many houses or seats in schools by future dates. Yet, for many, the arrival of a date, a *dead*line, can mean the arrival of the final loss of opportunity, a closing of the space in which hope and activity take place. This is notable in the new time of youth in Botswana—if it is a time of "waithood," to use the term favored by Alcinda Honwana (2012), what one waits for is not accession to a more powerful status in the form of adulthood. Social adulthood is desired in many respects, and 23-year-olds, who once considered themselves "just children," now complain about not being "heard" in family meetings (Setambule 2022). That kind of social adulthood, being "heard," might have come, in recent decades (including this one), in one's thirties or later, for those who had a successful career or had demonstrated leadership in organizations or a self-sufficient household. A fuller social maturity was not attained, in the twentieth century, until rather late in life, the outcome of successfully gaining recognition as an elder from one's own children and their children (Livingston 2003). However, as valued as being heard and the respect of full maturity might be, in the 2010s people of a certain age were waiting for the end of youth with considerable trepidation, as the end of youth means a closing of some kinds of opportunity, in particular the developmental aids offered by the government to those between the ages of fifteen and thirty-five.[5]

In the recent past (the 1990s, when I conducted much of my fieldwork; but see also Schapera 1940), youth was an open-ended state; people could occupy the social space of youth, and act as youth, into their sixties, at least situationally. The opportunities of youth were primarily associated with extending social connectivity, through romances, joining clubs and associations, evening singing and social life, contributing labor to community events, finding patrons, or furthering relationships with uncles and cousins in various ways (see Durham 2007, 2008). In the 1990s, young men committed suicide, too frequently it seemed, over failed romances, alienation from peers, and a feeling of scorn from or cruel treatment by their family, at least according to gossip and reports (lack of income fed into all these). While some young people started small business projects, including their own cattleposts (usually without cattle), ventures that might today be called entrepreneurial, the use of government subsidies and loans was more extensively within the compass of people well over thirty-five. Today, the government targets youth with special development programs, youth now being people under thirty-five. Youth up to thirty-five are eligible for tuition and a living stipend at a university,[6] grants to support business start-ups, internships in government and parastatal offices (deplored as inadequate but there nonetheless), as well as planned special housing opportunities. (Thato Setambule (2022) notes the shortcomings of many of these programs.) At thirty-five, these opportunities end and one enters the world of non-youth loans, government loans that are less generous for repayment and harder to access for the unconnected and untrained, or bank loans.

Youth, then, is not only the period of social opportunities, but now also the period of economic opportunities. Young people frequently talk of plans to apply for Youth Development Fund (YDF) or youth-targeted CEDA grants and loans with generous repayment (and forgiveness) terms, as well as talking of how they are thinking up new ventures (without sharing these ventures, though: idea theft was a serious concern), working with agency officers or hiring one of the many self-advertised consultants to craft formal business plans, or trying to round up a group of collaborators and locate the required office space. These elements mostly had deadlines specified in the application and loan conditions. Youth I met with in the 2010s were also busy applying for (and acquiring in a period of rapid allocation) plots of land for houses, typically in home villages far from where they lived in the cities, pursuing romantic relationships, and creating multiple flexible identities through Facebook and WhatsApp. They were registering nonprofits with the government, although they had yet to organize any nonprofit work; they were pounding the pavement with résumés in hand, looking for scarce—but sometimes materializing—jobs, preferably in the private sector, where they said salaries were higher, although benefits like pensions were fewer. While dishwashing at Nando's or waiting tables as a fill-in when staff did not show up, they tried to work out whether a small venture—a streetside car wash with cold drinks for sale, packaging hospitality soaps, a temp service, a cupcake business—could attract enough friends and relatives as customers to support itself and grow.

While, in their multiple concurrent ventures, there is an overlap with the "zigzag economy" that Jeremy Jones (2010) describes in the context of neighboring Zimbabwe—"making do" with various dispersed projects (see also Vigh 2006)—there are differences. The zigzag, making-do economies refer specifically to generating income; the ventures youth in Botswana contemplated relate to income, but also to social connectivities, possible good works, (possible) homes in distant villages that they will not use in the near future. In Botswana, too, people were more hopeful that one or more of their ventures might work out, even though they had watched those of peers and senior relatives fail over the decades. Throughout the 1990s, such failures in stock farming, arable projects, brickmaking, vehicle leasing, and general dealers and tuck shops, were rampant. By and large, discussing them with humor, concern, or schadenfreude, people noted that, at least for a time, those involved had enjoyed a business or material comforts bought on credit—and then they retrenched when their ventures failed or were repossessed.

Today, as younger youth are now pursuing business, jobs, relationships, plots for homes, and shell ("shelf" in Botswana) company registrations, I call them bricoleurs of the future, as they seek a wide range of opportunities, even though few will succeed. These opportunities are supported by the government, by family expectations, by church and club rotating credit, by peer networks (and loan sharks among them), and by hope, and the number and variety pursued, the entrepreneurial aspect, and the constant planning are new to people in their age range. These youth ventures should not be characterized with "cruel optimism," as in the United States (Berlant 2011); people expect many of them to fail, an eventuality they sometimes meet with humor, sometimes with angry suspicions of malevolence, sometimes (often, even) with resignation, simply turning to other or new ventures, and sometimes, but not inevitably, with cruel despair. Indeed, for many youth, it is better to wait, as things are still in motion, than to see the failure that has always partially cast a shadow over a project, as the chickens in a chicken farm die, as the captured ostriches escape through inadequate fencing, as patrons fail to materialize for a cake-baking business, as equipment is repossessed when loan payments are not made, as the employees signed on do not show up, as a critical computer breaks down when the rest of the capital has been spent on other things, as work stalls on building a house, as one's boyfriend drifts to other women or one's girlfriend marries a wealthier older man. (I also know of success stories!)

At thirty-five, however, people often either reconcile themselves to a life they have settled into (for some, a good life, for others a disappointing one), or continue to pursue new opportunities through the standard government development programs or week-long education or training courses, or through commercial or social-network loans, or new romantic relationships, which have long shaped post-youth citizen self-development. Waiting for development, then, takes place in two kinds of time: one, the openness of African time, with its space of self-development in the midst of a range of familiar failures and successes, and the other, the new punctuality of dates and clocks, associated with economic growth and yet also offering *dead*lines, endings. I turn to my anecdotes, to illustrate these temporal spaces.

Waiting, Yet Not Just Waiting: Four Vignettes

It is 1989. I offer a composite ethnographic vignette, based on many similar events.

> I sit in the ward *kgotla*—the chief's court in the village ward part of the urban village, where complaints were heard and government officers came to discuss new policies—and drag a small stick through the dirt around me, as do a couple of the women nearby, who are sitting, like me, on the ground. It is getting close to noon and some of the women are probably thinking of the midday meal that must be prepared, especially if someone in salaried (and clocked) employment is coming home for it. Men sit on chairs, upturned buckets, or old cinder blocks. I have been there, like several of the old men, for over two hours—I long ago learned that a meeting announced for 8 AM would never start before 10, at the earliest. While the men sit, gossiping about lost cattle, water levels at wells, or rumors of a sale of especially valued goats or sheep, women come and go. Some sit longer and others come for short periods to get away from the demands of the homestead and chat about whose cousin is where, whether a proposed marriage is still on, who is going to join the church group's visit to Twapewa at the hospital, how Annah's new

baby is (and whether the father's family has sent gifts), how Refilwe's ear was bitten by a cow at her in-laws' cattlepost, or how InaKanawa has harvested so many bags of beans, as well as talking about cattle and rain. If we are waiting for a case to be heard, the women may rehearse some of its history (one divorcing couple was said to have married with just chickens for bridewealth many decades ago). Business transactions are talked about; rides arranged to the hospital, where sick people must be visited, or to and from cattleposts; relationships reassessed as they change with childbirth or divorce. The government officer finally arrives hours late, or the other party to the court case is finally located and brought to the *kgotla*, and those who are still there enjoy the puzzle of whose cow the disputed beast is, or the entertainment of a dispute over shocking insults, or try to work out how to access the funds in this new agricultural scheme.

Although many of the Batswana are deeply concerned with government policies and their own failing agriculture, with disputes and frayed kin relations, with impending marriages or lost livestock—these things are important and worrisome—in some ways the time between, sitting and waiting, was also significant. E. E. Evans-Pritchard once wrote that for the Nuer "time . . . [was] a relation between activities," and not measured by clocks (Evans-Pritchard 1940: 100). In our *kgotla* waiting time, activities were indeed being put into relationships, distinguished and also brought together, the past sorted out with reference to the present (in gossip, in previewing court cases), the future explored (in plans spoken about or just thought through), and the present lived in (as an escape from chores, as pleasure in company, as just waiting). "Nuer are fortunate," Evans-Pritchard added (103).

Not everyone, of course, agreed that they were fortunate in the times between. Let us move ahead to the year 2000 to see a mix of reactions to time spent waiting. I am still fortunate, at least, in waiting as there is much in that time for the anthropologist to observe:[7]

> The Youth Day ceremony was delayed for hours, as the keynote politicians arrived late (typically), eventually explaining that they had been in "important meetings." The *kgosi* (chief) looked around at empty chairs set up in a large tent and asked where "the public" was. An organized group of youth that had marched through the city to the venue, who were not "the public" missed by the *kgosi* and were not invited to sit in the chairs roped off and under a tent, had not waited around. The few school-aged children at the ceremony, dressed in skimpy "traditional" costumes for choral and other performances that would punctuate the speeches, shivered and complained in the winter cold. During the long wait, they were chided by an older woman for "looking unhappy" and urged to be happy because "it is your day." Meanwhile, women and men from various government and nongovernmental agencies, who carried printed invitations and had chairs reserved with their names on them, drank tea and sat under the canopy, or drifted off to return to work.

I was invited to join those drinking tea and waiting; we chatted about the difficulty of getting visas to the United States and less consequential things. The woman sitting next to me, an office worker, looked at her watch repeatedly, but did not leave.

In this vignette from 2000, we see a variety of the ways in which people in a mixed urban crowd experienced waiting in Botswana at that time. Some were unhappy—but to act overtly unhappy in that situation was to be childish. Some did not wait at all but went on to other activities, either immediately, as in the case of the youth marchers, or as time passed and their office jobs became more appealing in the winter cold. Some were patient and some enjoyed the waiting period as it represented a chance to drink tea and chat with old and new acquaintances (like me). Unlike the wait in the village *kgotla*, however, there did not seem to be much talk aimed at gathering information, though my seatmate who complained about the US visa process perhaps hoped I would at the very least communicate the unfairness of the process to someone. People come and go; those in the space of waiting, however, are patient and quiet, or merry and chatting. If you are unhappy, you do not show it. While it might be that during our very long, cold wait for the minister and chief (no one, to my knowledge, believed their excuse about other meetings), people were "doing nothing," the printed invitations, the canopy and hot tea, and the roped-off chairs indicated that, sitting there, they were "doing something"—they were invited; their presence marked them as of significance to the event. Even the shivering children, who were clearly unhappy, were told that their presence was significant in making and marking the event. Although there is a common refrain among young people, in Botswana and elsewhere, that they are "doing nothing" (see Burke 2000; Dungey and Meinert 2017; Mains 2007; Masquelier 2019), those waiting (most not youth) on National Youth Day were doing something: they were making themselves into the kind of persons who sit under canopies or have days set aside for them. They were also making themselves subject to the minister and chief—but, in the persisting logic of the old Tswana polities, where it was said that *kgosi ke kgosi ka batho* (a king/chief is chief by the people—i.e., only with the recognition and support of the people), the minister and chief in 2000 were similarly subject to the appearance and waiting of "the public." And as the *kgotla* waiters (the public) made the community forum through presence, these waiters made a national day and, in some senses, the nation.

I am back in Botswana in 2014, for the first time since 2000. We are at a gathering of Herero, Nama, and others in a small dusty village in southwest Botswana, where Herero, Mbanderu, and Nama people from Botwana,

Namibia, and South Africa have come together to celebrate their identities and traditions. *Tiza ombazu*, says a vest I bought from fundraisers—"hold on to tradition"—and it strikes me that one tradition is hanging around waiting for events to begin. My old friend and I sit under a large tent with some hundred or more people as high winds threaten to tear it down (and eventually do). Choral and dance groups assemble and disassemble in the choking dust outside, horses are ridden back and forth, and my companion comments on the different outfits, laughing at the Nama ones, curious about Namibian Herero styles, complaining of the wind and dust. We talk briefly with Namibian women in stunning outfits. Hours pass. Suddenly, vehicles drive up and the President of Botswana arrives: he is precisely on time, exactly on schedule. He is, I am told by my companion, always exactly on time. I know from speeches and policy announcements that he connects punctuality with productivity and economic development. Perhaps from his days as head of the army, I think, or perhaps such comments point out that he is not living "in Tswana time," or, as is sometimes suggested about him, in Tswana culture.[8] He is visibly annoyed at the mysterious disappearance of a Nama children's dance group, who would eventually perform a thrilling polka for us. The program was then rushed and he left, again precisely on time, helicoptering off to a scheduled event in Tshabong (there is an election coming up).

Although I am still made to wait in 2014, sometimes for hours or even days in several government offices despite having appointments, in others I am told that this is a problem for the country and its development. The term "deadwood," popularized over the past twenty years or more to complain about government workers who attained their posts in the early days of the country when fewer qualifications were required and are now refusing to retire, lurks behind the complaints of the new younger elite. Yet, even members of that group who complained to me directly that African time was harming Botswana's development kept me standing in a rainy parking lot for over an hour, soon after confirming that they would pick me up for a dinner date.

It is 2017, my last visit and also my last vignette:

I have arranged to meet up with a young woman in her early twenties in one of the new malls now common in Gaborone and take her clothes shopping. I know she will not arrive at the designated time but get increasingly angry as texts arrive telling me she is walking to the (mini)bus, waiting for a bus, on the bus but now it is stuck in traffic, still stuck in traffic, and still stuck. I have already sussed out all the shops and chatted with some of the salespeople, watched passers-by from a bench, and think, after an hour, that I will just leave. In the end, I wait for over two hours. She shows up, laughing and apologetic and complaining about traffic. Where has she really been? Did she think I would wait two hours? I later find out that she has an occasional part-time job at the other end of the city from her shared one-room rental, which she was probably concealing from a wide circle of relatives (and me), and the traffic, and bus changes, actually had held her up as she traveled from work all the way to her room and then in another direction to this mall. If I had not waited, she probably would have window-shopped and then gone to meet friends in another part of town; indeed, we passed several young people she knows from university. For her, the time really was the relationship between activities, some of which emerged in the moment, others of which were scheduled; for me, it was measured, down to counting the 120 minutes of sitting doing nothing and thinking about activities I could have been doing.

Like so many others I knew, she lives by waiting, because waiting is the only path to the future. She is looking for a "real" job, one in an office, having finished her university degree recently, but such jobs are scarce; she is engaged in a romantic relationship and monitors her HIV status with periodic tests, recorded on a health card that she carries around; she is devising a variety of entrepreneurial options but needs to work out many details concerning sourcing, pricing, and labor, and so is waiting to submit applications for the youth loan programs; she goes to a lot of clubs, events, and parties, and I am one of the people who pay entry fees through small cash gifts. She is getting by, even if she is not getting much money; she feels that things will transpire here and there, and knows that certain things will not—much as I might, or might not, have been there when she finally got to the mall.

Creating the Meantime: The Modalities and Meanings of Waiting

This range of vignettes, spanning decades and set in different milieux in Botswana, illustrates the variety of ways in which people experience time in waiting times. Munn (1992) drew our attention to the various ways in which time is experienced by any one person, anywhere, and how anthropological attention can be drawn to one or another modality. Because time is experienced in dispositional ways—orientational, but also deeply affective—it will also have different qualities for different individuals in the same meantime. Here in Botswana, be it in the "fortunate" meantime between activities of the village, or in punctualities and productivities in the capital, or in the developmental and deadline-circumscribed times of designated youth, what we find is time in its "crosswise doubleness," as Clifford Geertz once described Balinese cockfights (1973a: 424), conjoining different registers and values.[9] Waiting, in Botswana, too, has divergent, overlapping, embodied, sensible meanings, which individuals bring to bear on a situation, or which can be seen in the ways different people occupy one temporal space.

Looking at the meanings of waiting in so-called African time in Botswana, we should keep in mind that meaning is pragmatic, and see waiting not only as something that happens, but also as an action. Part of that action is to create the meantime itself. While Victor Turner (1967) had agents mark out the betwixt-and-between from "normal" sociality, and had people move in and out from one to the other, we can also see the meantime as a space that is an ongoing work in progress in relationship to a past and a future, where all three need both to be delimited one from the other and brought into relationships with each other. I draw on Ricoeur's (2004) attempt to understand memory and forgetting as phenomenologically informed processes of relating pasts, presents, and futures, and also Munn's (2013) account of how people in pre–Civil War New York looked at construction that was going on—buildings being torn down and new ones being built—envisioning the new as already old, from the vantage point of a future they created to make sense of the present and the now-past.[10] The gist of both is that temporalities are relational, that temporal experiences, be they of past experience, present experience, or the future (anticipation), conjoin in a shifting, dynamic way that gives people some (albeit not open-ended) agency toward each. Waiting, as an activity, must, for a start, create a meantime, a time between, and in so doing demarcate a past that was different from the present and a future that is also distinct. It changes the "now" from something purely existential into a marked space in a specific temporal framework. This can be quite obvious: in speeches by ministers, chiefs, and politicians in Botswana—a developmental state—there is typically a reference to a past that is different from the present (only 6 kilometers of paved roads!), and to a future that is anticipated to be different as well (more connections to the electrical grid, or a diversified economy no longer reliant on minerals, tourism, and agriculture).

The temporal gap—the space between one time and another—is critical for social agency, whether for reproduction, exerting power over others, or social transformation, as Bourdieu (1977) argued. It is, perhaps, a feature of all agencies that agency is also affective (and affect is agentive: see Ahmed 2013 and see Durham 2002 for a culturally specific argument for Botswana). Although the term "waiting" implies a lack of agency and subjection to time imposed by others, the "meantime" gives us more scope to explore this temporal space and the things people do with it and within it. The term "waiting," however, draws our attention to the affective dimensions of waiting. Affect invites a range of interpretations (patience, impatience, anxiety and uncertainty or determination, dread or optimism, etc.), possibly because, as in the Balinese cockfights, it is crosswise double, as it is part of the various projects, engagements, and experiential moments that intertwine and pull apart in any event or moment.

We see this immediately in the *kgotla* meeting of 1989. When we consider the older men, sitting around in their chairs, we must question whether this is a meantime for them—that is, a time between a marked-off past and an anticipated future. They are, ostensibly, waiting for the government minister, but on any given day they are sitting there, waiting for the parties involved in a court case, another government official, the *kgosi* (chief), and sometimes they are waiting just to see if anything is going to happen. While they do do other things—going out to cattleposts to check on cattle, visiting the hospital or clinic, presiding over home disputes in their home compounds, enjoying the best plate of food—there is an everydayness to their sitting in the *kgotla*. They are waiting, though, and poised between things: perhaps they are waiting for an application for a tractor loan to be approved or denied, for a relative to arrive from Namibia or South Africa, for a pregnant wife or daughter to give birth, for bull semen to improve the herd, for the rains to finally come in yet another drought year, or just for the midday meal. If waiting for the court case, they will testify about having seen a missing cow or listen with delight as a reported insult (referring to genitals) is repeated over and over, or they may be curious about the social history of the disputed inheritance of a bed. One of them is scribbling figures in the margins of an old newspaper, working out a cattle trade or costing out a tractor scheme. However, waiting in the *kgotla* is not just waiting for the future: those waiting are enjoying gossip and company (reworking the past as they do so), displaying their current "traditional" knowledge, spending time that must be spent somewhere. The present seems as interesting as the past and future. Like many of the people at the Youth Day event, their presence in this waiting space is an assertion of worth, of value, of having a certain status. The older men in their chairs against the *kgotla*'s log walls are making themselves into the *kgotla* itself, the assembly of those who sustain order and define community.

The women are by and large in a meantime, a between-time. Some are there for a break from their household and are waiting until they have to return to prepare a meal or do the laundry: this is a pleasant between-time for them, one to be enjoyed for the gossip, relaxation, and company that it offers, but it will end with a return to the compound and the trials of managing the labor of the household. Others are genuinely there for the government official: there may be a village beautification council to join, or the recruitment of health visitors, or instructions on electrification or water reticulation, and his long delay in arriving is, for some, a nuisance because there are things that are waiting to be done at home. Some may be waiting for the court case in which they, like some of the men, are deeply involved—inheritance, divorce, insults, theft, other disputes—and they wait more intensely and in some anticipation of the case and its outcome. Unlike for the men, their waiting in the *kgotla* is not everyday. Like the men, they are waiting in multiple timelines: they may be waiting for the chief to sign an application form with an eye to a certain future, and at the same time they may be waiting as an enjoyed break after having swept the compound of devilthorns and debris.

One thing that you do not hear in the *kgotla*, generally, is anger or irritation at being made to wait, possibly for hours. (You do hear people wondering, with some pleasure, about the person who is not present for his or her court case.) In other venues, I heard people complain about being made to wait: they, like me, recognized that the waiting in those situations was an abuse of power. Making others wait in a government office violates the prevailing premises in those spaces of egalitarianism, whereby government officers are basically people no different from you, whose time is no more valuable than your own, and whose job is to serve you. I detected hints of resentment at National Youth Day, and skepticism about the minister and chief being in "other important meetings." To some extent, ministers are recognized as more important—a perception that President Ian Khama challenged through his own (powerful) insistence on absolute punctuality. But the *kgotla* is not an egalitarian space, or at least it was not in 1989. The women sit on the ground; only "important" or assertive educated women sit on chairs, but never the folding chairs used by the older men.[11] That the men sit and wait (or pass their time) and the women come and go, attending to other things, speaks to the inequalities and also simply the differences between genders and gendered spaces in village life. (Women compel others to wait in their households—especially when told to prepare tea or food for men or visitors.)

The ways in which time, authority, and respect are intertwined are evident an oft-repeated story in the Herero Ward at that time. Frederick Maharero, son of Samuel Maharero, who led the Herero rebellion in South West Africa (Namibia) in 1904 and led his immediate followers to settle under the Ngwato chiefs in Botswana, was sleeping. Tshekedi Khama, the Ngwato regent and an extremely powerful man in the larger British Protectorate, came to see him. Instead of waking the sleeping Frederick, Tshekedi sat for hours, waiting. People told this story to convey the respect people had for Frederick and the honor given by Tshekedi himself. Waiting is, in the *kgotla*, a recognition of the dignity of another, but it is especially potent when it is inserted into relations of authority and power, where waiting can simultaneously signal respect for authority but also invoke the equal power of waiter and awaited to create that relationship (as in the aforementioned phrase, *kgosi ke kgosi ka batho*).

We might, decades after I so often heard the story, reread this account as an act of *botho*—a term that, in the 2000s, has been officially flagged as a core value in Botswana; it is sometimes translated as "human dignity," the recognition of the worth of other people and of how one is enmeshed in humanity oneself. That waiting is today connected to *botho* is evidenced by something I witnessed in 2014: I was waiting to acquire a phone and phone card—which always required a long wait—at a shop in Gaborone with several others. As we waited, two young men (who seemed to be about seventeen or twenty at the most) entered and physically pushed two elderly men aside, such that they stumbled and needed to be caught. The young men went to the counter and demanded to be served right away. The shock in the room was palpable. A manager came and chased the young men away. To wait is expected and common and respects the *botho* of other waiters (and staff). Yet the young men's attack on the elderly, the resulting shock and dismay in the room, and the response by the manager showed how *botho* is inflected by issues of status, respect, and the authority associated with the elderly. It is no wonder, then, that the visible irritation, even anger, over waiting that was displayed by the president in 2014 and by the scolding woman in 2000 was directed at children.

What should we make, then, of my long wait for the young woman in 2017? I was frustrated: with limited time on a summer research trip, and in anticipation of giving her some pleasure but also learning about shopping among young people in the context of Botswana's new consumerism, I wanted to be doing something more productive than sitting around for hours. But what about her? I could speculate about my status within her group of relations, among whom waiting for arrivals and events and gradual improvements to houses or fields over long periods is not uncommon, though it is tempered by curiosity and indeed pressure about when this or that will be accomplished. I am more interested in her position in the official space of youth in Botswana, the meantime that has a deadline, where waiting is bound up with developmental orientations, but also with knowledge that this is a limited space and time. I will return to the wait she put me through.

She, and others I know like her, voiced impatience about many things. I ran into a man I knew in his mid- to late twenties waiting at the Ministry of Youth, Sport, and Culture, trying to submit an application for a YDF loan, for which he did not have all the required elements (proof of an owned or rented site was one hurdle, but the signatures of anticipated employees were the most difficult to obtain); when we met sometime later, he was still waiting—not for the response to the application, but for potential employees to agree to sign up. He was especially frustrated by the amount of time it was taking to get signatures; he was frustrated, too, by the long wait for YDF staff to provide assistance. Later, he would be frustrated by the long wait for the loan application to be processed. I do not know whether he ever got the loan: I do know he registered the potential business with the government and years later was willing to sell the registration as what they call a "shelf" company. He felt impatient, then, about a series of relationships with people he considered his peers (including the YDF staff). But his meantime and waiting with respect to this venture were ill-defined: the past was not quite past, but was still in the process of becoming—that is, he needed to find a site and gain documented rights to it, and he needed to convince relatives or friends to submit their names as employees of the business.[12] Only with these could he move into the meantime of waiting for the venture's possible future. Young people in focus groups led by a doctoral student from the University of Pretoria voiced similar frustrations in response to the requirements for YDF loans, focusing especially on the difficult paperwork and the need for a professional business plan (Setambule 2022). They were not so much waiting—that is, they had not set aside the past, in the form of applications, but were, rather, in the state of pursuing things.

I did not meet anyone who made it to the actual *dead*line associated with such loans: after five years, half of the YDF loan needed to be repaid (over time, and with no interest accruing; the government "forgave" the other half automatically).[13] As in the United States, most small start-ups fail before the fifth year. Deadlines might signal the beginning of repayment, but more often they were associated with failure. The government's internship program, which was aimed at giving young people work experience and was criticized for the long wait time between the submission of an application and the receipt of any response, was also heavily criticized for its *dead*line: at the end of the internship, youth wanted to be offered a job, but instead the internship ended and they were again unemployed.

However, my friend at the mall was at the beginning of the meantime of youth, between finishing school and finishing youth. Having recently completed her university degree, she was going to employment fairs and workshops held by the Botswana National Youth Council (about which she, most of her peers, and indeed the media and onlookers at large, were very skeptical) and had gone door to door with résumés. The first in her immediate family circle to go to college, she was also aware that a college degree was no guarantee of employment: the days when secondary school degrees (initially junior secondary, later senior) conferred automatic employment, especially in government service as the new country sought to "localize," were long gone. If she followed the path taken by many of her cohort, she would stop dropping off résumés, stop applying in person, and never submit the entrepreneurial projects she was devising (some of which sounded to me like they could potentially be very successful) to the YDF, where she feared her ideas would simply be stolen by government officers. She would start using her cellphone to search for jobs, spending more of her phone time on surfing for fun memes and videos to post on Facebook, and later simply post her qualifications on sites in the hope that someone would see them and contact her (cf. Setambule 2022). Or, possibly, she would get a job: some of her peers did, eventually, after persistent looking and knocking on doors, or through a relative's networking—and they got good office jobs at that. Or she would have a baby, receive support from a boyfriend and relatives, and eventually get married. (The average age of first marriage in Botswana in 2011 was thirty-five, but the rates of marriage were very low; her chances of marrying would probably be higher if she did not find a good job, as professional women in their thirties invested in houses and the sorts of things men typically wanted their wives to depend on them for.) It is possible she would make do with the intermittent waitressing job she was hiding from family, as well as gifts from boyfriends, her father (whose relationship with her mother was long over), and relatives, and hope, as so many did, that her own children would succeed in school and in the labor force and one day be able to build her a house.

This all sounds rather grim, and there is no doubt that disappointment, suspicion of being thwarted others, and pestering by relatives about her failures and dependency could be part of her future. Young men, under such pressure, sometimes took their own lives. Yet I would not describe my friend's life, or that of the many young men I knew or talked to, as characterized by "cruel optimism." Their meantimes were filled not with one plan or project but with many, some (many) in the social sphere, some that involved devising forms of income, some in church activities or NGOs serving orphans, some in building a home, bit by bit, on village land. The doing of these things could be as important as the desired futures and outcomes, much as sitting in the *kgotla* could be. The social projects should not be seen as secondary to economic ones: much literature has detailed how one's well-being in Botswana is the product of intersubjective and intercorporeal relationships. The only times I heard people say "I'm bored" (or, when speaking of other people, "she's bored") was in relation to the severing of significant relationships, and not the absence of activities or waiting for something—I'll be so bored, someone would say to me, when you leave for America. Boredom was associated with the absence of people, especially people with whom one was intimate and shared in an emotional exchange, and, connected to the emotional ties, from whom one received material support. Back in the *kgotla*, waiting for testimony in a case, the chief (who, to me, often looked bored), told me what he was doing: "I am always thinking," implying he was always thinking of his many business ventures in process or in the making, and possibly about his concurrent conflicting girlfriends. Youth in the 2010s, too, seemed to be always thinking, although their thoughts extended to things like how to get to a club or bonfire party, what set of clothing produced what kind of image for a particular encounter (social or professional or Facebook), who to ask for small sums of money that would add up to their rent or the entry fee for a party or the price of a tasty snack on the street, as well as how to register a shelf company or a nonprofit for future possible development. They knew several of these projects would fail. If they got that loan, or boyfriend, or party fee, they would enjoy its benefits until the deadline: the meantime of having a business office, or dancing to music. That was the way projects played out; that was why you needed to have several at any given time. You needed to be waiting, on some of them, on all of them, on the remaining ones and the new ones.

African Time

African time, the time spent waiting, is neither as unproductive as modern economists and rationalists, timeline-bound bureaucrats, the president and others make it out to be, nor is it simply that people do not care about clocks and deadlines. One could speculate that, at least in Botswana, a temporality that sees rewards in the meantime and anticipates ends may have roots in pastoralism and drought-land agriculture. In the 1980s, I heard many stories of families that had been fabulously wealthy in stock—one was known for the hundreds of goats and sheep it had, another for its ample cattle herd, another for the many bags of harvested beans it brought to the co-op. Then, suddenly, the stock was gone—disease and drought, poorly planned distribution, bad feelings within or without causing misfortune. The plow broke on the productive bean field; the senior male cashed in the cattle for a personal car; the goats died during one of Botswana's multi-year droughts. Beyond farming, people often acquired things through rent-to-own arrangements. Not infrequently, these items were repossessed when payments (deadlines) were missed: a whole household of furniture could disappear, or an envied TV (generating much humorous comment). In this kind of African time, things were always being waited for: they were producing and growing, generating jealousy or social benefits, or they were failing and disappearing, producing humor or sympathetic interest or anger. The meantime, this African time, was not suspended time; it was the time in which things happened.

The meantime of youth in Botswana is very much a time of things happening. In it, you can see a bit of the waithood that Honwana described in relation to African youth, in which people do do things, little creative things, but are not waiting for the outcomes of that doing; rather, they are waiting for something that will come from the outside—they are waiting for Godot. Botswana youth are waiting for the government internship program, for a YDF loan, for their résumés to be seen on the Internet and for someone to offer them a job. But that is not all of youth's meantime, a period now clearly delineated by the deadline of age thirty-five. They have multiple projects underway. The last thing they might want is to be fully and finally grown up, adult, or even an elder, too quickly, to be "a finished person", as adulthood is described in some parts of Africa (see Cooper 2018). Because it was always possible that, once they reached that point, there would be nowhere to go, or, at least, they would no longer be in the officially recognized and supported period of "developing themselves." More than one person said to me something along the lines of, "I'm now thirty-six [or older] and I can't get more schooling, I can't get the YDF loans, I'm stuck in my low-paid menial job." (These people were, nonetheless, still working on developing themselves, both economically and socially; I knew women in their forties, fifties, and sixties looking for spouses or applying to graduate or certificate programs, or starting chicken farms.) Like the Russians in their thirties studied by Anna Kruglova (2017), who were "already old" without ever having had their youth, the end of waithood could be a bitter end, not a beginning. For all ages, the end of waiting—the final meeting with the loan officer at the Ministry of Youth, the arrival of the dates for repayment, or the "achievement" of the age of thirty-six, when one is no longer officially a youth—may indeed signal a deadline: the death of opportunity, the end of the rich doing of open-ended anticipation and self-making, the end of African time.

Notes

1. There is, in fact, some debate about this. Political scientists debate whether Botswana is a "developmental state" or not (see Hillbom 2012, Taylor 2012; see also Good 1992, Gulbrandsen 2012, Maundeni 2002). This is mostly a definitional argument about the technical nature of the term, but it also relates to the extent to which Botswana has encouraged private "industrial" enterprise, whether there is "elite capture" of the state, and the relationship of the political to the bureaucratic domains. I use the term simply to indicate that the government has, successfully or not, been focused on various development programs, which benefit elites and other segments of the population in different ways. The focus on development programs, and the uneven success of these, is widely agreed upon, and people I worked with clearly experienced their state as a developmental one.
2. "Batswana" can mean citizens of Botswana (using the human plural prefix "ba-") or ethnic Tswana people. The government, which claims to be ethnically blind, of course uses the term to mean citizen. My research concentrated on Herero people from a large urban village; although an ethnic minority, most insisted they were both "Batswana" ("Ovatjuana" in the Herero language) and Baherero ("Ovaherero"). I also conducted research among Tswana and people of other ethnic backgrounds in Gaborone, the capital city. My in-country research spans the years 1988–2017.
3. I take the term from Thomas Csordas (2008) and refer to the ways, in Botswana, in which one's sentimental dispositions toward others can have a direct physical and environmental impact on them, whether it be positive or negative; their sentiments similarly affect one's own well-being.
4. There is considerable anxiety about the diamonds running out. It is also worth noting that, while typically seen as a "developing" country, Botswana is considered a middle-income country by the World Bank and has been for decades. A middle income is, not surprisingly, extremely unevenly received, with many with barely any income at all; those with income do redistribute it through family, associational, and friendship networks.
5. Youth ends at age forty for youth-focused agricultural development grants and loans.
6. Technically, these were loans when used at private universities, but people insisted to me that they rarely were repaid.
7. The indented material is adapted from Durham 2008.
8. Ian Khama was the son of Botswana's first, revered, president, Sir Seretse Khama, who married a British woman while in exile. Ian, the eldest son, was often accused during my earlier fieldwork of not speaking Setswana, and later of speaking it oddly; people also quietly wondered about his intimate life, as he did not marry. While his party won the elections, I (personally) did not think this was because of him; rather, it seemed to be due, in part, to the fracturing and squabbling of the opposition parties.
9. It is probably too much to call a cockfight a "meantime." But see Geertz 1973b on Balinese tempos.
10. Michael Ulfstjerne (2019) has also written insightfully about how the present becomes the past for those who look back from an as-yet-unrealized future, in China's (now-past) housing boom.
11. I was offered a chair at early attendance at *kgotla*, as a visiting White person and university graduate, but my preference for sitting with the women became well known after a short time.
12. I was never sure why this was such a challenge, but my first thought was that the people he was trying to bring in did not want other schemes they were involved in to be derailed as a result of their names being associated with this potential venture. However, there may have been past disputes weighing on them.

13. I am also uncertain as to how effectively the government pursued repayment. While tuition and living allowances for private tertiary educational institutions (as opposed to state ones) were supposed to be repaid—deducted in increments from paychecks for the employed—young people felt that the state did not follow through.

References

Ahmed, Sara. 2013. *The Cultural Politics of Emotion*. New York: Routledge.
Berlant, Lauren. 2011. *Cruel Optimism*. Durham, NC: Duke University Press.
Bourdieu, Pierre. 1977. *Outline of a Theory of Practice*, trans. Richard Nice. Cambridge, UK: Cambridge University Press.
Burke, Charlanne. 2000. "Dangerous Dependencies: The Power and Potential of Youth in Botswana." PhD dissertation. Department of Anthropology, Teachers College, Columbia University.
Cooper, Elizabeth. 2018. "The Importance of Being Serious: Subjectivity and Adulthood in Kenya." *Ethnos* 83(4): 665–82.
Csordas, Thomas. 2008. "Intersubjectivity and Intercorporeality." *Subjectivity* 22(1): 110–21.
Dungey, Claire Elisabeth, and Lotte Meinert. 2017. "Learning to Wait: Schooling and the Instability of Adulthood for Young Men in Uganda." In *Elusive Adulthoods*, ed. Deborah Durham and Jacqueline Solway, 83–104. Bloomington: Indiana University Press.
Durham, Deborah. 2002. "Love and Jealousy in the Space of Death." *Ethnos* 67(2): 155–80.
———. 2007. "Empowering Youth: Making Youth Citizens in Botswana." In *Generations and Globalization: Youth, Age, and Family in the New World Economy*, ed. Jennifer Cole and Deborah Durham, 102–31. Bloomington: Indiana University Press.
———. 2008. "Apathy and Agency: The Romance of Agency and Youth in Botswana." In *Figuring the Future: Globalization and the Temporalities of Children and Youth*, ed. Jennifer Cole and Deborah Durham, 151–78. Santa Fe: SAR Press.
———. n.d. "Batswana Must Develop Themselves: Self-Development in a Developmental State." Working paper in progress.
Evans-Pritchard, E. E. 1940. *The Nuer: A Description of the Modes of Livelihood and Political Institutions of a Nilotic People*. New York and Oxford: Oxford University Press.
Geertz, Clifford. 1973a. "Deep Play: Notes on the Balinese Cockfight." In *Interpretation of Cultures*, 412–53. New York: Basic Books.
———. 1973b. "Person, Time, and Conduct in Bali." In *Interpretation of Cultures*, 360–411. New York: Basic Books.
Good, Kenneth. 1992. "Interpreting the Exceptionality of Botswana." *Journal of Modern African Studies* 30(1): 61–95.
Gulbrandsen, Ønulf. 2012. *The State and the Social: State Formation in Botswana and its Pre-Colonial and Colonial Genealogies*. New York: Berghahn Books.
Hillbom, Ellen. 2012. "A Development-Oriented Gate-Keeping State." *African Affairs* 111(442): 67–89.

Honwana, Alcinda M. 2012. *The Time of Youth: Work, Social Change, and Politics in Africa*. Boulder, CO: Lynne Rienner.

Jones, Jeremy. 2010. "'Nothing Is Straight in Zimbabwe': The Rise of the Kukiya-kiya Economy 2000–2008." *Journal of Southern African Studies* 36(2): 285–99.

Kruglova, Anna. 2017. "Between 'Too Young' and 'Already Old': The Fleeting Adulthood of Russia's Split Generation." In *Elusive Adulthoods*, ed. Deborah Durham and Jacqueline Solway, 174–96. Bloomington: Indiana University Press.

Livingston, Julie. 2003. "Pregnant Children and Half-Dead Adults: Modern Living and the Quickening Life Cycle in Botswana." *Bulletin of the History of Medicine* 77(1): 133–62.

Mains, Daniel. 2007. "Neoliberal Times: Progress, Boredom, and Shame among Young Men in Urban Ethiopia." *American Ethnologist* 34(4): 659–73.

Makgala, C. John, and Phenyo Thebe. 2015. "'There Is No Hurry in Botswana': Scholarship and Stereotypes on 'African Time' Syndrome in Botswana, 1895–2011." *New Contree* 72 (July): 1–20.

Masquelier, Adeline. 2019. *Fada: Boredom and Belonging in Niger*. Chicago: University of Chicago Press.

Maundeni, Zibani. 2002. "State Culture and Development in Botswana and Zimbabwe." *Journal of Modern African Studies* 40(1): 105–32.

Munn, Nancy D. 1992. "The Cultural Anthropology of Time." *Annual Review of Anthropology* 21: 93–123.

———. 2013. "The 'Becoming-Past' of Places: Spacetime and Memory in Nineteenth Century, pre–Civil War New York." *Hau: Journal of Ethnographic Theory* 3(2): 259–80.

Ricoeur, Paul. 2004. *Memory, History, Forgetting*, trans. Kathleen Blamey and David Pelauer. Chicago: University of Chicago Press.

Schapera, Isaac. 1940. *Married Life in an African Tribe*. London: Faber & Faber.

Setambule, Thato. 2022. "An Exploration of Livelihood Strategies among Unemployed Youth in Botswana." PhD dissertation. University of Pretoria.

Taylor, Ian. 2012. "Botswana as a 'Development-Oriented Gate-Keeping State': A Response." *African Affairs* 111(444): 466–76.

Thompson, E. P. 1967. "Time, Work-Discipline and Industrial Capitalism." *Past & Present* 38 (December): 56–97.

Turner, Victor. 1967. *The Forest of Symbols: Aspects of Ndembu Ritual*. Ithaca, NY: Cornell University Press.

Ulfstjerne, Michael Alexander. 2019. "Iron Bubbles: Exploring Optimism in China's Modern Ghost Cities." *Hau: Journal of Ethnographic Theory* 19(3): 579–95.

Vigh, Henrik. 2006. "Social Death and Violent Life Chances." In *Navigating Youth, Generating Adulthood: Social Becoming in an African Context*, ed. Catrine Christiansen, Mats Utas, and Henrik Vigh, 31–60. Uppsala: Nordiska Afrikainstitutet.

Weber, Max. [1905] 2009. *The Protestant Ethic and the Spirit of Capitalism*, trans. Talcott Parsons. New York: W. W. Norton.

Chapter 8

Waiting Out the Rush
On the Durability of Wealth in Kenya's Coastal Sex Economies

George Paul Meiu

"If you get a lot of money very fast," Jadini, a man in his mid-twenties, explained in Swahili, "your mind will change completely. You will have a shock [*utapata shok*]. You will lose everything and return to zero." It was 5 April 2011. I had joined Jadini on Bamburi Beach, north of Kenya's coastal city of Mombasa, where he sold souvenirs to tourists. To attract foreigners to his beach stand, he wore a colorful traditional outfit associated with the "warriors" (*moran*) of Samburu, his ethnic group in northern Kenya. For the last four years, Jadini had migrated to the coast to make money in tourism. On that day, he and I sat in the shade, at the entrance of a tourist resort. We had joined four other young Samburu men, an elderly man from the coastal Giriama ethnic group, and a woman of Kamba ethnic origin, all of whom were selling different artifacts—fabrics, sculptures, and beadwork—at the beach. Jadini began talking about "fast money"—so-called *pesa ya haraka* or "money of the rush"—that is, money obtained quickly without substantial work, or, as Kenyans put it, "without sweating" (*bila kutoa jasho*). He wanted to convince the Giriama elder that the "shock" of receiving a large amount of money makes one lose self-control and spend mindlessly. I often heard Kenyans describe such money as "easy come, easy go" (using the English phrase).

The tourist season had just ended. Business was slow. Traders said that, in recent years, it had become difficult to make money at the beach. Tourist arrivals in Kenya had declined significantly following the post-election violence of early 2008. On the day I was visiting Jadini at the beach, six leading Kenyan politicians were arriving at The Hague to face the International Criminal Court on accusations of instigating the violence. To break the monotony of the long hours spent at an otherwise empty beach, men asked each other for news from The Hague. But the 2008 postelection violence was not the only reason tourism had declined. Growing security threats associated with the expansion of the Al-Shabaab terrorist organization at the border with Somalia, some 300 miles from Mombasa's north coast, had also conspired, of late, to keep international arrivals down.[1] My interlocutors hoped that tourism would soon recover. "We are just waiting [*tunangoja tu*]," one man said. "What else is there to do?"

As they waited for the few tourists from the nearby hotels to come out to the beach, these men talked extensively about money. The Giriama elder was unconvinced by Jadini's point about fast money causing a shock. So Rob, a Samburu man in his late thirties, stood up from under the shade of his souvenir display table, ready to tell a story. He had been migrating to the coast for nearly twenty years and had extensive experience with tourists. Pacing excitedly on the sand, he described how, some years prior, one white woman had paid him KSh 90,000 (US$900) for a rather ordinary wood sculpture of a giraffe. "At that time, tourists were not so knowledgeable about the prices of African art," he said. He had quoted this absurdly high price jokingly, not expecting the tourist to pay. But she did. Rob recalled:

> She told me to walk with her to the Barclays Bank, nearby. She took out four [bank] cards and withdrew her daily limit on each. When she put all that money in my hand—I am not kidding you—I started to shake [*nilianza kutetemeka*]. I could not believe all that money. That very night I boarded a *matatu* [public minibus] to go back home to Maralal [in Samburu district, northern Kenya]. I was scared to lose the money here, on the coast.

Jadini nodded. He understood Rob's reaction. Having experienced the shock of obtaining too much money too quickly, he had done a sensible thing by returning to northern Kenya, where his money would have been invested in livestock and kinship relations. This was how Rob coped with the danger of losing self-control and squandering cash: he opted to quickly reinvest in morally legitimate forms of social value; before, that is, the money evaporated. Turning to the Giriama elder, Jadini explained: "Believe me, *mzee wangu* [my elder], you cannot avoid a shock if you get all that money. That's a must [*hii ni lazima*]. That's the truth now. In that shock, with all that money, you will finish it all up without even realizing it. You just see it's all gone."

The elder waved his hand dismissively. "I won't get a shock. Why would I get a shock? I would put the money nicely in the bank and you will never see me at the beach again. If you budget the money neatly, you have it for a long time." Banking, budgeting, and planning, the elder suggested, were rational ways of preserving money, assuring its durability, no matter the timing of its arrival or its quantity.

Seeing the elder's skepticism, Rob decided to tell another story. "Let me tell you something, *mzee*," he said. "There was a time I had over one million [Kenyan] shillings in my account."

The elder now looked at Rob with surprise. That was a large amount of money that few ordinary Kenyans would ever have had at one time. Jadini and other friends had already told me that Rob had been a "millionaire." Like many other Samburu men, he had had intimate relationships with wealthy white women from Western European countries who had offered him large sums of money and expensive gifts. It was the first time, however, that I had heard Rob talk about his past himself. He continued: "Every time I would go to the ATM in Mombasa to withdraw money, I would first stop by the police station to hire an escort with a gun, for security. I'd pay him KSh 5,000 [US$50] and he'd go with me to the ATM." In a context in which most beach traders rarely made 5,000 shillings over the course of an entire month, Rob's ability to dispense this amount for personal security—however extravagant this may have seemed to his interlocutors—testified to the sheer magnitude of his wealth. During that time, Rob owned four *matatu* minibuses, which he employed in public transport, as well as a large villa in Mtwapa, a coastal town with some of the highest real estate values in the country.

"Now, I have nothing," Rob said. "It's all gone. And I am back at the beach."

"This money is the devil himself [*shetani mwenywe*]," Jadini concluded.

Shock. Rushed money. The devil himself. Rob's stories and Jadini's comments evoke the seductions of a speculative economy, its unpredictable yet miraculous possibilities of enrichment, its missed chances and uncertain triumphs. More and more poor Kenyans have migrated to the coast over the last few decades, hoping that, if they could be in the right place at the right time, they too would make money quicker than elsewhere. Though many people I spoke to blamed Rob's loss on his own wastefulness, his excessive drinking, and his partying, numerous others believed that the problem lay elsewhere: namely, in the nature of the rushed money. The elder disagreed with Jadini and Rob's understandings of this money. But, like everybody else, he also knew that young, good looking Kenyan men and women in coastal towns had a distinct advantage in acquiring wealth through sex, long-term relationships, and marriages with foreigners or wealthy locals. During my research on the coast, I collected numerous stories people told about various men or women who had become wealthy after an elderly white tourist fell in love with them or began paying them regularly for sex. Such stories emphasized not only how speculation and seduction brought about instant riches, but also—quite importantly—how their protagonists became rich one day, only to become poor again the next. What was it that made telling such stories an enjoyable pastime as people waited for such transformative opportunities to occur—or, in Rob's case, to *reoccur*?

Certainly, detailing instances of rapid transformations of fortune and carefully enumerating the wealth of the protagonists made such desirable possibilities real, experientially close, and palpable: it brought them more strongly into the everyday. Such stories were more than a pleasurable, if anxious, pastime. Those who told them also reflected on the ambivalent nature of wealth in the present, its dangers, and its seductions. They wondered how to handle fast money more efficiently; how to cope with the "shock" of obtaining too much too quickly; and how to participate in the otherwise uncertain rush of the coastal economies without losing one's self and one's money.

To track the implications of these questions ethnographically, I explore how the intersection of two contrasting temporal dispositions trouble attempts to produce value in Kenya's coastal sexual and tourist economies. The first such disposition is *the rush*. Coastal towns, like Mtwapa and the nearby resorts, are places of intense, albeit unpredictably shifting, flows of people, goods, and money. People migrate to such towns from all over the country, searching for different opportunities to make a livelihood; motorbikes and cars speeding in all directions attest to the rush of a space of intensified possibility (a bumper sticker on a passing truck announces "Total Confusion"); colorful commodities exchange hands quickly; large villa-type houses and apartment buildings emerge "overnight" only to be sold off, again and again; wealth materializes miraculously and often disappears as quickly as it arrived. The rush speaks of the visceral perception of a particular kind of global capital—one that, as James Ferguson (2007: 38) argues, is *"globe-hopping,* not *globe-covering,"* "neatly skipping over most of what lies in between." This is capital that comes and goes, "shocking" those it touches too quickly, too suddenly, before moving on. But the rush also describes people's urge to place themselves strategically in the path of unpredictable capital and to do so urgently and efficiently.

The second disposition is that of *waiting*. When one is well situated in a space of intensified possibility, whether that be at the beach or in a bar where one can meet foreigners, for example, "each person must wait for their own luck," as people say—*kila mtu angojee bahati yake*. Amidst the town's incessant rush—mobility, flexibility, investments—waiting practices play a central role in everyday life. To anticipate and access flows of money and commodities, men and women arrive from across Kenya, hoping to tap into the flows of "globe-hopping capital" and redirect it toward other places, such as, for example, their rural homes. To do so, sex workers and "beach boys" wait for hours—or, during "off seasons," for weeks or months—to meet wealthy patrons at the beach, in bars, or by the swimming pools in resorts; motorcycle cab drivers wait at crossroads to be hailed by travelers (and sometimes sexual patrons); and poor men and women often wait by the gates or office doors of the wealthy and influential to ask for money or work.

In this chapter, I explore practices of value production that emerge out of this dialectic of waiting and rushing. I outline, first, different ways in which people imagine and perceive the wait and the rush in relation to one another. Then, I demonstrate how the contradictions between these two temporal orientations generate new practices of managing and storing wealth. More specifically, I focus on attempts to "wait out the rush," that is, to produce durable forms of money and wealth in spite of the "shock" of the rush, in spite of the devilish nature of new wealth or "the devil himself," to use Jadini's phrase. My interlocutors on the Kenyan coast typically employed various strategies to prevent the quick loss of money. Even if, as I show, these strategies do not always overcome the contradictions of rushed money, they reveal how the dialectics of waiting and rushing shapes possibilities of value production in contemporary sex economies. I thus argue that understanding waiting and rushing relationally is important for conceptualizing how people imagine and contest money and durability in the present.

The Seductions of Speculation

With massive shifts in the global production and circulation of capital, speculative financial pursuits replace manufacturing capital and market liberalization diminishes constraints on the open circulation of goods and labor across boundaries. In this context, investments and opportunities for money-making connect discrete areas of the globe, while leaving others untouched, but their durability is uncertain: no one can predict just how long they will last. This has prompted new forms of migration, speculation, and entrepreneurship, myriad ways in which the marginalized have sought to put themselves in the way of capital and redirect money, goods, and opportunities toward their own regions, projects, and futures. Because flows of capital can easily cease or change path, producing new geographies of exclusion and inclusion, people everywhere imagine livelihoods amidst uncertainty and unpredictability

(Weiss 2007). Highlighting the speculative nature of neoliberal capital, Jean and John L. Comaroff (2001: 5) dub it "casino capitalism," a mode in which "production appears to have been superseded, as the *fons et origo* of wealth, by less tangible ways of generating value." This new mode of capital resonates with the logics, practices, and risks of gambling. It may appear that "gambling . . . has changed moral valence and invaded everyday life across the world" (ibid.). Middle-class Kenyans, development workers, and political and religious leaders are often critical of "gambling" as a mode of generating income, thus occluding just how much their own social and economic livelihoods are shaped by gambling-like speculations (Schmidt 2019). How then might we understand strategies of overcoming the rush in relation to what people describe as the contrasting forces of patient budgeting versus risky gambling, quick money versus durable wealth, or distinct space-time configurations of saving versus wasting?

The historical transformations mentioned above have also affected the nature of wealth as such, its perceived rhythms and temporalities, giving rise to new moral dilemmas. As a category of discourse and wealth, "fast money" has become, if anything, more pronounced globally in this late capitalist context (Osburg 2013; Walsh 2003; Znoj 2004). Discourses about ill-gotten money are certainly not new in Africa. The growing commodification and oppressive extraction of land, crops, and cattle have, since the advent of colonialism, generated new conundrums of kinship, respectability, and reproduction in which money plays a central role (see Bohannan 1955; Comaroff and Comaroff 2006; Hutchinson 1996). In *Bitter Money*, Parker Shipton (1989: 9) shows that, among Luo in western Kenya, "How money was obtained determines how it is classed; and how it is classed determines how people think it should be used." Thus, for example, the sale of resources associated with ancestors (land), European commodity extraction (gold), and masculine authority (roosters), to name only a few, represent causes generative of "bitter money." In coastal Kenya, such money has also been associated with "devil worship," witchcraft, sorcery, and the employment of *jini* spirits, in ways that associate particular currencies with negative forms of social value (McIntosh 2009; Meiu 2017; Smith 2008). In *For Money and Elders*, Robert Blunt (2019) argues that, since the 1980s, in Kenya, money—like gerontocratic authority—has become a salient object of popular suspicion, its value uncertain, its presence always potentially deceptive, devilish.

Coastal economies of sex and tourism, growing since the 1980s, only amplified the ambiguous qualities of money. In 2011, a coastal resident wrote in the national newspaper *Daily Nation*: "Many of my school mates at Kikambala Primary dropped out to become beach boys. Most of them hoped to hook up with rich tourists to support them." Suggestively entitled "Life Is Not a Beach: Time to End the 'Easy Money' Vicious Circle," this article decries young people's desire for quick money without serious work: "This mindset," the article continues, "that people can get easy money from rich tourists on the beaches . . . has caused a vicious circle of poverty from which many people are unable to break" (Daily Nation 2011). Discourses about the dynamics, rhythms, and unpredictable temporalities of quick money are always also discourses about morality, durability, and social reproduction: they debate the changing meanings of "work," proper forms of storing wealth, and the appropriate relation between accumulation and the life course.

In a context in which school education, employment, and the ability to save money were called sharply into question, those enriched through speculative schemes stood out: they appeared as both symptoms and causes of a perverse economy. This is evident not only in everyday talk and public opinion columns in national media, but also in the political spectacle of the state. Consider how, in early October 2018, police chiefs in Nairobi invited journalists and the public to witness them setting ablaze over three hundred gambling machines confiscated from city businesses. According to *The Star*, regional security chief Kang'ethe Thuku explained that these machines "encourage idleness and lack of productivity among the youths" (The Star 2018). Soon thereafter, police and government administrators across the country followed suit, burning gaming machines in big bonfires. A national ban on gambling passed by the Betting Control and Licensing Board in 2018 only amplified this trend. "These lottery joints," police officer David Kabena explained, "are . . . the major cause for the high dropout rate of school-going children and teenage pregnancies." Hence, the political spectacle of the public destruction of gambling machines can be understood as a ritual of national purification—targeted at the spirit of speculation characteristic of casino capitalism. The conditions of intelligibility for this political spectacle can be found in middle-class sensibilities of respectable work and wealth. They can also be found in political leaders' desires to produce an image of the state as invested in the securitization of youths as a demographic, by protecting their time and activities from the temptations of quick money, idleness, and wastefulness.

In the persistent absence of employment, however, young men and women continue to participate in speculative pursuits. Some of them acknowledge that something is wrong, not always with how they themselves produce money, but rather with the money itself. It is in this wider context that I propose to understand the quest of young men and women in coastal sex economies to devise new ways to "trick," as it were, money's devilish spirit—new ways, that is, to make it last. A central feature of this historical moment is thus the question of *durability* in a time of chronic *temporariness* (Mbembe in Shipley 2010: 659–60): how to produce forms of value that are lasting despite a growing sense of provisionality. Yet, it is important to remember that the condition of temporariness is by no means temporally uniform. Its rhythms alternate according to shifting possibilities, investments, and circulations. Thus, my ethnographic material prompts me to ask how people produce value at the intersection of two sets of affective dispositions and subjective orientations: the wait and the rush.

Trying to tease out subjective orientations and affective dispositions emerging in the neoliberal context, anthropologists have paid extensive attention to the central implications of waiting—as a set of practices, dispositions, and modes of relationality and temporality—in new kinds of social and economic value. Often, at the forefront of waiting practices, one finds young men—and sometimes women (Hansen 2005)—who are unemployed and find themselves with an excess of time on their hands (Ralph 2008). For many of them, waiting can result in feelings of uselessness, hopelessness, boredom, and devaluation (e.g., Jeffrey 2010; Mains 2007; Masquelier 2005; O'Neill 2017). Time in excess is thus often perceived as devalued time—it is time that cannot be converted into the exchange value of "labor"—and thus can be "killed," "past," or "wasted." Even so, anthropologists have shown that time in excess can also produce new forms of value. Michael Ralph (2008: 17), for example, argues that "If we define value as a meaningful consequence of human activity, transformed into social relationships that structure a system of production, we might begin to deliberate at greater length about how youth [use various kinds of waiting practices]." Waiting practices generate new forms of intimacy and social capital that, if mobilized at the right moment, can be converted into cash (Newell 2012).

The temporalities of waiting are, nevertheless, relational: one can only understand oneself as waiting, being left behind, and bored in relation to others who speed up, move on, and progress (O'Neill 2017: 15–17). More attention needs to be paid then to the relationships between myriad forms of waiting, dwelling, and rushing, and their mutually constitutive implications. Rosalind C. Morris (2008) argues that, for many unemployed men and women in South Africa—who, like many others, are waiting around for opportunities—the rush has become a dominant dimension of their lived world: a rush to insure life and death against risk, a rush to achieve even minimal forms of dignity. If the rush has characterized South African economies at least since the rise of mining industries in the early twentieth century, in the present the rush of capital is more strongly tied to the temporalities generated by risk discourse: in particular, panics and the related haste to speculate on possibilities, security, and value. Drawing on Morris's work, I ask: how do people position themselves to anticipate the rush of capital? What do they do as they wait? How and when do they choose to rush themselves, to make the rush happen? And, if successful, how might one dwell in success—how might one "wait out the rush" and emerge from it with wealth? These are questions about the production of durability at the intersection of waiting and the rush.

Kenya's Coastal Sex Economies

The possibility of young men and women acquiring spectacular wealth by engaging in various forms of transactional sex is not new in Kenya. Luise White (1990) shows how, as early as World War I, in colonial Nairobi, women who engaged in transactional sex often amassed much more wealth than male labor migrants. This allowed them to invest in livestock, the bridewealth payments of their male kin and dependents, or the farms of their rural families. Later, such wealth also allowed women to become central players in Nairobi's housing market. As White argues, "full-time prostitution and women's use of their earnings . . . to establish themselves as household heads seem to have been widespread in Nairobi and coastal towns" (1990: 50). Since the 1920s, the international port economy of the coastal city of Mombasa attracted numerous labor migrants from across the country (Cooper 1987). The economic possibility of this labor economy also brought to town young women who engaged in various forms of transactional sex, whether as "prostitutes" or "temporary wives" (Gachuhi 1973). Similarly, young men on the coast engaged in sex-for-money exchanges with senior men or women who would become their intimate patrons (1973: 7). Gill Shepherd (1987: 251) notes that "While they are still young, homosexuals bask in their glory, boasting of their lovers and sometimes making a good deal of money." One gay man interviewed in the 1950s, Shepherd points out, "proudly showed . . . his Post Office Bank book with a credit balance of over 600 [pounds] in it, a huge sum at the time. Another owned at least 150 [pounds] worth of jewelry given him by admirers. The financially astute are able to buy a house and as they get older they can begin to live from renting rooms out" (251). Urban sexual economies have thus long sustained the possibility of enrichment, often expressed in real estate as an idiom of durability.

What has changed in the last quarter of the twentieth century is, in part, the scale and magnitude of the sexual economy. With the spectacular

Figure 8.1. The rush of life in Mtwapa, Kenya, 2017. © George Paul Meiu.

rise of tourism to Kenya, which began in the mid-1970s, migrants from across the country have moved—seasonally or for long periods of their lives—to the coast, seeking employment or informal sources of income in and around the port and beach resorts, with their nightlife (Mahoney 2017; Schoss 1995). This has also led to the proliferation of forms of intimate attachment (Kibicho 2009; Omondi 2003). Brothel and street sex workers, strippers and call-out escorts, beach boys and pimps, as well as male and female tourists, are some of the key social actors who form the vast networks of tourist-oriented sexual exchanges on the Kenyan coast. Men and women from Germany, Italy, England, the Netherlands, and the United States travel to Kenya seeking, among other things, cheaper sexual services, the realization of stereotypical fantasies with racial Others, adventures, and the anonymity of a foreign place. Whereas many tourists hire sex workers for one-time sexual encounters, many others engage in long-term relationships with locals, supporting them with money and gifts for longer periods of time (Kibicho 2009). African elites, both from Kenya and elsewhere on the continent, also joined the vast clientele of those engaged in transactional sex on the coast.

I began doing fieldwork on the Kenyan coast, in the town of Mtwapa, in 2008, when I joined Samburu men from northern Kenya on their seasonal trips to the coast. Mtwapa—a township of nearly 50,000 people (in 2009), north of Mombasa (see figure 8.1)—has become infamous, since the late 1980s, as a haven for all kinds of transactional sex. As, from the 1980s, retirees mostly from Germany, Switzerland, England, and Italy bought land and built houses in what had initially been a small set of Giriama villages, Mtwapa quickly turned into Kenya's infamous "sin city." Expatriates—known among residents as *Kenya Kimbo*, that is, "the cooking fat of Kenya" (Kimbo is a local brand of cooking fat)—fueled a large market of casinos, discos, nightclubs, and real estate. In 2008, a Kenyan journalist said that Mtwapa was a place of "unforgettable fun, sin and loads of cash" (Standard 2008). Animated by strippers, exotic dancers, streetwalking sex workers, gays and lesbians, and tourists, Mtwapa, he wrote, "comes to life, with sin that can put Sodom and Gomorrah to shame." By 2011, administrators of the Kilifi and Mombasa districts, at the borders of which the town is located, fought over its territorial incorporation, in no small part because of the revenues from the sex economy. The possibility of making money through transactional sex with foreigners but also wealthy Africans—whether through one-night stands, long-term relationships, or even marriages—attracted many young Kenyans to Mtwapa.

Men like Jadini and Rob (whom I introduced at the beginning of this chapter) migrated twice every year to tourist resorts, renting rooms in Mtwapa and selling artifacts and dancing for tourists in nearby beach resorts. Most of these men hoped to meet white women for one-night stands or long-term, long-distance relationships. Those who were successful built houses, bought cars, traveled to Europe, and established themselves as influential "big men" in the north (Meiu 2015; 2017). Since 2015, my research has shifted to exploring the livelihoods of women and gay men in sex work. Like my Samburu interlocutors previously, many of these men and women came to Mtwapa as migrants or migrant settlers from "upcountry" (*barani*). Others were "coastal people" (*wapwani*) from neighboring towns and villages. While, overall, relatively few became wealthy, the wealth and stories of the lucky few circulated widely and informed the desires of the many who continued to wait in and around Mtwapa for similar opportunities. More often than not, such wealth never materialized. Waiting for life-transforming opportunities, men and women talked at length about such wealth.

The Rush before the Crash: On Fast Money

"If you're lucky, here, it is easy to get rich fast," said Vivian, a 35-year-old woman, in 2017. She had lived in Mtwapa for the past seventeen years. Vivian, my research assistant Mary, and I were talking over cold sodas in a small street-side restaurant on Mtwapa's main road. We had met Vivian earlier that week, during a visit at a local NGO that supports women involved in sex work. Vivian, who identifies openly as a *dem ya rodi* (street lady) or *malaya* (prostitute), worked as a peer educator for this NGO. As we slowly sipped our drinks, Vivian talked to us about troubles with fast money. Like Rob, Vivian had also been wealthy in the past. "Life goes up and down here," she said. "When things go up, I too do well. When things go down, I struggle."

Vivian arrived on the coast from a village in western Kenya for the first time in 2000. She had dropped out of school and decided to move to Mtwapa, where her older sister was living with a white man. Upon arrival on the coast, she learned that her sister had recently moved to Europe. Vivian worked for one month as a housemaid, but because the work was hard and poorly paid, she quit her job and made friends with young women in sex work. Thus, as she put it, "I entered prostitution" (*niliingia umalaya*). A few years later, Vivian met an elderly white man from Switzerland. "I was beautiful at that time," she recalled. "I was not as big as I am now. I would dress smart and attract many clients." The Swiss man not only supported her financially but also decided to build her a house. "At that time," Vivian said, "I was living with friends in a small shack in a squatter area." Squatter land is land designated for temporary use by poor families; no permanent structures can be built on it. "The white man asked me: 'Is this your land?'" Vivian said. "I was so happy he was going to build me a house, so I said yes. He asked: 'Do you have a title deed?' I said yes." So, the man built her a spacious self-contained three-bedroom house. But soon after the house was finished, the city evicted Vivian and demolished the large concrete construction. When the Swiss man found out that Vivian had lied, he broke up with her. And so, Vivian concluded, "I returned to poverty" (*nilirudi kwa umaskini*).

When Vivian mentioned the area in which the Swiss man had built her a house, I recalled walking through an adjacent neighborhood in 2008. Some Samburu migrants had taken me there to show me the "cursed wealth" (*mali ya laana*) of Mtwapa. I remember looking in awe at large concrete villas—two- or three-story houses—all allegedly built by foreigners. The walls of many of these houses had large vertical cracks down the middle. A few had come crashing down. Most of them were no longer inhabited. I remember saying to my companions that perhaps landslides were responsible for the destruction. But, no, they reassured me, there was nothing wrong with the land. The houses cracked and began falling down because they were built with "money of sorcery" (*pesa ya uchawi*). Young Kenyan men and women had involved witch doctors (*waganga*) or even *jini* spirits in securing rich foreign partners and thus obtained money to build these structures. Vivian remembered those houses vividly. "The problem is that this money is cursed," she said. "It is hard to make it stay put. Even if you build with it, it won't last."

Concrete houses were important idioms not only of wealth but also of durability. Owning such houses, along with the land upon which they were built, was an important element of middle-class success. Unlike the more temporary wood-and-clay dwellings of poor urban dwellers, constructions of concrete offered a sense of permanence—they made a more solid claim to a future. As the price of real estate had climbed spectacularly in Mtwapa in recent years, such homes seemed like the safest kind of investment. Nonetheless, my interlocutors pointed out, such structures were themselves permeable to the moral conjunctures of their production. For Vivian and others, the image of cracked concrete houses crashing down was emblematic of a form of wealth that was itself problematic: quick money that, even if converted into tokens of durable wealth, such as houses, would not acquire the permanence that its owners desired.

In April 2011, I asked Jadini, whom I introduced in the beginning of this chapter, if he really thought that the dangers of fast money lay in the money as such. He said,

> Yes, I felt that thing myself. Because I am just fine before I enter Western Union, before I go inside. But after, I come [out], I'm like stupid. I am not able to do a budget, nothing. If I got the money like that, before I arrive at [the bar], already one thousand or two thousand [shillings] are gone. Because I meet friends: "How are you? Here, take some [money]!" Or, I meet people at the bar. [The banknotes] go away one by one. Or I run into someone else who is hungry or something. So, that's true. Everyone sees that that money is evil [*mbaya*]. I can say to myself "I won't give it out." But that is very difficult. . . . If I wake up, I go there to the ATM and take twenty thousand or thirty thousand [$250–350] and I go with it to the bar. If it finishes, I run back to the ATM and take out [more]. So, there is nothing that you can save.

According to Jadini, fast money makes people "stupid," it makes them lose their mind, leaving them unable to budget or control the pace of their consumption or the redistribution of the money. Instead of the person controlling the money, the money appears to control the person. Jadini's point—just like his earlier claim that "this money is the devil itself"—echoes Michael T. Taussig's (1980: 17) argument that, in Latin America, beliefs about money being controlled by the devil are "collective representations of a way of life losing its life," a way of speaking of "what it means to lose control over the means of production and be controlled by them." According to Jadini, such money is "evil." Even if stored in a bank, the knowledge of its presence prompts the person to return, over and over again, to the ATM, until the money is gone. Jadini's words reveal the idea of money that resists the individual's capacity to "budget" it, a practice I discuss below. They also displace agency away from apparently rational consumers who know they should budget. Many of my interlocutors used the English verb "to budget" in Swahili sentences to describe how money that resists saving and planned spending is inherently evil, cursed. Sociality also played an important role in such narratives: one usually needs others to prevent such wasteful behavior, but Mtwapa's social life was itself understood as dangerously extractive. Everybody in Mtwapa is thought to want "to extract" (*kutoanisha*) from others.

I asked Jadini what "polluted" the money. While working in northern Kenya among the families of Samburu migrants to the coast, I had heard numerous people say that money was polluted by its origin in sex and sorcery (Meiu 2017: 157–69). Jadini disagreed. "Whether you went to the witchdoctor or not," he said, "it does not matter. Whether you slept with a woman for it or she just gave it to you like that, it does not matter. You lose it just the same."

"Why is that?" I asked.

"You don't know where this money comes from. Sometimes I have to tell the white lady: 'I want this money now or I will finish it with you.' So, she starts crying, crying. That's why you cannot get any help out of this money."

The fact that the money is not "earned," given with a good heart, but extracted, Jadini suggested, might also compromise it. But he also suggested that the ambiguous origin of the money among white people is troublesome. Kenyans who seek white partners, he explained, cannot know how the latter acquired their money and why they are richer than them. "People say that the money of the whites is not bad. But then why do so many people [who obtain that money] turn mad? At the last minute, you lose everything. And you find out you have AIDS. Many people have AIDS here. They say you have to watch out for this money of the whites [*pesa ya wazungu*], because it will destroy you."

Then Jadini concluded: "You can make houses, everything. And then, the last minute, you have nothing because you did not sweat for this money." As if echoing middle-class discourses of respectable work, he framed money produced through one's own sweat as morally distinct from that produced through sex. Now, Jadini said, he hoped to meet a white woman who could take him to Europe, where he could find work and sweat for his own money. Vivian, too, found the money she made as a peer educator with NGOs more helpful than the fast riches of the sex economy. But this money was not enough to transform one's life.

Imagining Durability, Waiting for the Rush

A central preoccupation of those waiting for opportunities in coastal sex economies was imagining how an inherently problematic type of wealth could be made durable. Recall the opening of this chapter, when Jadini and Rob talked about fast money in ways that not only reproduced the fantasy of miraculous possibilities in everyday life, but also drew on a collective repertoire of known cases to devise permanence in wealth. One day in August 2008, Jadini, Saruni, another man, and I were having breakfast at a small street restaurant in Mtwapa. Saruni had been coming regularly to the coast for the past twelve years. So far, however, he had not met a European woman to help him with money. Jadini, on the other hand, had recently arrived on the coast. He had been fired from his job in Nairobi and decided to look for a white girlfriend. As we ate, Saruni gestured toward a large building across the street. It was a three-story lodge with a bar and a restaurant called Kandara. His story went somewhat like this:

> Kandara had belonged to a Kikuyu woman called Nyambura. She had migrated to the Mtwapa from upcountry as a poor, but young and beautiful woman, sometime in the late 1960s. Nyambura was a clever and enterprising woman. She went to a Swahili sorcerer and purchased a *jini* spirit. With the help of the *jini*, she soon became the secret lover of Kenya's first president, Jomo Kenyatta. Throughout the years, Kenyatta visited her on the coast and gave her lots of money. With this money, Nyambura bought land along the main road in Mtwapa and also built the Kandara lodge and several houses. But Nyambura never married and she could not have children. Seeing that she was very rich and without offspring, she adopted and raised some street children who used to hang out at the back of her lodge. When she died, the children inherited all her wealth. In return, they buried her in a mausoleum-like grave that people in Mtwapa still marvel at when passing by her former estates.

This story hints at the complex interconnections of sex, money, and miraculous possibilities that characterized everyday life—especially waiting practices—in Mtwapa. It speaks of the high concentration of economic possibility in this town. It is a story about chance, luck, and rapidly shifting economic statuses; a story of how those who are poor today can become rich by tomorrow. While Nyambura became wealthy through her intimate relationship with Kenyatta, the street children she adopted became rich, as luck had it, because they happened to be in proximity to Nyambura at the right time. It was this proximity to the rich—to foreigners, big men, and those intimately related to them—that held life-transforming possibilities for migrants like Saruni and Jadini.

Stories like this one also had a particular appeal for the two men as they regularly returned to Mtwapa and waited to run into similarly fortunate conjunctures. Here, waiting was oriented toward the rush—its promises, pleasures, and miraculous possibilities. The fantasy of durability was central to this story: Nyambura certainly did wrong by employing sorcery to seduce the president. Long after she died, some people still spoke of "Nyambura's goats" (*mzubi wa Nyambura*) that walked up and down the town's main road causing deadly accidents: "Those are not goats," Saruni assured me, "they are Nyambura's *jini* drawing blood." Despite the ambivalence of negative forces perpetuating themselves in Nyambura's surviving wealth, men like Saruni admired Nyambura for having amassed so much power and perpetuated her lineage and name in time.

Vivian had known Nyambura personally—*Mama Nyambura*, she called her. "She only died ten or so years ago," Vivian recalled. "She was our mother, the mother of all the prostitutes. She had built a large estate and she was renting out her apartments only to prostitutes, because she knew they would pay. And she also looked out for us." Vivian knew that, like her, Nyambura had come to the coast from upcountry as a young woman and soon thereafter "entered" prostitution. But in Vivian's story, Nyambura, who could not have children, had taken a younger woman—also a sex worker—as her "wife" (traditionally, women-to-women marriages were common in East Africa) to birth in her name. The woman, who was of Kamba ethnic origin, had several children with a male lover, who was also Kamba. Later, she and this man decided to kill Nyambura. But Nymabura found out about their plans. "So, when that Kamba with her lover were getting ready to leave on a trip," Vivian said, "Nyambura told them: 'You will never come back.' They had a car accident and died." Nyambura, Vivian implied, used sorcery to kill them. But, clearly, Vivian's sympathies, like those of Saruni, lay with Nyambura. Although Nyambura had used sorcery, she did so to protect herself and her offspring. Somehow, in helping others, Nyambura succeeded in converting evil means into moral good and she made her "fast" money last. She thus secured morally positive forms of social reproduction: a lineage that continued her name and business, fame, and the recognition that came with a large cement grave attesting to her former grandeur. Indeed, everyone in Mtwapa had heard of Nyambura and the neighborhood around her former lodge is now known as Nyambura's Village.

Nyambura's story—in its various versions—played an important role in the imagining of durability *despite* the rush of an uncertain economy. And it was precisely as people waited for the rush and to find their ways into it that such stories had particular appeal. Waiting was productive in terms of the envisioning of strategies of value preservation for when the rush took over.

Waiting Out the Rush: Durability in Times of Flux

Not everybody was lucky enough to establish intimate relationships that generated substantial wealth. What is more, even those who were successful were often not able to hold on to their wealth. Vivian, who had lost her house and money after her Swiss partner left her, was convinced that the "money of sex" was the work of the devil. "This is money that it is hard to budget. You keep spending and, at the end, nothing is left." Jadini was in a similar situation. When I met him again in 2011, Jadini had had two simultaneous relationships—one with an English woman and the other with a Swiss woman. For a while, he had been doing very well. But after the women found out about each other, they left him. Jadini could no longer afford the luxurious apartment he had been renting. He moved into a simple room without water and electricity in a poor neighborhood of Mtwapa.

Learning how to wait out the rush then became an important pursuit for those involved in the sex economy. A popular saying goes, *Haraka haraka haina baraka*—"The rush, the rush brings no blessing." Indeed, as we have seen, a common perception among the Kenyan middle class is that young people lack the patience (*subira*) to work and acquire things gradually. Instead, they want to obtain things quickly. In March 2017, I heard a local police officer complain in a public speech in Mtwapa that "We have been offering training for youths to start various businesses . . . But very, very much these days, youths lack that patience to do business, to work. They only want those rushed things [*vitu vya haraka*]." But while local leaders and elders wish to inculcate patience in the acquisition of resources, many young men and women I spoke to sought better strategies to hold on to resources they acquired quickly. "Waiting out the rush" can thus mean several things. It is, first, an attempt to resist the incitement to consume or, at least, to do so excessively—indeed, it is a kind of patience. It is also an attempt to resist redistributing money to others, who would constantly ask for financial support. It is, furthermore, about preserving wealth despite the "shock" of its sudden acquisition. To some extent then, "waiting out the rush" is comparable to what Ghassan Hage (2009: 101) describes as "waiting out the crisis," or waiting to escape a situation of "stuckedness," as both efforts seek to recuperate an "ability to snatch agency in the very midst of its lack." Below I distinguish three strategies for seeking to produce durable wealth amidst the rush.

Figure 8.2. House fortified with a concrete brick fence and a large gate, Mtwapa, 2017. © George Paul Meiu.

First: enclosure. Once they found wealthy partners, men and women in sex work often moved into luxurious neighborhoods or rented, purchased, or built expensive houses. They also drove wherever they needed to go, rather than walking. These may seem like wasteful practices; at least that is how other, poorer town residents saw them. However, for those engaged in them, these practices were the opposite. They were central strategies of money preservation. Large gates, high fences, and driving rather than walking granted them more privacy. These modes of being in space and time prevented their poorer friends from seeing them and constantly demanding money. For young men, like Jadini, Rob, and Saruni, therefore, the practices of containment associated with enclave-like homes with locked gates and loose watchdogs or speedy cars with fogged-up windows (preventing acquaintances and friends from seeing that the driver has seen them but refused to stop) were not generated by a desire to be selfish and greedy. Rather, these practices constituted active attempts to defer actions and interactions that could lead to the loss of their wealth; they were attempts to literally prevent the quick flow of money. Men and women also used a sense of spatiotemporal closure to deter other people from becoming involved in their private lives, generating more gossip and envy that could prompt others to use sorcery against them or, as often happened, negatively affect their relationships with wealthy intimate patrons. Thus, young wealthy men and women tried to "stop time" through spatial closure and sustain their wealth, making money outlast the rush. Ironically perhaps, expanding wealth in time necessitated "stopping time" through concrete spatial practices that deferred intense social interaction and therewith the redistribution and depletion of wealth.

Second: the rural repatriation of capital. Another strategy I have described elsewhere (Meiu 2017) was the repatriation of capital from the coast to migrants' places of origin. Recall Rob who, upon receiving a large amount of money from a tourist, decided to board public transport and return to northern Kenya the very same day, to invest his money in cattle and kinship. Many migrants hoped that, once home, their family and kin would prevent them from spending money wastefully and guide them toward the right kinds of investments. This belief was so strongly engrained that the Samburu Moran Association, an ethnic organization that helped migrants in Mtwapa manage their finances, would only disburse their savings on the day they were returning home. To receive their savings, migrants had to show that they had already purchased a bus ticket for upcountry. To be sure, in rural areas, this money gave rise to new contestations over durability, respectability, and value. Meanwhile, on the coast, not everybody had the option of repatriating wealth. Vivian's parents in western Kenya, for example, severed their relationship with her when they saw her on national television speaking as an activist sex worker. For many other women and gay men who had run away from home, going back and investing in social ties elsewhere was not an option. So, they developed other strategies.

Third: microfinance groups. Since the 1990s, German, Dutch, American, and Kenyan NGOs in Mtwapa—many of them Christian "faith-based organizations"—initiated programs to "rescue" women (and, to a lesser extent, gay men) from sex work. These included microfinance projects meant to teach bookkeeping, accounting, time management, and other entrepreneurial skills. Small loans to start businesses (accompanied by strict repayment schedules) were intended to convince beneficiaries to abandon sex work. These NGO workers tried to discourage sex workers from participating in the speculative economy of the rush and instead sought to inculcate in them a Protestant ethic of labor, distinctly infused with the logics of budgeting, saving, and slow, gradual growth. In the ideology of such developmental reformist practices, "gambling" was in moral opposition to "working" and "budgeting." A graffiti mural along a highway in Mombasa captures this idiom quite saliently (see figure 8.3). It states: "Development: Plan the Budget" (*Maendeleo: Panga Budget*), as if to say "if you want development—that is, progress through wealth—you must learn to budget."

Development workers in Mtwapa encouraged women to open and manage their own small businesses and accumulate wealth gradually. In national development discourses, waiting in low-paying, manual jobs

Figure 8.3. Graffiti mural: "Development: plan the budget." Mombasa, Kenya, 2017. © George Paul Meiu.

in the "informal sector"—the *jua kali* or "hot sun"—figured as a middle-class ideal of work that disavows the rush and gambling as perverse. According to this logic, gambling—speculating on the rush—is the choice made by those who do not want to work and prefer "easy money." Many of these development programs have failed: as it turned out, small businesses also participated in the economy of the rush after all. "It was up and down, up and down, until you had to abandon that business," Vivian said, recalling her own trade selling plastic dishes by the roadside.

Interestingly, however, sex workers did adopt and rework the techniques of the NGOs, if not to leave sex work as such, to transform the temporal dynamics of value production in sex economies. If the money of sex was to wait out the rush, they reasoned, it had to be diverted through the channels of microfinance projects. Thus, they initiated so-called *chama* groups of twenty to twenty-five participants. These are informal accounting and lending groups that employ the logic of microfinance. Every week (sometimes twice a week), participants deposited money with an "account-keeper." Then, once every month, one member could request a loan from this common account for a particular project (e.g., children's school fees, home renovations, a life-course ceremony, etc.). While such rotating credit groups are certainly not new—indeed, they previously played an important role in colonial African cities (Shipton 2010)—in the contemporary context, people understood the role of such groups to include, among other things, an ability to tame the troubled temporalities of rushed money. The groups worked to redirect people from "gambling" to "budgeting." By rerouting money through channels of sociality and reciprocity, they sought to "rescue" it from the turbulence of the rush—indeed, to inculcate in money the waiting dispositions of durable wealth. Vivian said: "*Chamas* are very important. Without them money would not stay. You would lose it fast." Note how "rushed money" must be made to "wait out the rush." Because one type of waiting—waiting *for* the rush—is so uncertain and long, the other type—waiting *out* the rush—becomes necessary as a disciplining technique. According to this logic, if one is to emerge from the rush with some wealth, one better reroute the money of sex through the collective socialities of *chama* budgets and loans—a money laundering of sorts. As Vivian explained to me, by participating in *chamas*, men and women hoped to literally stop time and halt the exhaustive consumption of money in order to imagine how to best convert their wealth into durable goods and relations.

While those engaged in practices of enclosure, the repatriation of resources to rural homes, and/or microfinance groups hoped these strategies would prolong the durability of their savings, in reality, things were more complex. For example, while producing closure through spatial and temporal containment might indeed have been efficient in delaying, if not preventing, too quick a redistribution of money, sustaining such practices—including cars, homes with security, or lives in gated communities—required large expenditures of cash. Similarly, if the repatriation of wealth to ethnic rural areas meant investing in seemingly durable ties of kinship, in the end, relatives in economically marginal rural areas could quickly exhaust migrants' resources. More importantly, however, if these strategies of money preservation were indeed ways to cope with the contradictory temporalities of the wait and the rush, the lived experience of pursuing these strategies reproduced—albeit in different, new forms—similar contradictions. For instance, if budgeting in *chama* groups meant delaying personal expenditure because one had to wait for one's turn to spend, disbursements of money were still very much perceived as a rush. "When your turn comes and you receive the money from the *chama*," Vivian admitted, "you must go quickly and do what you promised to do. Otherwise, if you stay with that money in your pocket, you will lose it fast." There are echoes here, once more, of the "shock" of quick money, even if it has been "laundered" through microfinancial planning. Similarly, rural areas could experience intermittent remittances of money from migrants as rushed money, money that comes suddenly and dissipates quickly.

Conclusion

New attempts to wait out the rush to prevent the depletion of wealth are themselves outcomes of a dialectic of myriad forms of rushing and waiting in Mtwapa's sex economies. Therefore, I have argued, one can only understand the temporalities of waiting relationally, in terms of their intersections with other spatiotemporal orientations, including those of the rush. These practices reveal not only that waiting is anticipatory, but also that it is relative—its meanings inscribed through the affective deployment of different temporalities and rhythms of social action.

For many young men and women from rural Kenya, coastal sex economies held the potential of radically transformed fortunes and livelihoods. Intimate relationships with foreign tourists and sometimes African elites presented unprecedented opportunities to gain wealth, build houses, buy cars, and lead independent, luxurious lives. Nevertheless, my interlocutors pointed out, "fast money" or "money of the rush" was problematic in more ways than one. This was money that would not last. It could "shock" its recipient into mindless spending and the tangible tokens of value into which it could be converted—concrete houses, for example, which are otherwise quintessential media of durable wealth—would slip away or come crashing down. As people positioned themselves to anticipate the rush of foreign capital—through rich lovers and partners—they often spoke at length about how such wealth could be tamed, made to last, and stretched out over longer periods of time. The desire to dwell as long as possible in the success of the rush led many to devise new ways to more securely store the devilish money of the rush. Whether living in enclosed compounds or driving cars to avoid redistributive requests, reorienting wealth from the coast to rural economies, or redirecting money through the socialities of communal microfinance projects, people involved in transactional sex sought to resist the temporariness of wealth as such. Even if these strategies were themselves uncertain, they offered people a sense of agency, a way to feel like they controlled money rather than being controlled by it.

The pursuit of durable value in a time of chronic temporariness brought the space-time of waiting and that of the rush into a dialectical relationship, generative of new modes of producing and storing value. But because these new modes of value preservation were themselves uncertain and remained speculative, they did not offer definitive solutions to struggles associated with the unpredictability of the rush. Instead, they amplified debates over durability and intensified the desire to find ideal modes of producing such permanence. These quests and contestations, as we have seen, enveloped vastly different media—houses, land, cars, ATMs, and grave memorials—and myriad domains of social life, including beach trade, sex work, neighborhood alliances, and relations to tourists and NGOs. The desire to wait out the rush—itself a rush against risk and speculation—was, in turn, a speculative pursuit, redefining the meaning of work, durability, budgeting, and gambling. Thus, I have argued, anthropological studies of waiting should also take into consideration the myriad temporal and spatial organizations emerging at the intersection of waiting and rushing, an intersection that has redefined the meanings of social value.

George Paul Meiu is Professor of Anthropology and Chair of the Institute of Social Anthropology at the University of Basel. His research focuses on sexuality, gender, belonging, and citizenship in Kenya. His book, *Ethnoerotic Economies: Sexuality, Money, and Belonging in Kenya* (University of Chicago Press, 2017), was awarded the 2018 Ruth Benedict Prize and the 2019 Nelson Graburn Prize by the American Anthropological Association. His work has also appeared in the *American Anthropologist, American Ethnologist, Cultural Anthropology, Ethnos, Anthropology Today,* and in edited volumes on tourism, sexuality, Africa, and the history of anthropology. He holds a PhD in Anthropology from the University of Chicago.

Note

1. Later that year, in September 2011, one British tourist would be killed and another kidnapped from the Kenyan island of Kiwayu, near Lamu, a major tourist destination.

References

Bohannan, Paul. 1955. "Some Principles of Exchange and Investment among the Tiv." *American Anthropologist.* 57: 60–70.
Blunt, Robert W. 2020. *For Money and Elders: Ritual, Sovereignty, and the Sacred in Kenya.* Chicago: University of Chicago Press.
Comaroff, Jean, and John L. Comaroff. 2000. "Millennial Capitalism: First Thoughts on a Second Coming." *Public Culture* 12(2): 291–343.
———. 2006. "Beasts, Banknotes and the Colour of Money in Colonial South Africa." *Archeological Dialogues* 12(2): 107–32.
Cooper, Frederick. 1987. *On the African Waterfront: Urban Disorder and the*

Transformation of Work in Colonial Mombasa. New Haven, CT: Yale University Press.

Daily Nation. 2011 "Life Is Not a Beach: Time to End the 'Easy' Money' Vicious Circle." Nairobi, 23 February.

Ferguson, James. 2006. *Global Shadows: Africa in the Neoliberal World Order*. Durham, NC: Duke University Press.

Gachuhi, J. Mugo. 1973. "Anatomy of Prostitutes and Prostitution in Kenya." Working paper, University of Nairobi. Nairobi.

Hage, Ghassan. 2009. "Waiting Out the Crisis: On Stuckedness and Governmentality." In *Waiting*, ed. Ghassan Hage, 97–106. Melbourne: Melbourne University Press.

Hansen, Karen Tranberg. 2005. "Getting Stuck in the Compound: Some Odds against Social Adulthood in Lusaka, Zambia." *Africa Today* 51(4): 3–16.

Hutchinson, Sharon E. 1996. *Nuer Dilemmas: Coping with Money, War, and the State*. Berkeley: University of California Press.

Jeffrey, Craig. 2010. *Timepass: Youth, Class, and the Politics of Waiting in India*. Stanford, CA: Stanford University Press.

Kibicho, Wanjohi. 2009. *Sex Tourism in Africa: Kenya's Booming Industry*. New Directions in Tourism Analysis. Farnham, UK: Burlington.

Mahoney, Dillon. 2017. *The Art of Connection: Risk, Mobility, and the Crafting of Transparency in Coastal Kenya*. Berkeley: University of California Press.

Mains, Daniel. 2007. "Neoliberal Times: Progress, Boredom, and Shame among Young Men in Urban Ethiopia." *American Ethnologist* 34(4): 659–73.

Masquelier, Adeline. 2005. "The Scorpion's Sting: Youth, Marriage and the Struggle for Social Maturity in Niger." *Journal of the Royal Anthropological Institute* 11: 59–83.

McIntosh, Janet. 2009. *The Edge of Islam: Power, Personhood, and Ethnoreligious Boundaries on the Kenya Coast*. Durham, NC: Duke University Press.

Meiu, George Paul. 2015. "'Beach-Boy Elders' and 'Young Big-Men': Subverting the Temporalities of Ageing in Kenya's Ethno-Erotic Economies." *Ethnos* 80(4): 472–96.

———. 2017. *Ethno-Erotic Economies: Sexuality, Money, and Belonging in Kenya*. Chicago: University of Chicago Press.

Morris, Rosalind C. 2008. "Rush/Panic/Rush: Speculations on the Value of Life and Death in South Africa's Age of AIDS." *Public Culture* 20(2): 199–231.

Newell, Sasha. 2012. *The Modernity Bluff: Crime, Consumption, and Citizenship in Côte d'Ivoire*. Chicago: University of Chicago Press.

O'Neill, Bruce. 2017. *The Space of Boredom: Homelessness in the Slowing Global Order*. Durham, NC: Duke University Press.

Omondi, Rose Kisia. 2003. "Gender and the Political Economy of Sex Tourism in Kenya's Coastal Resorts." Working paper. Tromsø, Norway.

Osburg, John. 2013. *Anxious Wealth: Money and Morality Among China's New Rich*. Stanford, CA: Stanford University Press.

Ralph, Michael. 2008. "Killing Time." *Social Text* 26: 1–29.

Schmidt, Mario. 2019. "'Almost Everybody Does It . . .': Gambling as Futuremaking in Western Kenya." *Journal of Eastern African Studies* 13(4): 739–57.

Schoss, Johanna H. 1995. "Beach Tours and Safari Visions: Relations of Production and the Production of 'Culture' in Malindi, Kenya." PhD dissertation. University of Chicago.

Shepherd, Gill. 1987. "Rank, Gender, and Homosexuality: Mombasa as a Key to Understanding Sexual Options." In *The Cultural Construction of Sexuality*, ed. Patricia Kaplan, 240–70. London: Tavistock Publications.

Shipley, Jesse Weaver. 2010. "Africa in Theory: A Conversation Between Jean Comaroff and Achille Mbembe." *Anthropological Quarterly* 83(3): 653–78.

Shipton, Parker. 1989. *Bitter Money: Cultural Economy and Some African Meanings of Forbidden Commodities*. Washington, DC: American Ethnological Society Monographs.

———. 2010. *Credit Between Cultures: Farmers, Financiers, and Misunderstanding in Africa*. New Haven, CT: Yale University Press.

Smith, James H. 2008. *Bewitching Development: Witchcraft and the Reinvention of Development in Neoliberal Kenya*. Chicago: University of Chicago Press.

Standard. 2008. "Toy-Boys and Mtwapa's Property Boom," Nairobi, 28 August.

Taussig, Michael T. 1980. *The Devil and Commodity Fetishism in South America*. Chapel Hill: University of North Carolina Press.

The Star. 2018. "Nairobi Security Chiefs Destroy Over 300 Illegal Gaming Machines." www.the-star.co.ke/news/2018-10-05-nairobi-security-chiefs-destroy-over-300-illegal-gaming-machines. 5 October (accessed 15 December 2019).

Walsh, Andrew. 2003. "'Hot Money' and Daring Consumption in a Northern Malagasy Sapphire-Mining Town." *American Ethnologist* 30(2): 290–305.

Weiss, Brad. 2004. "Introduction. Contesting Futures: Past and Present." In *Producing African Futures: Ritual and Reproduction in a Neoliberal Age*, ed. Brad Weiss, 1–19. Leiden: Brill.

White, Luise. 1990. *The Comforts of Home: Prostitution in Colonial Nairobi*. Chicago: University of Chicago Press.

Znoj, Heinzpeter. 2004. *Heterarchy and Domination in Highland Jambi: The Contest for Community in a Matrilinear Society*. New York: Kegan Paul.

Afterword

In Slow Time

Thomas Hylland Eriksen

Perhaps a good place to start is in the domain of the *entrepreneur*. In the Introduction to this book, the editors remind their readers that the word is composed of *entre* (between) and *preneur* (from *prendre*, someone capable of grasping, grabbing, or taking). The entrepreneur, in its original meaning, was someone who was able to identify and profit from the gaps, the spaces between. In classic anthropological studies of entrepreneurship, these cunning individuals were able to bridge formerly separate spheres of activity—e.g., labor and money in traditional societies—for the sake of profitability, carrying out conversions to their own benefit.

Entrepreneurs need not be economic actors. They can also cross the boundary between the worldly and the transcendent, or between fast and slow time. Entrepreneurs are experts at finding and filling niches left vacant or ignored by others. The meantime, the theme of this immensely evocative and rewarding book, can be regarded as such a niche. It may drag on in excruciating ways, but it can also be an open temporal space that enables reflexivity, stimulating the imagination and opening a window of opportunity. Yet the conflicting temporalities that are engaged through entrepreneurship may also clash. The window of opportunity may well slam shut when you are halfway through, leaving you in a sorry state of stuckedness (Hage 2009).

Although this book is not a collection of articles about the pandemic, building as it does on a conference held two years before the onset of the pandemic, it cannot be read independently of the intervening events and the continuing looming shadow of Covid-19, in its many permutations and multiplicity of meanings.

Perhaps more than anything else, this book suggests the possibility of meaningful lives outside the straitjackets of fast capitalism and state regimentation, but also that the dance between the fast and the slow continues—indeed, that too much slowness inevitably produces a yearning for speed and, probably, vice versa.

The early 1980s saw the triumph of neoliberalism in the so-called free world and, almost immediately, the category of the *yuppie* was introduced as an ambivalent designation of "young aspiring professionals"; efficient, goal-oriented individualists of both genders, poster children of the new era. A few years later, the Cold War ended and capitalism progressed from being merely dominant to becoming virtually hegemonic. The middle and upper classes of the world were encouraged to do as much as they could as fast as possible. The 1990s was the decade in which the Internet and the mobile phone changed our lives. It was the era of the tyranny of the moment (Eriksen 2001). Cheap calls (Vertovec 2004) and affordable travel contributed to shrinking the world and enhancing efficiency in the realms of production and consumption, while the container ship ensured a spectacular growth in world trade.

Forty years after the election victories of Ronald Reagan and Margaret Thatcher—in March 2020, to be precise—the message conveyed by the political elites was suddenly turned on its head. While the gospel of neoliberalism equated freedom with individual choice and framed accelerated lives as unanimously good, we were now told to slow down. In fact, people were told to do as little as possible, leading to catastrophic effects for the global precariat and inconveniences for the global middle and upper classes. Non-essential shops and restaurants were closed, air travel was reduced by more than 90 percent overnight, work was either scarce, lost, or done from home. Authorities stated that all non-essential travel was either inadvisable or illegal and shopping—even for groceries—was restricted. The physical world slowed down perceptibly for the first time in many years. Waiting became the air that we breathed: waiting for things to change, workplaces to reopen, tourists to return, flights to resume, friendly hugs and handshakes to come back. The stories about waiting narrated in this book resonate with the state in which many unexpectedly found themselves for a period of time that dragged on much longer than anyone had expected. The staccato rhythms of everyday life, from strict lockdowns to gradual reopenings and new lockdowns, resemble some of the life-worlds explored in the chapters of this book.

Waiting is symmetrically tied to efficiency. For waiting to be a burden, there first has to be agreement that time is a scarce resource to be filled with profitable or useful activities. Decades ago, a friend from Trinidad visited me in Oslo. At one point, having seen the rhythm of my everyday life, he exclaimed: "Why you working yourself to death, man?" I stopped momentarily, sat down, and had a couple of beers with him, resuming work when he had gone to bed. Some of us never learn.

In social settings that are not saturated by the gospel of neoliberalism, waiting has its own qualities. The slow openness of the *entretemps*, the meantime, offers opportunities as well as limitations; it can be active or passive. People often wait for something better, but fear something worse. The bracketed temporality of the meantime produces uncertainties that can be as liberating as they can be frightening, depending on the circumstances.

The range of stories and empirical cases in this book is nothing less than astonishing, from waiting for dialysis and a longer future, to the meantime—or *mean time*, as Martin Demant Frederiksen has it—of people who suddenly found themselves stuck in limbo during the pandemic—from the tension between punctuality and "African time" in rural Botswana to the seemingly interminable, yet inherently meaningful wait for sovereignty among nationalist fighters in Western Sahara. In the chapter about Costa Rica, Sabia McCoy-Torres describes the shifting temporalities, between fast busyness to slow contemplation, experienced by workers in the tourist sector of Puerto Viejo. Her account resonates with the neoliberal European life cycle, wherein affluence in time often corresponds with material scarcity. It is a sign of the times that being overworked and super busy, with few gaps left to be filled with fun, mere languishing, contemplation, or intense immersion in art, should be considered a mark of success in this kind of society. Without romanticizing material scarcity, it needs to be pointed out that the materially less successful, with their steady supply of *entretemps*, can sometimes lead more fulfilling and meaningful lives, whether or not they subscribe to ganja-fueled Rasta time. Or, rather, that an alternation between fast and slow time adds layers of meaning to life unfamiliar to those who know nothing about empty time that can be filled with anything. When there are no temporal gaps, nothing new can take place because there is no flexibility.

Interestingly, the chapters and *entretemps* in this collection, notwithstanding their thematic sprawl and stylistic variation, speak to many of the same concerns. This could indicate that universally human themes are being addressed, but it could also mean that we live in a world where most life-worlds are partly shaped by many of the same forces. Arguably, both are true. Like the fragrant Rasta time of Costa Rica, the *fada* tea drinking in Niamey initially comes across as a defiant activity, a form of resistance and opposition to the dominant ethos of efficiency and time budgeting. Yet it turns out that even the seeming passivity and aimlessness of the *fada* collectivities may help their participants to secure successful careers, as well as improving security in the *quartier*. It is precisely this indeterminacy of the meantime that makes it such a fertile field for explorations not only of the contemporary world, but also of the human condition. Futures are fundamentally uncertain; they may be "stolen," as in Frederiksen's (2013) ethnography from Georgia or in Greta Thunberg's stern accusations on behalf of the children of the world, but they may also be invested with hope (Appadurai 2007), even if that hope has faded, as in Mark Drury's account from Western Sahara. The meantime, while often boring and uneventful, is kept alive through excited anticipation, as among Misty L. Bastian's ghost hunters, but it can also be a slow, empty time of stuckedness, a widespread source of frustration among refugees waiting to be allowed to move on and restart their lives (Jacobsen, Karlsen, and Khosravi 2021).

The state of stuckedness is not about the restless habitus encouraged by neoliberalism or the faith in growth and development presupposed by modernity. It concerns something more fundamental, beginning with the temporality of the human body. One linear temporality shared by all humans is the fact of their ageing and eventual death. Being forced to remain indefinitely in a state that precludes growth and development is unpleasant and feels unnatural to human beings everywhere. Female PhD students in anthropology are often asked, in the field, about their children, and if they respond that they are single and childless, they may be treated as children themselves, even if they are in their early thirties, since they seem to be stalled in their development, stuck, as it were, in a state of innocence and ignorance. This is a main reason that not all times can be meantimes. The meantimes are bittersweet, ambiguous (or amphibious?), bracketed breathing spaces that enable anything to happen only because nothing in particular happens, and therefore attain their meaning in the context of more eventful times, past and future.

Thomas Hylland Eriksen is Professor of Social Anthropology at the University of Oslo. His recent and current research concerns local perceptions of and responses to accelerated global change, which he speaks of as *Overheating* in his eponymous 2016 book. The aim is to develop a holistic analysis of a world caught between continued growth and long-term survival.

References

Appadurai, Arjun. 2007. "Hope and Democracy." *Public Culture* 19(1): 19–34.
Eriksen, Thomas Hylland. 2001. *Tyranny of the Moment: Fast and Slow Time in the Information Age*. London: Pluto.
Frederiksen, Martin Demant. 2013. *Young Men, Time, and Boredom in the Republic of Georgia*. Philadelphia, PA: Temple University Press.
Hage, Ghassan, ed. 2009. *Waiting*. Melbourne: Melbourne University Press.
Jacobsen, Christine, Marry-Anne Karlsen, and Shahram Khosravi, eds. 2021. *Waiting and the Temporalities of Irregular Migration*. London: Routledge.
Vertovec, Steven. 2004. "Cheap Calls: The Social Glue of Migrant Transnationalism." *Global Networks* 4(2): 219–24.

Index

A
able-bodiedness, 150, 151, 152, 162
ableism, 152, 155
addiction,
   and damage to body, 156
   hashish, 102
   substance, 127, 136
   to tea, 127, 134
   See also amphetamines
adulthood, 13, 14
   adulting, 13
   as being, 13 (*see also* becoming)
   as finished person, 190
   desirability of, 175
   and gun violence, 152
   and social expectations, 133
advance care planning, 121
affect/affective, 47, 86, 173, 182
   affective anticipation, 59, 41n5
   affective dimension of waiting, 3, 6, 29, 183, 201
   affective economy, 40
   and agency, 183, 215
   and time, 78, 84, 86
Afro-Caribbeans, 17, 71, 75, 76, 80, 85–86
   and greatness, 79 (*see also* Rastafarianism)
   and migration, 88
afterlife/afterlives, 3

of violence, 158
of war, 157
Agamben, George, 30, 31
agency, 6, 39, 70, 73, 79, 87, 183
   and antidiscipline, 138
   and money, 207, 215
   and stuckedness, 210
   temporal, 18, 140, 143, 150
   See also wound: agency of
amnesty of undocumented migrants, 26–27, 32, 34, 35, 38, 40
amphetamines, 142. *See also* addiction
Appadurai, Arjun, 7, 12, 28, 39, 59, 132, 222
apprehension, 169
aspirations, 7, 174
   and future perfect, 60n5
   collective dimension of, 17, 28, 29, 39, 40
   decolonial, 93
   and power, 14
   space of, 132, 133
Auyero, Javier, 12, 28, 59, 140, 143, 150

B
Babylon, 72, 73, 82
Bargu, Banu, 100, 110n9
becoming, 10, 13, 16, 105, 187
betwixt-and-between, 9, 183. *See also* liminality

black stamp (*Kŏmŭn dojang*), 26, 40. *See also* deportation
Blackness, 81, 82
Blunt, Robert, 135, 199
bodybuilding, 128, 130
boredom, 2, 6, 19, 28, 117, 133, 170–71, 201
   as absence of people, 189
   and low tourist season, 74, 78
   as price paid by ghost hunters, 66, 68
   remedy for, 134
   as suspended time, 12
   and youth, 13, 19
botho, 186
Botswana National Youth Council, 187
Bourdieu, Pierre, 7, 9, 183
Bourgois, Philippe, and Jeff Schonberg, 156
Boyer, Florence, 143

C
capital, 39, 178, 198, 199
   daytime, 141
   and displacement, 132
   flows, 87, 198
   nighttime, 123
   repatriation of, 212
   rush of, 197, 201
   social, 201
   See also wealth
Casey, Edward, 44, 45
Certeau, Michel de, 15, 135, 138–39, 141
Christianity, 12, 118
   Christian NGOs, 212
   and liminality, 67
chronos, 6, 71, 87
civic engagement, 127, 142
contemplation, 70, 78, 82, 87, 221
Covid-19 pandemic
   and boredom, 170
   and dialysis patients, 122
   lockdown, 19, 169, 170, 171, 220
   meantime of, 1, 2, 122, 170–71, 219, 221
   and scholarship, 19–20, 220
   and slow living, 19
   and urgency, 19, 168–69
Crapanzano, Vincent, 10, 155, 157
crip theory, 150
crip time, 18, 148–64

crisis
   of global political authority, 95, 107
   and gunshot trauma, 155
   as low season, 83
   management of, 72
   normalization of, 14, 59 (*see also* suspension)
   in places of fieldwork, 169
   as real estate bust, 49, 53, 56, 58
   See also waiting out the crisis
crosswise doubleness, 182, 183

D
dates, 10, 11, 104, 175, 178, 181, 190
daytime, 135, 136
   capital, 141
   conventions, 133, 134, 141
   diurnization of night, 142 (*see also* nighttime)
dead, 63, 66–67
deadlines, 11, 15, 175–76, 178, 182, 186–190
deadwood, 181
death, 1, 67, 115, 155, 222
   counts, 2, 122
   of opportunity, 190
   preparation, 14
   prolonged, 115
   and rush, 201
   slow, 154, 155
   staving off, 115
debt, 13, 17, 19, 44, 47, 52–55, 57, 59, 60n3
decolonization, 92, 93, 94, 106
   as immediate goal, 107
   stranded in, 107, 108
   as unresolved event, 95
   UN Special Committee on Decolonization, 107
deferral, 3
   aimless, 143
   time deferred, 71, 76
deportation,
   refuge from, 29–30
   regime in Korea, 26, 27, 29, 37
   threat of, 30, 31, 34
   untimely, 38
   See also black stamp
development, 32–33, 48, 50, 101, 174, 181, 222

development (*cont.*)
  developmental state, 174, 175, 183, 191n1
  discourses, 51, 174, 212
  expectations of, 12, 86
  failure of, 58
  limits of, 76
  nostalgia for, 86
  organizations, 134
  and present continuous, 51
  programs, 44, 53, 176, 178, 191n1, 213
  reports, 48
  self-development, 178
  shifts in, 85
  and tourism, 76
  underdevelopment, 75
  uneven, 74
Dewachi, Omar, 155
dialysis, 18, 117–21
disability, 119–21, 148–64. *See also* ableism, crip theory, crip time, wheelchair life
disengagement, 171
displacement
  of Greek and Turkish Cypriotes, 47
  of indigenous and African people, 80
doing nothing, 6, 14, 38, 55, 59, 180, 182
durability, 198, 200, 201, 202, 206, 216
  debates over, 212, 215
  fantasy of, 209
  of money, 19, 196, 214
  of opportunities, 198
  and real estate, 202
duration, 4, 68, 134
  awareness of, 134
  dissolution of, 11
  durational enjoyment, 134
  durational ethic, 132
  emptiful, 16
  as experience, 14, 133
  See also gap, meantime, temporality

E
economy
  bartering, 75
  drug, 74
  gig, 15
  and insecurity, 129, 130, 155
  Nigerien, 131, 132
  nighttime, 136
  "no economy," 83
  of the rush, 196, 209, 212, 214
  of waiting, 29, 40
  Ordos, 43, 44, 45, 47, 52, 57
  perverse, 200
  scriptural, 144n5
  sexual, 202, 204, 207, 211 (*see also* prostitution, sex work)
  South Korean, 30, 33
  temporal, 7
  tourist, 17, 70, 76, 86 (*see also* tourism)
  zigzag, 177 (*see also* zigzag capitalism)
education
  advanced, 174
  and better future, 28
  and ethnic identity, 32
  and job security, 131
  as prequalification for labor visa, 41n3
  and social mobility, 131
  as solution to poverty, 133
egalitarianism, 185
embodiment. *See* disability
entrepreneurship, 14–15, 36, 174, 198, 219
  bricoleurs of the future, 177
  entrepreneur, 4, 15, 19, 32, 43, 56–57, 219
  laoban (business owners), 32, 38, 39
  See also tactic, zigzag capitalism
entretemps (interludes), 16–17, 18–19, 221
epistemology,
  of the everyday, 69
  and Rastafarianism, 72, 78, 88
  spiritual, 71
ethnography
  space between of, 16, 17
Evans-Pritchard, E. E., 7, 179
exclusion,
  and bare life, 31
  economic, 70, 75, 82
  and forgiveness, 80
  historical, 76, 81
  of Korean Chinese from Overseas Korean Act, 30
  as racism and ableism, 152
  of undocumented migrants, 31
  zones of, 10, 12

F

fada (tea circles), 18, 124–44. *See also* bodybuilding, nocturnity, teatime, vigilantism
Fischer, Michael, 3, 13
freestyling, 82. *See also* music: and Rastafarianism, *Nyabinghi*
future, 2, 6, 12, 18, 27, 28, 29, 40, 41n5, 44, 60n5, 68, 70–71, 92, 170, 179, 189
   apocalyptic, 154
   certainty of, 52, 58
   in gift exchange, 6–7
   incurability as lack of, 121, 151
   indeterminacy of, 4, 51, 133
   and the meantime, 16
   near, 12
   quest for healthier, 115–116, 120, 150–51 (*see also* hope: and sickness)
   as reward for waiting, 173, 182–83
   trace of futures past, 93
   unattainable, 11, 93, 94, 108, 125, 127, 129
   vanishing of, 54
   See also futurity
futurity, 4, 6, 14, 16, 67. *See also* future
   curative terms of, 151

G

gambling, 199, 200, 212, 213–14, 216
   lottery, 38
   See also rush, speculation
gangs, 128, 130
   gang violence, 157–58
   See also fada and *palais*
ganja
   as medicine, 87
   as psychic stimulation, 70
   See also marijuana
gaolidai (informal, high-interest lending), 49, 52, 53, 54. *See also* loans
gap
   disappearance of, 221
   and ethnography, 3, 16, 17
   in Kula ring, 7
   and social agency, 183
   as dense time, 10
   as space of experimentation, 3
   as space of the possible, 4, 7
   strategic, 9
   temporal, 2, 3, 4, 10, 15
   See also meantime, waiting
Garvey, Marcus, 77
Geertz, Clifford, 182, 191n9
ghost hunting, 17, 63–68
ghost cities, 48, 60n2, 60n6
   lenweilou (buildings with rotten tails), 58
Gilroy, Paul, 77, 128

H

Hage, Ghassan, 7, 8, 10, 12, 13, 46, 47, 55, 210, 219
Honwana, Alcinda, 13, 175, 190
hope, 6, 8, 12, 16, 18, 28, 44, 117, 141, 177, 222. *See also kairos*, optimism
   as acceptance of that which cannot be changed, 73
   as affective economy, 40, 41n5
   foreclosed by deadlines, 175
   and precarity, 173
   orienting the future, 7, 12, 17, 98, 103
   and sickness, 122, 150, 160–61
   spaces of hope, 132–33
human rights, 33, 93, 94
   activism, 95, 107, 108, 111n7
   discourse, 95, 100, 103
   oversight, 97, 103, 104
   protest, 100
   training, 104, 106
   violations, 99, 109
Hurricane Katrina, 149, 158–59

I

immobility, 27, 29, 40, 41, 83–84, 93, 127
   as asset, 18, 129, 139
indeterminacy, 3–4, 13, 70, 222. *See also* uncertainty
inertia, 54, 170, 171. *See also* boredom
infrastructure
   boom, 17, 45, 47–52, 53–54, 57, 58–59, 192n10
   bust, 17, 44, 45, 47, 54, 57, 59 (*see also* ghost cities)
   fada as anticipatory, 18, 133, 138, 143
   of nighttime, 135
   as sign of progress, 51
   post-boom, 55, 57, 58, 59
intercorporeality, 174

J
Jansen, Stef, 59
Jeffrey, Craig, 8, 28, 59, 72, 201
Jeffrey, Craig, and Jane Dyson, 15
Jones, Jeremy, 15, 177
"just sitting," 18

K
Kafer, Alison, 151, 152
Kafka, Franz, 46
kairos, 5, 15, 71, 74, 83, 87. *See also* hope, optimism
Kenyatta, Jomo, 208
kgotla (chief's court) meetings, 172, 178, 179, 180, 184, 185, 189, 191n11
kidney disease, 115, 120, 122
  end stage, 121
  transplant, 120
Korean wind, 17, 26, 28, 29, 32–33, 39, 40. *See also* migration: labor
Kruglova, Anna, 190
Kula, 4–6, 7

L
Lazar, Sian, 94, 95, 98–100, 103, 105, 106
Lee, Jooyoung, 157
liminality, 3, 9, 14, 27
  of midnight, 141
  of overlapping war and peace, 94
  of waiting, 27, 31, 39, 40, 46, 57
Livingston, Julie, 156, 157, 158, 176
loans, 44, 49, 57, 176, 178, 184, 186–87, 190, 191n5, 191n6, 212. *See also* microfinance, *gaolidai*, Youth Development Fund
  and rotating credit groups, 177, 213–14
long-term acute care hospital (LTACH), 161
Lorde, Audre, 73

M
Madrid Accords, 92
Malinowski, Bronislaw, 4–5, 7
manners, 34, 35, 36
marijuana, 18, 70, 71, 87. *See also* ganja, *puro*
masculinity, 128, 132, 133
Mauss, Marcel, 6, 7, 10
Mbembe, Achille, and Janet Roitman, 14
McRuer, Robert, 150

meanplace, 44
meantime, 2, 6, 8, 12, 13, 16, 58, 221
  between boom and bust, 57
  of deportation, 27
  and *entretemps*, 16, 17
  and music, 86
  and socialized dispositions, 9
  topography of, 60
  See also gap, waiting
methicillin-resistant *Staphylococcus aureus* (MRSA), 148
microfinance, 212–14, 215. *See also* loans
migration, 6, 28, 29, 32, 33, 40
  labor, 17, 27 (*see also* Korean wind)
  margins of, 39
  policy, 37 (*see also* Overseas Korean Visit-Work Visa)
  as social remittance, 36

Mitchell, David, and Sharon Snyder, 152
mobility, 11, 12, 27
  and disability, 151, 153
  transnational, 40
  and waiting, 40
  See also education, Korean wind
money
  quick, 200 (*see also* rush, temporality of wealth)
muktessabat (gains through political struggle), 104–06
Munn, Nancy, 7, 8, 71, 94, 174, 182, 183
Musharbash, Yasmine, 134
music
  electronic reggae, 51
  emotional dimensions of, 84, 87
  and Rastafarianism, 18, 77–78, 82 (*see also* freestyling, *Nyabinghi*)
  and temporal disjuncture, 86
  and the meantime, 86, 189
  Muslim prayer, 124

N
National Youth Policy (Bostwana), 174
National Youth Day (Bostwana), 180, 185
Navarro-Yashin, Yael, 47
nighttime, 125, 129, 134, 135
  as anti-structure, 136
  at the *fada*, 142
  military watches of, 145

Index

negative social value of, 142
nightwork, 136

O
O'Neill, Bruce, 138
optimism, 183. *See also* hope, *kairos*
    cruel optimism, 16, 177, 188
Overseas Korean Act, 30
Overseas Korean Visit-Work Visa, 32
overstanding, 72, 81, 84, 87. *See also*
    raising consciousness

P
palais, 130. *See also fada*, gangs
paranormal research, 63–68. *See also*
    ghost hunting
pastime, 52, 131, 132, 197
patience, 11, 154, 183, 210
    as combination of urgency and
        restraint, 143
    and crip time, 148, 149
    cultivation of, 9, 117, 132, 133, 150,
        161, 162
    and ghost hunting, 17
    lack of, 210
    and prison time, 163
    as work, 162, 163
Patwá, 80, 82
place. *See also* time and place
Polisario Front, 18, 91, 92, 98, 104, 105,
    107, 108, 109, 110n3
Pratten, David, 129
present, 40, 51
    continuity of, 44, 80
    continuous, 51, 52, 54, 59
    and lack of progress, 76
    and overstanding, 72 (*see also*
        overstanding, raising consciousness)
    as meantime, 8
    as space of reflection, 78, 80, 82 (*see
        also* temporalities: Rasta)
    suspension in, 78, 93, 155 (*see also*
        wound: chronic)
    See also gap, meantime
Procupez, Valeria, 9, 132, 143, 150
progress, 4, 11, 151
    expectations of, 13
    idealized narrative of, 51
    measurements of progress, 105, 175
    medical histories of, 154

shifting sense of, 98
as urban growth, 51
through wealth, 212
See also development
prostitution, 202, 205, 209. *See also* sexual
    economy, sex work, transactional
    sex
punctuality, 10, 175, 178, 181, 185, 221
puro, 69, 81, 83, 87. *See also* ganja,
    marijuana

R
racism, 75, 80, 81, 152, 155
raising consciousness, 69–87. *See also*
    overstanding
Ralph, Laurence, 157–58
Rastafarianism (Rasta)
    and greatness of Afro-descendants, 81,
        86 (*see also* Afro-Caribbeans)
    Nyabinghi, 82
    See also epistemology
remittances, 29, 33, 35, 214
    social, 36
resignation, 12, 170, 177
Ricoeur, Paul, 173, 183
rush, 19, 194–216
    rushed money (money of the rush), 19,
        196, 198, 213, 214
    rushed things, 210
Russo-Georgian war, 19, 169
Rutherford, Danilyn, 106, 107

S
Samuels, Ellen, 151
Sahrawi Arab Democratic Republic
    (SADR), 18, 91–109, 110n3
Sahrawi political activism, 9, 92, 99–108
    intifada, 95, 96, 101, 108
Say, Jean-Baptiste, 15
Scott, David, 93, 95, 106, 107
security work, 127, 137, 138, 142. *See also*
    surveillance, watchfulness
self-affirmation, 72, 132
sex work, 204, 205, 211–13, 216. *See also*
    prostitution, transactional sex
Smith, Adam, 15
social invisibility, 160
sociality, 47, 125, 130
    and betwixt-and-between, 183
    and competition, 144n4

sociality (*cont.*)
  of the economic boom, 59
  enriched by waiting, 173
  and money, 207, 214
  in pandemic, 2
  as remedy for despair, 127
  and surveillance, 141
  and the meantime, 8
sovereignty, 18, 103, 107, 109, 221
  compromised, 106
  Moroccan sovereignty over Western Sahara, 109
  negative, 107
  Spain's view of sovereignty over Western Sahara, 110n2
space of exception, 30, 31
speculation, 6, 13, 49, 70, 84, 160, 197–200, 216. See also gambling
spirit, 65, 66
  jini, 199, 205, 208
  spirit communication, 65
  See also ghost-hunting
Strathern, Marilyn, 16, 17
stuckedness (or stuckness), 13, 47, 55, 133, 134, 173, 210, 220, 222
subjunctive mood, 160. *See also* uncertainty
surveillance
  informal, 136, 139, 142, 143 (*see also* sociality)
  nighttime, 143
  of "proprietary powers," 139
  state, 96, 101, 102, 104
suspension, 2, 8, 12, 46
  between war and peace, 18, 94
  liminal, 9
  of law, 30
  of predictable future, 4, 11, 14
  of progressive time, 71, 78
  of time, 12, 47, 67–8, 70, 86, 87, 141, 173, 190
  See also gap, meantime

T
tactic, 128, 139, 143
  political, 95, 104
  temporal, 3, 9, 15, 47, 140–41 (*see also* zigzag capitalism)
tea, 56, 97–98, 125, 127, 141, 142–43, 172, 179, 180, 185, 221

teatime, 132, 134, 143
technology
  of alertness, 142
  and development, 51
  dialysis, 116 (*see also* time: machine-made)
  medical, 19, 156
  of paranormal research, 65
  and speed, 11
  timesaving, 11
temporality/ies
  of activism, 98, 99, 103, 105–6, 108
  anthropological concern for, 5, 6, 12
  boundaries and intersections of, 2, 3, 13, 17, 20, 67
  chronic, 154–55, 156 (*see also* crip time, present: undying)
  day/night, 85, 129 (*see also* nighttime)
  of development, 55, 70–71, 72, 76, 86, 174
  and heterotopia, 132
  historical, 70–2, 78, 79, 80
  of hope, 7, 150 (*see also* hope)
  normative, 63, 148, 150–51, 154, 163, 222, 60n5 (*see also* time: curative)
  overfilled, 68
  of pastoralism, 190 (*see also* time: Nuer)
  of precarity, 13, 138
  purposeful, 125, 143
  Rasta, 70–71, 73, 78–79, 82, 84–85, 214, 221
  relational, 183
  seasonal, 71, 78 (*see also* tourism)
  "split bodies and split time," 38, 39
  suspension of, 2, 70, 86, 87
  of waiting, 3, 8, 13, 17, 64, 201, 215 (*see also* waiting)
  of wealth, 199 (*see also* capital: unpredictable, gambling, money: quick, rush)
  See also duration, meantime, teatime, time
temporariness
  chronic, 201, 215
  of wealth, 215
  permanent, 39
time
  attritional, 94–95, 98, 99, 100, 103, 105, 106, 109

Index   231

as burden, 6, 133
bureaucratization of, 11, 12, 46, 59, 119
  (*see also* deadline)
capitalist, 10, 72 (*see also* nighttime)
of caregivers and health care
  providers, 18, 120, 121
chronicity, 154, 155
clock time, 19, 153, 173
curative, 151 (*see also* temporalities: of
  cure)
dead, 11, 72
of insecurity, 135
"it is time," 122
machine-made, 115 (*see also*
  technology)
management, 1, 18, 125, 212
musical, 84
narrative, 160
Nuer, 7, 179 (see temporalities: of
  pastoralism)
open-ended, 6, 7, 16, 116
and place, 44–45 (*see also* place)
rupture in, 77
"slow time," 4, 19, 20, 220–21
as substance of reciprocity, 7
as tactic, 9, 15 (*see also* tactic)
See also duration, meantime,
  temporality
torture, 96, 101, 102, 103, 108
  scars, 155
tourism, 44, 194
  cyclical, 71
  economic role, 69, 76, 85, 183, 199
  ghost, 64
  rise and decline of, 195, 203
  seasonality of, 69–74, 76, 78–9, 83, 85
transactional sex, 202, 203, 204, 217. *See
  also* prostitution, sex work
Tsing, Anna, 3, 58
Turner, Victor, 3, 9, 183

U
uncertainty, 44, 99, 125, 132–33, 183, 198
  anthropological preoccupation with,
    46, 47, 59, 173
  engaging with, 12, 15, 40, 142 (*see also*
    entrepreneurship)
  of chronic wound, 150, 158, 160–61,
    162
  of migration, 29

and the possible, 3, 9, 17, 19, 39,
  68–69, 221
and the present continuous, 51–52,
  54–55, 58
and subjunctive time, 161
See also subjunctive mood,
  unpredictability
United Fruit Company, 75
Universal Negro Improvement
  Association, 77
unpredictability, 63, 198
  of rush, 196, 197, 215
  unpredictable capital, 197
  unpredictable temporalities, 15, 39,
    40, 200
  of visa regulations, 39
  See also uncertainty
unemployment, 126, 132, 175
  and the creation of *fadas*, 127–29,
    132–33
  as exclusion from progress, 4
  government initiatives against, 175,
    187
  and the nighttime economy, 136
  seasonal, 71, 76
  and waiting practices, 9, 27, 201

V
Van Dijk, Rijk, 135
violence,
  and Covid-19 regulations
  debt-related, 55, 59
  between *fadas*, 128
  and fight for self-determination
    in Western Sahara, 93, 100, 102,
    105, 109, 110n7 111n11
  gun, 149, 151, 152, 158, 160,
    165n1
  post-election, 194–95
  and quest for self-realization,
    128
  and racial inequality, 81
  and security work, 137
  state, 152
  symbolic, 151
  urban, 126, 157–58, 162, 164
  war, 155
  See also vigilantism
vigilantism, 126, 130. *See also* violence:
  urban, '*yan banga*

W

waithood, 13, 175, 190
waiting
  as basis for action, 27, 28, 40, 47
  bias, 6, 46, 59
  as burden, 220
  chronic, 12, 27, 39, 54
  as *chronos*, 6
  and delaying the future, 13–14, 32
  as emptiful duration, 16
  existential, 10
  for something, 3, 94, 163
  human condition of, 8, 46
  as inactivity, 6, 10, 14
  "just," 27
  as *kairos*, 5, 15
  in legal limbo, 30, 39, 40, 46
  as naturalized mode of being, 28, 29, 41
  politics and poetics of, 28, 39
  relational character of, 5, 6, 8, 10, 28, 141, 161, 198, 201, 215
  situational, 140
  as time work, 8
  as "total social fact," 10
  universal experience of, 6, 46
  work of, 8, 29, 150, 158, 161, 162
  See also boredom, gap, meantime, patience
"waiting out the crisis," 10, 12, 132, 211
"waiting out the rush," 196, 202, 210, 213–16
watchfulness, 8, 139, 140
  watchful sitting, 132. *See also* security work, surveillance
wealth, 45, 55, 204, 212
  bridewealth, 179, 202
  concrete houses as, 206
  durable, 198, 210, 214
  generational, 76
  hidden wealth of debtors, 54
  instability of, 197–98, 215
  managing, 211, 215
  new, 50, 53, 198
  as quick money, 206
  from sex, 196, 202

Weiner, Annette, 7
Western Sahara, 18, 91, 99
  claims by Mauritania, 110n2
  conflict, 93, 95, 107, 109
  future of, 92
  international attention on, 99
  Moroccan-occupied, 92, 94, 95, 100, 107, 108
  natural resources of, 102
  self-determination in, 103, 106, 109
  Spanish colonialism in, 91–92
wheelchair life, 149, 152, 162
Whyte, Susan, 160
witchcraft, 199
Wool, Zoe, 157
Wool, Zoe, and Julie Livingston, 154, 155
wounds, 18, 148, 149–63
  agency of, 156
  bedsores, 153, 161
  gunshot, 148, 153, 157, 164
  as nexus of care, 156, 165n4, 165n6
  social wounds, 155
  tumor, 156, 157
  and uncertainty, 160
wounded warriors, 157

Y

'*yan banga*, 126, 128, 137. *See also* urban violence, vigilantism
youth, 13, 14, 105, 129, 141, 173, 176, 177, 178, 188, 190
  age range, 176, 186, 191n5
  and gun violence, 165
  meantime of, 187, 190
  as opportunity, 19, 176
  and sociality, 130
  as threat, 127
  and unemployment, 126, 175
  and waithood, 175

Z

zigzag capitalism, 15. *See also* entrepreneurship, tactic, zigzag economy

www.ingramcontent.com/pod-product-compliance
Lightning Source LLC
Chambersburg PA
CBHW051538020426
42333CB00016B/1987